EDDIE JORDAN
FULL THROTTLE

EDDIE JORDAN FULL THROTTLE

Lessons from a Life of Motorsport, Money and Mischief

KEITH O'LOUGHLIN

QUERCUS

First published in Great Britain in 2025 by Quercus
Part of John Murray Group

1

Picture credits (in order of appearance): 1 – Keith Sutton's private collection;
2, 5, 10, 11, 16, 17 – Jordan private collection; 3 – LAT Images;
4 – ZUMA Press Inc./ Alamy Stock Photo; 6 – Instagram; 7 – Ercole Colombo;
8 – Michael Cooper/ Allsport; 9 – Frederic Nebinger/ Palais Princier;
10 – Oli Scarff/ AFP via Getty Images; 13 – Christian Retaggi;
14, 15 – Courtesy of Keith O'Loughlin

A CIP catalogue record for this book is available
from the British Library

HB ISBN 978-1052945-000-2
TPB ISBN 978-1-52945-001-9
EBOOK ISBN 978-1-52945-003-3

Typeset in Minion by CC Book Production

Printed and bound in Great Britain by Clays Ltd, Elcograf S.p.A.

MIX
Paper | Supporting
responsible forestry
FSC
www.fsc.org   FSC® C104740

Papers used by Quercus are from well-managed forests and other responsible sources.

Quercus
Carmelite House
50 Victoria Embankment
London EC4Y 0DZ

John Murray Group
Part of Hodder & Stoughton Limited
An Hachette UK company

The authorized representative in the EEA is Hachette Ireland,
8 Castlecourt Centre, Dublin 15, D15 XTP3, Ireland (email: info@hbgi.ie)

In memory of EJ – who raced through life with heart, humour, and unstoppable drive. This is for the man who made the world louder, bolder, and infinitely more fun.

You were one of a kind.

FTB.

Keith O'Loughlin

Contents

Part I – *The World of EJ*

Contents

Contents

Part II – *The Jordan Code:*
25 Principles to Live and Lead

Contents

Contents

Part III – *Side Roads and Legacy*

Contents

Appendices

Preface

I am honoured to have been asked to write this preface, as not only was I fortunate enough to know Eddie Jordan, I also enjoyed the privilege of his friendship for many years.

Eddie had an extraordinary ability to connect people. He made connections that turned into opportunities, friendships, and memories that endured. Believing deeply in giving back, he channelled his energy into supporting numerous charitable causes, whether in Monaco or beyond. He participated, he gave, and he encouraged others to do the same.

As someone who has always championed sport and the arts, I admired Eddie's equal passion for both. Whether in the paddock, behind a drum kit, or on a stage, Eddie was a performer in the best sense – joyful, mischievous, and always generous. He was a regular and enthusiastic participant in our Saint-Tropez to Monaco charity bike rides – never the quietest cyclist in the group, but always one of the most determined and generous in spirit.

In many ways, Eddie became an ambassador for Monaco. Wherever he was in the world, he spoke about Monaco with affection and pride, making people want to be part of it.

He loved Monaco, and Monaco loved him back.

Our friendship was also bound by heritage. Eddie's Irish roots and my own connection to Ireland through my mother, Princess Grace, gave us a shared cultural affinity. His legacy is more than his Formula 1 record. It is in the people he championed, the underdogs he backed, the mischief he encouraged, and the sheer sense of life he brought to everything he touched with such generosity.

This book captures so much of who Eddie was – the lessons, the laughter, the risks, the rewards, and his humanity. It is a fitting tribute to a man we all miss, and whom I was proud to call a friend.

HSH Prince Albert II

Foreword

This book is a testament to the success of Eddie's life. It contains tributes from all sorts of incredible people who were inspired and motivated by him. It is written from the heart, out of love for Eddie and all he gave us, by Keith O'Loughlin. It is written for the benefit of the Eddie Jordan Foundation, whose mission is to keep Eddie's legacy alive – helping those he always believed were out there somewhere, and who might need just a little bit of help at the crucial moment, even if he himself can no longer be physically present.

All of us who have contributed to this book want to share the gift of Eddie – because we saw how he brought out the best in people. We all felt like better versions of ourselves when he was around. Through the Foundation, the sincere hope is that he will continue to give to those with a spark of creativity or that ounce of talent, who only need a slight push or the sense of permission to fulfil their true potential. They will become his greatest tribute.

In this book, you'll also find an explanation of The Jordan

Code: 25 Principles to Live and Lead. Those of us who knew Eddie well are quite surprised to hear he had any code, let alone one with 25 principles! So now you're beginning to understand. Eddie had no real rules, no boundaries, and no reason not to do what you wanted. And that's exactly why we loved him. Deep down, people don't want to be constrained. They want the freedom to express themselves, to live life to the fullest. EJ would ask you, quite directly, "Why don't ya just fookin' do it?" It's a good question. It may be the biggest question of all.

This book won't do anything for you. You have to do it all yourself. But by reading it, you may absorb some of the EJ philosophy that might just empower you to venture into a world of complete freedom – the Infinite World of Eddie.

To call it a philosophy might be misleading. I doubt Eddie ever thought of it that way. He just did what felt right in the moment. He listened to his gut, his soul, his finely tuned survival instincts. He didn't let convention contain or restrict him. He saw straight through the hypocrisy of those who wanted to hold him back because he wasn't playing the game the way it was "supposed" to be played. These people are the begrudgers. Eddie saw through them. He saw what he wanted and went after it. To hell with the begrudgers! Or, more succinctly – as only Eddie could put it – FTB. You can guess what the "F" stands for.

In his life, Eddie achieved a staggering amount and he did it from virtually nothing. So how did he manage that? He certainly wasn't born in Monaco – though he did end up living there. Monaco has many famous residents, but Eddie didn't just hide away, counting his millions. No, he brought EJ to the Principality and became close friends with so many, not least HSH Prince Albert. Eddie could, as Kipling put it, "walk with Kings – nor lose the common touch".

And that's the point. Society is riddled with hierarchies – constant, subtle reminders to "know your place" or climb above others. This book is about how not to let that define you, or limit your life. Be yerself, was Eddie's way. But who is yerself? You'll have to find out for yourself. And it starts by stepping out into the world and breaking a few of your own rules.

Knowing Eddie Jordan was like being in a private club. But in EJ's club, everyone was welcome. The only rule? Don't be a killjoy. If you weren't bringing something to the party, the party would leave you behind, so you'd better keep up.

Eddie was a whirling dervish, a small tornado, an electron that never came to rest – energizing every room and everyone in it. "Faster Than Life," Bono once called him, and that about sums him up. But he was also many other things. One moment, he'd be babbling from topic to topic, seemingly off track, and then suddenly – bam! – he'd land exactly on what needed to be said.

Sometimes he was uncouth, it's fair to say, but when the word finally came out, we were all grateful he'd said it – so we didn't have to.

And then, just as suddenly, he could speak in hushed tones – your counsellor, your confidant, your closest friend, your therapist. The next minute he was a stern, matter-of-fact businessman, explaining the seriousness of your situation. Then he'd be playing spoons with a musician in a beach bar. And when you thought you were playing golf with him, you'd find him in the bushes – looking for any golf balls, not just his. He always liked to come out ahead. He was, shall we say, unpredictable. But never boring. Always enjoying himself. Always able to see the absurdity in the moment.

My son, Oliver, has Down's syndrome. He and EJ had a special bond. Eddie saw that Oliver cared about who you are, not what you are. Oliver has no concept of fame or money, but he has an instinct for good people – and he instantly liked Eddie. Maybe it was the funny face?

One day we were at a party at Eddie's house in Spain, and Oliver decided he liked Eddie's Crocs. So he took them. Eddie thought it was hilarious. That kind of cheeky, unfiltered behaviour? That was exactly the sort of thing Eddie approved of. Maybe, in that moment, he realized he'd met his match. And to be fair, Oliver did look better in them – but that's not the point of the story.

Before Eddie left for South Africa – to be with his family for what he must have known was his final chance to fight the illness – he made sure that part of a deal he'd helped me with went to our charity, HALOW, which helps young people like my son live a fuller life.

We met at his London flat for a curry, just him, his sons, and a few close friends. Eddie was frail, thin, and clearly very tired. He had already been fighting this disease for some time. But still, he made this gesture of friendship. There must have been countless things on his mind, but he made sure this was done. It was on his list. Just in case.

It's impossible to capture Eddie Jordan in full. He was too big, too complex, too brilliant. For those of us lucky enough to have known him, there is deep sorrow that he is gone – but great joy in the remembering. And for those who never met him, this book holds a generous dose of his essence. I hope when you finish it, you'll wish you had known him. I'm sure you will.

And if one day, many years from now, someone writes a book about you – filled with stories of love, laughter, and admiration from everyone you touched – then you'll know your life was well spent.

FTB, EJ.

Damon Hill OBE

A Word from Marie

This book captures Eddie's unique way of approaching life and business. When I think about how he operated, one quality stands out above all the rest.

Eddie never took "no" for an answer, as those who knew him well will confirm. He would start by asking a straightforward question – if that wasn't agreed to, he would then ask in a slightly different way, and he would go back again and again until he got his agreement in some form.

Also, he was often asking for outlandish things to begin with and then reaching more normal territory by the end and ending up by getting what hc had originally wanted or expected. I witnessed this many many times, used in various different scenarios. A great lesson in never giving in after the first hurdle.

This was all natural for Eddie and there was no planning or strategy. Just normal business and the thrill of pulling off another deal!

Miss you, with all your mischief.

Introduction

This book didn't start as a tribute. It started as a few scrappy notes – business ideas, sharp lines, and wild stories picked up from time spent with Eddie Jordan. But like everything with Eddie, it didn't stay small. It grew. It picked up speed. It got loud. It became something else.

Not a business book. Not a racing memoir. Not a self-help guide. Something messier. More honest. More useful. This is a book of principles – tested in chaos, sharpened through risk, and lived at full throttle. You won't find academic theories here. What you will find is instinct, conviction, and a way of moving through the world that doesn't wait for permission. And always grounded in fun.

It's not about what Eddie achieved – though that list is long. It's about how he did it. Why he did it. And how you might too.

This book is for the doers, the risk-takers, the people who think sideways. It's also for anyone who needs a push – to believe more, to bet bigger, or to stop playing by someone else's rules. It's a reminder that life doesn't come with a manual – so you might as well write your own.

Eddie didn't go to university – but he probably learned more than most who did. Because learning isn't confined to lecture halls or diplomas. It's a mindset. A hunger. An openness. Eddie had a rare instinct for asking sharp questions, really listening, staying curious, and picking things up fast. He was always learning – and always interested. And while he was known for taking shortcuts, they weren't to cut corners. They were to get to the goal quicker. This book can be your shortcut manual – if you're ready to move.

At the centre is The Jordan Code – 25 principles that shaped how Eddie led teams, made deals, built trust, backed talent, and stayed real. They're not commandments, they're rhythm and feel. Eddie didn't live by bullet points – he lived by instinct. But those instincts left a pattern. That's what this book is about.

Inside, you'll find stories from garages and boardrooms, backstage and broadcast booths, boats and startups, bike rides, late-night chats, and bold moves. They come with laughter, heart-break, wisdom – and plenty of unexpected detours.

You'll also hear from the people who knew him – teammates, drivers, friends, partners, and musicians. People who were in the room when it got loud, and stayed when it got hard. Their reflections remind us that success isn't about titles or trophies. It's about the energy you bring, and the permission you give others to be bold.

To make it practical, there's a digital companion – *The FTB Hub* – filled with exercises, reflections, and prompts to help you apply the ideas. Whether you're building a business, leading a team, or just trying to live with a little more intent, it's there to help you turn inspiration into action.

Introduction

But let's be clear: this book isn't about trying to be Eddie. No one else ever could be. It's about learning from the way he moved – with urgency, loyalty, rhythm, and mischief. He didn't separate business, life, and fun – and neither does this book.

You don't want to be Eddie Jordan – there was only one. But you can learn from him, just as he learned from others – often the hard way. His success speaks for itself, and the principles here reveal much of what powered it. Eddie didn't just build a career – he built a life, rich with family and enduring friendships.

Whether you read this book from cover to cover or just dip in when you need a push, we hope it stays close. We hope it earns your scribbles, your coffee stains, and a few corners folded down. You'll find repetition – that's intentional. This book is meant to be used, not simply read. It will make you laugh, think, and reflect in equal measure. Some stories have been shaped for clarity, others are told exactly as Eddie told them – poetic licence and all. But every one of them is true in spirit.

At its core, this is a book about belief. Belief in ideas. Belief in risk. Belief in people – especially when it's not the obvious choice. Eddie built his life on backing people before they'd proven anything, often before they believed in themselves.

When he passed in March 2025, there was a minute's silence at the Chinese Grand Prix. Across the world, people paused – not only in silence, but in recognition. They thought of him, and universally they smiled, feeling the spark he left behind. For a man who made the world turn that little bit faster, he would've loved that tribute.

As part of writing this book, it was extraordinary to see how many lives Eddie had lived – and how many people's lives he touched. The number who called him their best friend, or one of their closest friends, was remarkable – a reflection of his rare ability to connect, listen, and make people feel seen. Everyone who met Eddie came away with an experience and a story. That's what people remembered. That's what made them smile.

He gave his time and energy freely, yet no one ever felt they were asking too much. And he never made you feel like he was rushing to the next thing. One-on-one, you had his full attention. In a group, he lit the room – made everyone feel like something electric could happen at any moment.

And finally, 100 per cent of my royalty earnings from sales of this book will be donated to the Eddie Jordan Foundation – supporting programmes that unlock potential, ignite creativity, and create opportunity for young people who just need one person to back them. Please scan the QR Code below or visit www.ej.foundation and get involved.

Thank you for reading. I hope this book inspires you – so you can inspire others.

Welcome to the ride.

FTB.

Keith O'Loughlin, May 2025

FTB

What's FTB? FTB stands for "F*** the Begrudgers".

Simple as that. It was Eddie's mantra and motto and features throughout this book.

This book is about momentum. It's about showing up. About betting on yourself. About making something out of nothing – and doing it without waiting for permission.

But to do that, you have to ignore the noise.

The cynics. The critics. The ones who talk and never do. The ones who say, "That'll never work," or "Who do you think you are?"

You know the type.

They've got no skin in the game, but they've always got something to say. Eddie had a name for them: Begrudgers. And his answer? Always the same: FTB.

He had FTB tattooed on his wrist! And he wore it with pride and shouted it from the rooftops. And that is how he lived.

Because the truth is – if you try to do anything big, bold,

or different, they'll come for you. Not because you're wrong, but because you're *moving.* And movement scares people who've stayed still too long. These are the people who want to slow others down to their pace. Jealous and begruding, they drain the energy from people and things.

Eddie never waited for the world to clap before he acted. He built teams, backed talent, made deals, told stories, raised hell, and helped thousands – all while staying true to his rhythm. And along the way, he tuned out the doubters.

Not with anger.

With action.

FTB isn't about aggression. It's about belief. It's about commitment.

Believe in your vision.

Believe in your team.

Believe in your rhythm.

Believe that being *fully yourself* is not only allowed, it's the only way to live!

So, this book isn't just about business. Or racing. Or drumming. Or deals.

It's about building your life around *your voice* – not theirs.

It's about being your best.

And every time the noise gets loud?

Just smile.

And remember:

FTB.

Let's go . . .

Eddie Jordan

A Full-Throttle Life Timeline

From Bray to the grid to global boardrooms –
always at full tilt.

1948–1970s: Born with Rhythm and Rebellion

- **1948**: Born 30 March in Dublin, raised in Bray, County Wicklow
  - Educated at Synge Street CBS – numbers came naturally, authority less so
  - Joins the Bank of Ireland – leaves to chase speed and freedom
  - Races in Formula Ford and Formula Atlantic, winning the 1978 Irish Atlantic Championship.
- **1978:** Married Marie McCarthy, who remained by his side for life.

1980s: The Maverick Manager Emerges

- **1980**: Launches Eddie Jordan Racing – the proving ground for raw talent
  - Gives early drives to Martin Brundle, Johnny Herbert, Jean Alesi, and Ayrton Senna.
- **1989**: Briefly sells a stake to Warburg Pincus, but later buys it back (for a fraction of what they paid him for it) – refuses to let go of the vision.

1990s: Shakes Up F1 with Jordan Grand Prix

- **1991**: Debuts in F1 with the now-iconic Jordan 191
  - Gives Michael Schumacher his first F1 race
  - Known for culture, charisma, chaos, and competitiveness.
- **1998**: Achieves maiden win – a dramatic 1–2 at Spa.
- **1999**: Jordan GP finishes third in the World Constructors' Championship.

2000s: New Stages – Music, Media, and Money

- **2005**: Sells Jordan GP – the team becomes Midland, later Force India, and eventually Aston Martin.
- Plays drums in V10 and Eddie and The Robbers, performing with Bryan Adams, Mike Rutherford, and Texas.
- Joins BBC F1 as a pundit – colourful, outspoken, and beloved.

- Guest-hosts BBC's *Top Gear* during its transitional era.
- Appointed to the board of Citibank Private.

2010s: Elder, Explorer, Entrepreneur

- **2012**: Awarded an Honorary OBE for Services to Charity and Motorsport.
- **2013–14**: Circumnavigates the globe aboard the sailing yacht *Lush* in the Oyster World Rally.
- **2022**: Receives the Freedom of the City of London
  o Mentors young entrepreneurs, investors, and athletes.

2020s: Still Moving the Needle

- **2022**: Makes a £3 billion bid for Playtech.
- **2023**: Launches the *Formula For Success* podcast with David Coulthard
  o There are 110 episodes, featuring icons from F1, sport, business, and music.
- **2024**: Continues to act as a TV pundit and commentator
  o Guides Adrian Newey's move from Red Bull to Aston Martin.
  o Second fastest in a 120km cycle race in the over-70s category, Cape Town Cycle Tour race.
- **2025**: Helps lead the revival of London Irish Rugby with his son, Kyle Jordan.
  o Passes away on 20 March 2025, aged 76. Tributes pour in from across the world.

Eddie Jordan: Achievements

Eddie Jordan's achievements span motorsport, business, media, and music – all powered by instinct, energy, and fearless belief. Here are the key highlights of his extraordinary journey:

Motorsport

Founder of Jordan Grand Prix (1991–2005)

- Created one of F1's most beloved and overachieving independent teams.
- Debuted on the F1 grid in 1991 – with almost no budget – and finished fifth in the Constructors' Championship in its first season.
- Gave Michael Schumacher his first F1 drive (Belgium, 1991).
- Achieved the team's first win in the 1998 Belgian Grand Prix, a 1–2 finish with Damon Hill and Ralf Schumacher.
- Won three subsequent F1 races:
  - o 1999 French Grand Prix – Heinz-Harald Frentzen
  - o 1999 Italian Grand Prix – Heinz-Harald Frentzen
  - o 2003 Brazilian Grand Prix – Giancarlo Fisichella.
- Finished third in the Constructors' Championship in 1999 – beating McLaren in one race and Ferrari in another.
- Sold the team, bought it back for a fraction of the price, and sold it again.

Talent Spotter Extraordinaire

- Launched or accelerated the careers of many great drivers including:
  o Michael Schumacher
  o Damon Hill
  o Rubens Barrichello
  o Eddie Irvine
  o Ralf Schumacher
  o Jean Alesi
  o Giancarlo Fisichella.

Known for:

- Bringing colour, chaos, and creativity to a grid that was growing increasingly corporate.
- Outperforming bigger, better-funded teams through culture, hustle, and heart.

Broadcasting and Media

BBC F1 Pundit (2009–15)

- Became the charismatic, unfiltered voice of F1 coverage.
- Beloved by fans for his candid insights, bold predictions, and unpredictable energy.

it_Top Gear_ Pundit (2016)

- Channel 4 F1 Team Member (2016 onwards).
- Continued as a respected media figure and go-to voice in F1.
- Often credited with asking the questions others wouldn't.

FFS Podcast with David Coulthard (2023–25)

- Recorded over 100 episodes.
- One of the most popular sports podcasts in the world.

Music

Founder of Eddie and The Robbers
- Performed regularly as a drummer, including with celebrities and professional musicians.
- Played gigs across Europe and the Middle East, often combining racing weekends with music events.

Known for:
- Playing with the likes of Bryan Adams, Texas, and Chris Rea.
- Making music part of his brand and energy wherever he went.
- Pulling out spoons at any possible moment and kicking off a music session.

Business and Deals

Entrepreneurial Spirit

- Made shrewd deals throughout his F1 career – including licensing colour rights (e.g. "Jordan Yellow" to DHL).
- Turned Jordan GP into a launchpad for sponsorship innovation – with brands like 7UP, Benson & Hedges, and Puma.

Bids and Business Ventures

- Involved in a headline-making £3 billion bid for Playtech (2022).
- Lead acquisition of London Irish and Bezier Rugby Clubs in 2024/25.
- Supported major businesses, startups and causes in sports, hospitality, and tech.

Mentorship and Legacy

Mentor and Backer of Underdogs

- Advisor and mentor to the winning 2014 Ryder Cup team and Captain Paul McGinley at Gleneagles. Also performed with Eddie and The Robbers at three Ryder Cups.
- Believed in raw talent over polish – often backing people before the world saw their potential.
- Known for mentoring musicians, entrepreneurs, yacht captains, and young broadcasters.

Philanthropy

- Champion for young people through education, mentorship, and creative opportunity.
- Long-time and passionate supporter of CLIC Sargent, the UK's leading charity for young people and families affected by cancer.
- Founder, supporter, and patron of Amber Rocks charity for disadvantaged young people.

Eddie used his platform in Formula 1, music, and media to raise awareness and funding for all charities.

Cultural Icon

- Brought Irish flair, humour, and chaos into one of the world's most precision-driven sports.
- Remained grounded and loyal to his roots, even as his global influence grew.
- Recognized not just as a team boss but as a character, connector, and culture-maker in F1 and beyond.

Awards

- Awarded the OBE (Officer of the Order of the British Empire) for Services to Motorsport and Charity in the 2012 New Year Honours list.
- Honorary Doctorate of Law – University of Ulster (2002).
- Honorary Doctorate of Philosophy – Dublin Institute of Technology (2003).
- Autosport Awards – Gregor Grant Award (2009) – Lifetime Achievement Award.
- Motorsport Industry Association (MIA) – Outstanding Contribution to Motorsport Award.

PART I

The World of EJ

1

Chaos in the Blood

How a kid from Dublin built a global legacy
by never asking permission.

Born into Motion

There's a certain kind of chaos that lives in the blood – a refusal to sit still, a hunger for movement, a need to turn friction into fuel. Eddie Jordan had it from the very beginning. He was never built for stillness, never made for systems. His spirit was a cocktail of adrenaline, instinct, mischief, and motion. And though he didn't know it then, that exact mix would one day take him from the backstreets of Dublin to the front row of Formula 1.

Born on 30 March 1948 in Ireland's capital city, Eddie came into a post-war world still shaking off its scars. His family was working-class, devoutly Catholic, and tightly woven – full of characters, contradiction, and warmth. He grew up in Bray, a coastal town just south of Dublin, surrounded by the kind of raw, unfiltered Irish energy that shapes the sharpest minds and the toughest skins.

From a young age, Eddie showed signs of being wired differently. He was curious. He was fast. He was cheeky. He got into fights, into trouble, into places he probably shouldn't have – and out of them, just as quickly. He had a flair for humour and a disarming ability to charm adults who were initially ready to punish him. Mischief didn't seem like rebellion in Eddie's hands – it seemed like art.

School was always going to be a problem. At Synge Street CBS, a stern Christian Brothers school in Dublin, discipline came before expression. Eddie learned early on how to take a hit – metaphorically and sometimes literally. But what the Christian Brothers didn't understand was that they weren't beating misbehaviour out of him, they were simply sharpening his sense of who he *wasn't*. He wasn't someone who would follow orders without question. He wasn't someone who accepted the world as it was handed to him.

He was someone who needed to move.

Even as a child, motion fascinated him. He took apart bicycles to see how they worked. He raced down hills with reckless glee. He played football not for tactics, but for the thrill of running past someone who underestimated him. His friends noticed it too – there was always a streak of "more" in Eddie. More noise. More risk. More laughter. More dreams. He was someone who, even in his early years, had the brightness, contrast, and definitely the volume knobs turned up to the max.

That streak wasn't born of ego, it was born of urgency. He could feel the world pulling at him – not to sit still and get a trade, but to push forward, even if he didn't know what he was pushing towards. He often said he was trying to fit three times more into every day than others, and he did this from an early age.

When he landed a job at the Bank of Ireland after school, it seemed like a win. A stable salary. Clean suit. Pension. For most Irish families in the '60s, it was the dream. But for Eddie, it felt like a cage. The quiet hum of calculators, the predictable small talk, the uniform days and tighter nights – they weren't just boring, they were suffocating. He used the bank as a launchpad for his future.

When someone called looking for a car loan, Eddie would smile and say he might be able to get them a better car than they'd planned – maybe even one from his own "stock" out back. And if he didn't have it, he'd go and find it. The name of his side hustle? Honest John Car Sales – a cheeky little operation he ran with his childhood friend, Mick Tunney. Classic Eddie: always dealing, always thinking one step ahead.

He didn't last long in the bank.

In 1966, Eddie went to Jersey for a summer – chasing a bit of sun, a bit of work, and a taste of something different. He worked nights in the Bristol Bar and days at the electricity company, but it was in the downtime between shifts that something sparked.

Karting.

A low-slung machine, hugging the tarmac, buzzing with potential. It wasn't glamorous, but it was fast – and it gave Eddie his first real taste of racing. The rush. The rhythm. The roar of competition. Everything clicked.

After leaving his banking job behind, he'd stumbled into something that felt more like destiny than diversion. In those early karting sessions on the island, he discovered the balance between chaos and control – a feeling that would define the rest of his life.

Go-karts might not sound like much but for Eddie, they were pure magic. Racing stripped to the bone: reflex, grit, feel, balance. No million-dollar engines. No sponsors. Just you and the corners. Man and machine.

And in that simplicity, he found everything he needed to begin.

He dove into it with the same reckless commitment he brought to everything. In those early days, karting was raw. Circuits were patched together. Mechanics were often drivers' mates. Safety was minimal. But the talent? The hunger? The stakes? Real. Eddie felt at home.

From karts, he moved into Formula Ford and was competitive, and then moved on to Formula Atlantic, winning the Irish National title in 1978. He raced in the UK and across Europe, against drivers who had far more funding but often less nerve. He didn't have a factory behind him. What he had was feel. He could sense a line, an opening, a braking point, before most drivers could spot it on a map.

Still, he knew the limits. The higher up he went, the clearer it became: he wasn't going to make it to Formula 1 as a driver. He didn't have the reflexes of a Senna, the composure of a Lauda. But that didn't disappoint him. It *freed* him. As Eddie told it, Niki Lauda pulled him aside one day and said, "Eddie, you are a good driver, but look around you. You are in a sport with me, James Hunt, Emerson Fittipaldi, and there is a new French driver coming through called Alain Prost. You are not going to make it as a driver. Sorry. I know you have great experience in commerce. You should start your own team." Eddie wanted to compete and win at whatever he was doing, not make up numbers. And just like that, Eddie Jordan – former bank clerk, former karting rebel, wannabe rock star with some success as a driver – began his journey as a team boss.

Because Eddie wasn't here to be famous. He was here to be *in it*. And if that meant stepping out of the car and into the garage then fine, he'd build something that *lasted*.

He started to see the sport as more than competition – it was opportunity. Who built the teams? Who got the sponsors? Who discovered the drivers? Who made the real decisions?

In 1980, with barely enough cash to rent a trailer and zero reputation in the paddock, Eddie formed Eddie Jordan Racing. His goal wasn't to be the biggest – it was to be the most *alive*. The team was built in his image: fast, gritty, energetic, loud, and loyal.

He ran it like a band. You didn't join for a pay cheque, you joined because you wanted to make music with him. Mechanics worked overtime without being asked. Drivers listened to him like he was their brother and their coach. Everyone pulled in the same direction because Eddie made it *fun*.

In 1983, he gave a seat to a young, electric Brazilian talent named Ayrton Senna. It was a glimpse into Eddie's real genius: *talent spotting*. Senna dazzled in British Formula 3 under Eddie's stewardship. Later, Eddie would repeat this magic over and over – with drivers like Martin Brundle, Johnny Herbert, Jean Alesi, Damon Hill, and of course, he infamously gave Michael Schumacher his first drive in Formula 1. He didn't wait for the obvious talent to show up polished, he saw it raw and shaped it.

Those years weren't easy. Sponsors came and went. Parts broke. Engines failed. There were crashes, lawsuits, money troubles. But the team survived because it had one thing most others didn't:

spirit. Eddie's teams felt like family. And that feeling couldn't be bought.

He kept it scrappy. While bigger teams focused on margins and technology, Eddie focused on people. He knew every mechanic's name. He took drivers to dinner. He shared hotel rooms to save money. There were no egos. No walls.

Just momentum.

The Making of a Leader

Eddie Jordan didn't become a leader the traditional way. He didn't study it. He didn't inherit it. He became one by sheer force of personality, resilience, and vision.

In those early years of team management, he learned how to lead by doing everything wrong – and then figuring it out. He made mistakes with money, with hiring, with logistics. He underestimated rivals. He overpromised. He scrambled.

But he never panicked.

That calm in chaos would become his trademark. "Everything's gone wrong? Grand. Let's have a beer, fix it, and go again."

He learned that leadership wasn't about control – it was about trust. If you trusted people, they performed better. If you gave them a little room, they gave you back loyalty tenfold. Eddie wasn't a micromanager, he was a conductor.

And when things went right, he didn't take the credit. He gave it away – to the driver, the mechanic, the guy who stayed up all night. That humility, wrapped in humour, made him beloved.

He also learned to deal – fast. Sponsors didn't line up at his door. He had to chase them, convince them, charm them. He pitched in pubs, in paddocks, in boardrooms. He made people believe – in him, in the dream, in the car. He hustled and hustled and hustled.

What he built wasn't only a team – it was a way of thinking.

It said: You don't need the biggest budget to make the biggest noise.

It said: You can laugh and still win.

It said: We're not here to survive, we're here to shake things up.

It said: It's the race, the competitive edge, the challenge that you remember. Not the trophy.

By the end of the 1980s, Eddie Jordan Racing was more than a small outfit. It was a proving ground. A place where futures were made. A brand. A tribe. A movement.

And Eddie? He was now far more than a former driver.

A leader with nothing to lose.

A rebel with a following.

A man about to bring that chaos – the same chaos that once raced through the streets of Bray – to the most elite grid in motorsport.

Formula 1 was coming.

And Eddie Jordan was already on the way.

> *"I wasn't supposed to get here.*
> *But the thing is, I never asked who was*
> *doing the supposing. I just went."*
> *– Eddie Jordan*

2

Becoming Eddie

How personality became Eddie's business weapon.

The Birth of a Character

Eddie Jordan didn't step into the world of motorsport with a strategy manual. He stepped in with a personality – and that was the playbook.

In a sport driven by engineering, data, and precision, Eddie was pure theatre. The hair, the shirts, the voice, the sparkle in his eye – it wasn't an affectation. It was Eddie, turned up to the max. From the earliest days, he knew that if he couldn't outspend the big teams, he could outshine them. Visibility would become his most powerful tool.

Back in Dublin, Eddie had always been known as a character. He could tell a story, sell an idea, or calm a situation with a smile. He made people laugh, but he also made them lean in. He had that rare gift of magnetism – you remembered him, even if you didn't remember why. He took up playing music to get the girls when he was younger: "I wanted to be different and saw that the guys in the band always had girls chasing after them. So I took up drumming."

When he entered the motorsport business, he realized quickly that the paddock was full of stiff suits, whispered deals, and clenched jawlines. Eddie would be the opposite – loud, open, full of colour and chaos. He wore gold watches and Hawaiian shirts while others wore grey. He played music in the garage. He joked with the press. He danced when others sulked. He used colourful language with a smile. He had an incredible aptitude for numbers, and in a sport where it's all about lap times and milliseconds, he was in his comfort zone.

And it worked.

Formula 1 is about entertainment. He got out of banking because it was boring . . . he wasn't going to bring boring to the world of Formula 1.

People started talking about him – and that talk brought deals, drivers, and attention.

Eddie claimed, "We all robbed each other in those days. I robbed off the other teams and they robbed off me. And then we would have a laugh about it after the race."

Personality as a Strategy

Eddie wasn't trying to be different. He *was* different. But he was smart enough to know that difference was an asset. He turned personality into performance.

He built relationships in places others overlooked. He charmed sponsors who hadn't even considered motorsport. He found drivers not only based on lap times, but on attitude, hunger, and chemistry.

In business, people often talk about the power of brand. Eddie *was* the brand. And before "authenticity" became a corporate buzzword, he had already proven its power. What you saw with Eddie was what you got – for better or worse. And that made him trustworthy. He wasn't hiding anything. He was also a natural leader who inspired his team, and they became friends – many of the drivers actually lived with his family: the Jordan team was just the extended Jordan family.

This authenticity let him operate across borders and boundaries. He could hold his own in a corporate boardroom one hour, then share a pint with mechanics the next. He had no hierarchy in how he treated people. Status didn't impress him. Character did.

For Eddie, being yourself wasn't a luxury, it was the foundation of everything.

In 2002, Deutsche Post had just acquired a small logistics outfit called DHL, and they were keen to boost the brand's visibility through their sponsorship of Jordan Formula 1. They called Eddie with a request.

"Eddie, we want to increase our sponsorship next year – but we need the car to be white."

"Of course," Eddie replied with a grin. "If you pay me enough, you can have it any colour you like."

But first, Eddie made a courtesy call to Nigel Northridge, Head of Marketing at Benson & Hedges – the team's long-time title sponsor.

"Nigel, we're thinking of switching the car to white next year. It's going to look brilliant."

"Sorry, Eddie. That's a deal breaker. If the car's not yellow, we walk. Have a look at the contract."

Eddie had a problem. The DHL money was too good to walk away from – but so too was Benson & Hedges. So, he called Deutsche Post back.

"Sorry, I can't agree to it," he said. "Because I don't believe in the DHL brand."

Pause. "But . . . I do have an idea. Let me come to your next board meeting and pitch it."

"No outsiders are allowed," came the reply.

"Then there's no deal."

A few hours later, the phone rang again. "Fine, you can come. Here's the time and date."

Eddie showed up at the meeting in full Jordan team kit – bright yellow – carrying ten neatly-bound presentations. As the Deutsche Post board looked on in bemusement, he began.

"Turn to page one. You'll see eight white vans – one of them is DHL with a red flash, the rest are FedEx and your other competitors. Next page – six white vans, two yellow ones for DHL. Now planes – same story. White everywhere, with a couple of yellow blips."

Then he delivered the punchline: "I want you to change DHL's main colour from white to yellow – and then I'll put you on the car."

The room was stunned. This wasn't on the agenda. The board literally couldn't compute the suggestion. They said they'd consider it – but it was unlikely. Later that same day, Eddie got the call: "It's a Yes. We have agreed to change DHL to yellow."

Cool and calm, he replied, "Great. Thank you." Then he hung up the phone and roared with excitement, "Another robbery pulled off! Love it!"

The cherry on top? Eddie negotiated a royalty deal for "Jordan Yellow" – meaning DHL paid him for years, even after he sold the Formula 1 team.

"There's nothing sweeter," he liked to say, "than the bit you steal."

I was watching a football match with him on TV in 2024 when an ad came up for Coldplay's upcoming tour, with "Yellow" being the theme song as DHL were sponsoring the tour. He just looked at the advert and beamed.

That was Eddie.

Building the Culture Around the Character

As Eddie's presence grew, so did his influence. Drivers wanted to race for him. Engineers wanted to work for him. Sponsors wanted to be associated with the energy he brought.

He created a culture at Jordan Racing that mirrored his own vibe: bold, fast, creative, loyal, and a little bit wild. It wasn't just about lap times – it was about atmosphere. People smiled more at Jordan. They played music in the garage. They danced in the rain at Spa. They celebrated small wins like they were titles.

This environment bred loyalty. People worked harder for Eddie not because they were scared but because they *cared*. He made it personal. He asked about your kids. He remembered your birthday. He'd sit on the garage floor with you after a bad race and drink a beer.

At the same time, he demanded excellence. If you dropped the ball, you'd hear about it – loudly, colourfully, and immediately. And then it was done. Move on. You got a second chance. And a third. Because Eddie knew that the best people weren't perfect, they were human. And if you backed them long enough, they'd repay you with brilliance.

Ireland Rooted, Not Limited

Through all the chaos, colour, and international stages, Eddie Jordan remained unmistakably Irish. Not in a token way – in a lived, daily way. He brought Irish grit and mischief to every deal, every track, every city. He didn't just represent Ireland; he *embodied* it – the rhythm, the resilience, the irreverence. Even at the peak of running Jordan Formula 1, with millions on the line and teams scattered across the world, he rang his mother Eileen every morning at 8 a.m. on the dot. It wasn't ritual. It was respect. It was grounding. Eileen, like Eddie, had a fierce personality – witty, warm, and utterly unbothered by anyone's status. People who met them both said the same thing: the apple didn't fall far from the tree. And Eddie was proud of that. He would say, tongue-in-cheek with a huge grin, "She was hard . . . unlike me."

He stayed true to his roots – not out of obligation, but out of joy. He waved the Irish flag on global stages not to limit himself, but to lift the flag higher. He promoted Irish talent, gave Irish stories a global voice, and brought the nation's soul with him whether he was in Monaco, Melbourne, or Mumbai. But he was never confined by geography. He didn't let being Irish box him in – he used it as a launching pad. A rhythm. A swagger. A story that started in Bray but belonged to the world.

The Eddie Jordan Experience

Outside of racing, Eddie's life bled into music, media, and moments. One lane was never enough. He played the drums in bands, with Chris Rea, Bryan Adams, Texas, and Mike + The Mechanics. He had his own band, originally called V10, then upgraded to Eddie and The Robbers. He hosted events. He built a network that stretched from race circuits to rock concerts.

This cross-pollination made him more than a team boss. It made him a storyteller, a host, a connector. People came to him for more than deals; they came for energy and advice. For advice. For access to a world that felt more *alive* when Eddie was in it. He didn't hide his flaws. He swore too much, stayed out too late, trusted people too easily. But he owned those flaws with the same confidence he carried into every meeting. That vulnerability made him real. And in a world full of masks, that realness made him powerful.

By the time Jordan Grand Prix arrived on the Formula 1 grid in 1991, Eddie was already a legend in the paddock – and not just for his antics. He had built a team, a movement, and a message: be yourself, bet on people, and never apologize for either.

When he stepped out in Phoenix, Arizona, that day, he knew that he had achieved something nearly impossible, but it became just the first in a series of amazing milestones.

What began as a character trait had become a business weapon. Eddie brought personality – and then turned it into strategy.

"You can buy engines. You can buy data. But you can't buy chemistry. People either believe in you or they don't. I gave them someone to believe in."
– Eddie Jordan

3

Jordan Grand Prix –
The Impossible Startup

How a fearless outsider took on Formula 1
with charm, guts, and belief.

The Decision to Go Big

By the end of the 1980s, Eddie Jordan had built something real. His team had become a factory of future champions, a magnet for hungry talent, and a haven for gritty racers. Eddie Jordan Racing was respected – but that wasn't enough. Not for Eddie.

He wanted to go further. He wanted Formula 1.

It was a mad idea. Formula 1 was the Everest of motorsport – expensive, political, ruthless. Getting there required a level of funding, infrastructure, and influence that Eddie didn't have. But he had one thing that others didn't: *momentum.*

He looked around and saw an opening. The turbo era was winding down, and a new ruleset was making the sport more accessible. He sensed that with the right package – a decent engine, a nimble chassis, and a brave heart – it might just be possible to survive. To belong. To compete.

So, he jumped.

In 1990, Eddie announced that his team would enter the 1991 Formula 1 World Championship. The motorsport press laughed. The established teams sneered. People whispered behind his back: "He's got no money. No facilities. No experience at this level. No chance."

Eddie smiled – and got to work.

He said, "The only reason I started with Jordan Grand Prix was because I was unemployable elsewhere. So, the only person that would employ me was myself."

> *"Everyone told me I couldn't do it.*
> *That's how I knew I had to."*
> – Eddie Jordan

Building the Dream (with Duct Tape)

Jordan Grand Prix was born in Silverstone, in a modest industrial estate near the circuit. The team's early home was more warehouse than factory, more hopeful than high-tech. But it was filled with people who believed.

Eddie hired designer Gary Anderson to build the car – the Jordan 191. It would become one of the most beautiful and balanced Formula 1 cars ever made. Powered by a Ford HB V8 engine, the 191 wasn't about brute force, it was about flow. Elegance. Precision.

Eddie didn't have the budget to match McLaren or Williams,

but he knew how to hustle. He worked day and night securing sponsors, making promises, and rallying suppliers. His charisma was at full throttle. Meetings ended in handshakes. Doubts melted under the weight of his conviction.

He pulled in deals from Total, Goodyear, and 7UP – who agreed to become the title sponsor after a dazzling pitch. The livery that resulted – green, blue, and white – would become one of the most iconic colour schemes in Formula 1 history.

Mechanics slept on floors. Staff worked triple shifts. Every penny was stretched. But something rare was happening: a *real team* was forming. One built not just on contracts, but on belief.

When Jordan re-signed with Ford in 2003, Ford agreed to be contracted into giving Eddie a car of his choice. Once the ink was dry, Eddie said, "I will have a DB9 please, for my wife Marie." Ford owned Aston Martin at this stage, and replied that he could have any Ford, but that didn't extend to cars from other group-owned brands. There was some negotiation back and forth and, soon after, Marie picked up her DB9. Another robbery, as he would say.

A Star is Born – And so is the Storm

Jordan Grand Prix made its debut at the 1991 United States Grand Prix in Phoenix, Arizona. The world expected disaster. Instead, they saw competence, calm, and pace.

Andrea de Cesaris and Bertrand Gachot were the team's first drivers. Both were quick, both were edgy. The car – the Jordan 191 – turned heads with its smooth lines and nimble handling.

Points started coming in. Respect followed. It is still lauded as being one of the most beautiful cars in Formula 1 history.

Then came the twist.

In August 1991, when Bertrand Gachot was jailed for a pepper-spray incident with a taxi driver in London just days before the Belgian Grand Prix, Eddie moved fast. He brought in a little-known German rookie named Michael Schumacher. The 22-year-old stunned the paddock by qualifying seventh on his debut, having never raced at Spa. A clutch failure ended his race early, but his arrival lit up the sport. Within a week, he was gone – poached by Benetton. Eddie had found a star. And lost him just as quickly.

The Madness of Making It

Despite the Schumacher saga, Jordan finished fifth in the Constructors' Championship in its debut season – ahead of teams with double the budget and ten times the experience. It was one of the greatest rookie seasons in Formula 1 history.

But the chaos never stopped. Every season brought new challenges – budget crises, legal battles, crashes, technical upgrades, driver dramas. Yet Eddie never lost the joy. He kept the energy alive with jokes, dancing, wild interviews, and loud shirts.

He was never afraid to speak his mind. He took jabs at Fédération Internationale de l'Automobile (FIA) decisions. He mocked rival teams. He defended his drivers fiercely. He wasn't trying to fit in, he was trying to shake things up.

Eddie's office became a shrine to madness: drums, trophies,

crazy artwork, and half-empty wine bottles. Deals were done on the phone, in pubs, on flights. Loyalty was the currency. Fun was the atmosphere.

He didn't merely survive in Formula 1 – he *thrived* in his own way.

What Jordan GP Really Meant

Jordan Grand Prix was more than a team – it was a way of life.

It said: You don't need to be born into power to win. It said: You can build something meaningful with heart, humour, and hustle. It said: Be yourself – loudly and the right people will find you.

Through the 1990s, Jordan GP became a fan favourite. It was because of the spirit – not just the cars, results, or drivers. Because Eddie had done the impossible. He had taken a wild idea, built it with charisma and chaos, and carved out a permanent place in the most elite racing series on Earth.

And somehow, through all the madness, he was still smiling.

4

Culture Over Control

*How Eddie Jordan led from the heart,
not from a handbook.*

A Team That Felt Like a Band

In the sharp, competitive, money-soaked world of Formula 1, most teams functioned like corporations. They had layers of management, strict codes of conduct, and a hard line between drivers, engineers, and executives. Jordan Grand Prix was nothing like that. It was closer to a band on tour – loud, emotional, fiercely loyal, and forever improvising.

From the very beginning, Eddie made it clear that culture mattered more than protocol. He didn't lead through control, he led through connection. He wanted to build a team that laughed together, partied together, bled together, and occasionally broke things together – but never turned on each other.

He knew that when people feel safe, they take risks. And when they take risks, great things happen.

At the heart of it all was a simple rule: do what works. If it made the car faster, do it. If it didn't, don't. That guiding instinct ran through every part of the operation – from design choices to race strategy to who they brought into the garage. No long memos. No bureaucracy. Just clarity, speed, and trust.

The Power of Permission

One of Eddie's greatest leadership gifts was *permission.* He gave people room to be bold. A junior engineer could pitch a wild idea. A mechanic could redesign a workflow. A driver could speak his mind.

This created a culture of initiative. People didn't wait to be told what to do – they *wanted* to contribute. They felt seen, trusted, and important. That trust ran deep. It wasn't something you earned through titles, you earned it through effort and honesty.

Eddie didn't care about formalities. He cared about intent.

The Fun Was the Fuel

At Jordan, fun wasn't a reward, it was the engine. There were garage singalongs, beer after victories, nicknames, pranks, and dancing. It wasn't childish – it was *human.* Eddie believed that joy produced better work than fear ever could.

There were moments when the team would lose – badly. A crash. A retirement. A blown strategy. But Eddie never exploded. He'd deliver a truth bomb, sure. But then he'd laugh, slap your shoulder, and say, "Right, now fix it and let's have a pint."

That kind of leadership created resilience. People didn't hide from mistakes. They fixed them. Fast. Together.

Loyalty is a Two-Way Street

People stayed at Jordan longer than they had to. Drivers returned. Engineers stuck around. Even when they could have chased higher salaries elsewhere, many stayed for one reason: *Eddie had their back.*

He defended his people. In public and private. He didn't throw anyone under the bus. If someone failed, he took the hit too. And when someone succeeded, he gave them the spotlight.

That kind of loyalty wasn't manufactured, it was earned. And in a cut-throat sport, it made Jordan Grand Prix feel like a home.

Chaos and Chemistry

It wasn't always perfect. There were flare-ups. Mistakes. Party hangovers that bled into race prep. But that was the cost of real culture. It was messy, human, and alive. Eddie knew you could control a team into mediocrity; or let them breathe their way into greatness. He chose the latter. Jordan Grand Prix was never the richest, never the most polished – but it was often the most alive.

*"You can lead with fear, or you
can lead with fun. I chose fun."*
– Eddie Jordan

5

Eddie the Mentor (Talent, Loyalty, Mischief)

How Eddie Jordan found greatness in the raw and the rough, and backed it like no one else.

Seeing What Others Missed

In a sport defined by data, speed, and polish, Eddie Jordan trusted something different – instinct. He could walk into a pit lane and, within minutes, identify a kid with something special. It wasn't only about the stopwatch – it was about the story. It was about how they carried themselves. How they listened. How they grinned. How they didn't flinch.

Eddie wasn't looking for perfect drivers, he was looking for *unfinished stories*. He was looking for youthful hope with talent yet to be refined, polished, nurtured, and mentored. People with rawness and hunger, not yet dulled by politics or corporate polish. He knew that greatness often came disguised – rough round the edges, with no PR team and a second-hand helmet. But Eddie could see through all that. He saw the *spark*.

Michael Schumacher was just 22 when Eddie gave him a chance at Spa in 1991. One test session, that's all it took. "He had that look," Eddie would later say. "That quiet menace. You just *knew*." Schumacher's seventh place qualifying stunned the paddock. It cemented Eddie's reputation as a talent spotter with unmatched instinct.

Damon Hill was already in Formula 1 with Brabham, but was struggling to break through in a meaningful way. Eddie saw something deeper: maturity, discipline, and a will to grow. Though he didn't give Damon his first drive, Eddie gave him belief – and eventually a platform to be seen. That belief stayed with Damon all the way to his world title.

Then there was Ayrton Senna. Before he was the icon, he was a young Brazilian sensation in need of a seat. Eddie saw magic in him. He watched Senna test for Jordan and was transfixed – not only by the pace, but by the focus, the hunger. "He looked like he belonged in the car more than anywhere else on Earth," Eddie said.

Eddie Irvine had the flash. The attitude. The rawness. Martin Brundle had the smarts and grit. Rubens Barrichello had heart and humility. Giancarlo Fisichella had a rare balance of fire and finesse. In every case, Eddie didn't only see a driver – he saw *a journey*, and he helped launch it.

Eddie didn't rely on consensus. He didn't need ten data points or a scouting committee. He had a gut instinct sharpened by years in the trenches – in the garage, at the bar, in the race truck. And when he believed in someone, he didn't hesitate.

He gave chances no one else would. He pushed people to believe in themselves before they had results. He didn't wait for them to be ready, he *made* them ready.

He trusted talent before the world saw it. He believed that the best leaders surround themselves with go-getters and do-ers – the kind of people who didn't wait to be asked, they just got on with it.

"You are the sum of the people closest to you," he'd often say. "So choose well."

And when it came to hiring, he was crystal clear: Hire people smarter than you – then get out of their way. No micromanaging. (he may have struggled with this sometimes . . .). No ego. Just space, belief, and a clear runway to perform.

That's what made his teams work – in racing, in business, and in boats. He backed the person, gave them room, and trusted them to deliver. And they almost always did.

And that's the kind of mentor who changes lives.

"You don't wait for the world to notice talent. You notice it. You back it and then make the world notice."
        – Eddie Jordan

Loyalty First, Always

In the high-stakes world of Formula 1, loyalty can be scarce. But with Eddie Jordan, it was non-negotiable. Loyalty wasn't just a leadership quality – it was his operating system. If you earned Eddie's trust, you had it for life.

That trust went both ways. He stuck by his drivers during difficult spells, whether they were nursing a broken car or a broken confidence. When Rubens Barrichello endured a run of bad luck and setbacks, Eddie didn't bench him or spread blame.

He backed him, publicly and privately, and gave him the emotional runway to rebuild.

For Eddie, loyalty wasn't measured by podiums – it was measured by presence. He showed up for people. If a driver's family was unwell, he sent support. If a mechanic's morale was low, he'd share a pint and a story. He made himself available, human, real.

Long after drivers moved on to bigger teams or retired, they kept in touch with Eddie. Many credited him with more than career starts – he shaped who they became. His belief in them lingered, long after the helmets were hung up. They still looked to him like an Elder of the sport.

This loyalty extended beyond racing. Eddie mentored young entrepreneurs, musicians, and engineers with the same dedication. He offered guidance, introductions, and encouragement, not because it was strategic but because it was *right*.

He maintained friendships and offered advice without conditions. When people hit rock bottom – financially, emotionally, professionally – Eddie didn't disappear. He picked up the phone. He opened doors. He reminded them who they were.

He believed that loyalty, like belief, must be unconditional to be real. It's what made his teams feel like families. And it's what made him more than a boss.

He was *Eddie*. And once you were in his circle, you were in for life. He used the phrase "bangle". You were strapped to his wrist like a bangle.

> *"I don't care how fast you are if I can't trust you.*
> *But if I can trust you, I'll back you 100 per cent."*
> – **Eddie Jordan**

Mischief as Mentorship

Eddie Jordan never gave a motivational seminar. He didn't believe in PowerPoints or personality tests. His mentorship came with a wink, a jab, a joke – and more wisdom than you could fit in any training manual. He led with mischief. And somehow, it worked. He made you feel like anything was possible and you could play the biggest part.

For Eddie, levity was a leadership tool. He instinctively knew when someone was wound too tight, drowning in expectation or doubt. He'd defuse it with humour, often aimed at himself. "Look at me," he'd say, pointing at his untamed hair and louder-than-life shirt. "You think *you* feel pressure? I've got sponsors to entertain and socks older than you."

He'd throw in pranks – harmless ones – just to remind his crew and drivers that they were human. He believed laughter sharpened focus, not distracted from it. When the mood in the garage got too heavy, Eddie would burst in with a drumstick from a takeaway chicken joint and use it as a pretend radio mic. "Right, lads, who's about to make history today?"

He'd rib his drivers before lights out. "Try not to hit anything, but if you do, do it with flair." With journalists, he spun answers into punchlines. But underneath the charm was a deep message: don't take yourself too seriously – take the *work* seriously.

And when someone really screwed up? Eddie rarely yelled. He'd pause, throw a look, maybe raise a brow, and drop a one-liner that said it all: "If you were any slower, we'd have to change the sport to fishing." The message landed, without shame or resentment.

His mischief was medicine. It kept spirits high. It made tough days manageable. It reminded everyone that this wild, beautiful, unforgiving sport was still *meant to be fun*.

And for those lucky enough to be mentored by Eddie Jordan, that fun became fuel – for confidence, for connection, and for courage. He believed in you and communicated his conviction to your capability, so that you couldn't not feel like you could take on the world.

> *"Everyone knew the rules and I drove people hard.*
> *We worked hard and we played hard."*
> – Eddie Jordan

Mistakes Were Welcome

Eddie Jordan didn't fear mistakes, he welcomed them. In his world, failure wasn't a sign of weakness – it was proof that someone was *trying*. And trying, in high-pressure motorsport, was often the difference between mediocrity and mastery.

He created an environment where people weren't paralysed by perfection. Mechanics could try new solutions. Engineers could pitch untested ideas. Drivers knew they could take a risky line – not to be reckless, but to grow. As long as the intention was bold and the commitment total, Eddie had their back.

When things went wrong – and they often did – Eddie's response was rarely fury. He leaned in with questions: "What went wrong? What do we learn? What do we do next?"

He knew that overreacting to mistakes made teams freeze.

Innovation would stop. Risk-taking would vanish. Instead, he turned errors into a culture of *iteration* – try, fail, learn, adapt. Repeat.

One young engineer recalled burning out a crucial electronic component during testing. "I thought I was done," he said. "I'd cost the team time and money. But Eddie just looked at me and said, 'That's what happens when you try something new. Now make it better.' And I did."

For Eddie, mistakes were data. Feedback. A necessary chapter in the story of progress. He was allergic to blame culture. If someone screwed up out of laziness or ego, sure – they got a talking-to. But if they failed trying to win? That was different.

This philosophy shaped his entire leadership ethos: trust the people, support their growth, and let them earn confidence the hard way.

He believed that brilliance wasn't born fully formed. It was shaped through failure – raw, painful, messy – and then forged into strength.

That's what made him a mentor.

Not because he had all the answers.

But because he let you find yours.

> *"If you're not making mistakes, you're not pushing hard enough. We're not here to be cautious – we're here to be great. Winning takes finding an edge. That takes courage and risk."*
> – **Eddie Jordan**

Beyond the Track

Eddie Jordan's impact didn't stop at the chequered flag. While the world knew him as a race team boss, those closest to him understood something deeper: Eddie mentored people well beyond racing – in business, music, media, and even sailing. Wherever there was passion, energy, or creativity, Eddie saw opportunity. Not for profit, but for *people*.

In the business world, Eddie quietly advised founders, startups, and investors, often over a lunch or a drink. He didn't drown them in spreadsheets, he challenged their mindset. "Back yourself first," he'd say. "No one else will until you do." Entrepreneurs left conversations with Eddie with ideas and with *fire*.

That fire extended into major business moves too. In 2022, Eddie partnered with friend Keith O'Loughlin in a bid to take over Playtech – one of the world's largest gambling technology firms – with a bid of over £3 billion. The bid was bold, strategic, and disruptive, reflecting Eddie's trademark willingness to challenge the status quo. Though the bid ultimately didn't succeed, it showed that Eddie was still hungry to lead at the highest level – and still believed in betting on vision, not only valuation.

Eddie also passed the entrepreneurial spirit onto his family. In 2025, he partnered with his son Kyle and businessman Daniel McKeown in a bid to take over the London Irish rugby club. The goal was to restore the club's fortunes through fresh energy, commercial nous, and cultural leadership. While the outcome was still in the balance, the move reflected Eddie's lifelong belief in backing underdogs, building community, and taking brave swings – especially when family is involved.

Musicians, too, found a champion in him. He helped young bands with exposure, funding, or just the belief to keep going. As a drummer himself, Eddie understood that rhythm was more than sound – it was *connection*. He hosted jam sessions, shared stages, and gave artists the courage to perform their truth. For Eddie, a garage band had the same spirit as a pit crew – raw, united, and alive.

One of the most enduring and personal examples of Eddie Jordan's mentorship came in the form of a young street musician named Luca. Eddie first encountered Luca busking on the streets of Dublin when he was still a young man himself – long before the fame, the TV lights, or the Formula 1 grid. Something about Luca's raw talent, the way he played guitar with soul and passion, resonated deeply with Eddie. He mentored and played music with Luca for decades. Over the years, they performed together at events, parties, and stages around the world – a symbol of Eddie's belief that friendship and music, like racing, are built on rhythm, respect, and trust.

He mentored presenters and journalists in the broadcast world. Many who came through the BBC and Channel 4 paddocks credit Eddie for helping them find their voice. His advice? "Don't just talk about the sport – *feel* it. Then let the audience feel you."

And in sailing, Eddie found a new kind of racing – one defined not by laps, but by wind, water, instinct, and trust. He supported sailors emotionally and creatively, treating oceanic navigation with the same reverence as track strategy. To him, both were tests of nerve and character.

What united all these areas was Eddie's relentless *curiosity*. He didn't care what field someone worked in, he cared whether they gave a damn. Whether they were bold. Whether they needed someone in their corner.

Eddie was that someone.

His mentorship wasn't formal, it was personal. He picked up the phone. He sent a text. He showed up. And in doing so, he reminded people of what they were capable of – not with applause, but with *belief.*

"Talent is talent – whether it's behind a wheel, a drum kit, or a boardroom desk. You just have to give oxygen."
– Eddie Jordan

"Formula 1 drivers are selfish. They only care about themselves. I'm ok with that. They have to be that way – otherwise, they don't have the edge to win."
– Eddie Jordan

The Schumacher Bet

In the summer of 1991, Formula 1 was buzzing with anticipation and uncertainty. That's when Eddie Jordan made the boldest call of his career – and one that would change the face of motorsport forever.

When Bertrand Gachot, one of Jordan Grand Prix's two drivers, was abruptly jailed, it left Eddie in a crisis: the Belgian Grand Prix at Spa-Francorchamps was just days away, and he needed a replacement. Fast.

Enter Michael Schumacher.

Eddie the Mentor (Talent, Loyalty, Mischief)

Schumacher had never raced in Formula 1. He had only a brief test under his belt – one outing for Jordan at Silverstone. But Eddie had seen something special. Word had reached him through Mercedes insiders, and the test confirmed what instinct had already told him: the kid was electric. Fast. Calm. Composed. Almost eerie in his focus.

Michael told Eddie he knew the Spa circuit well – but in truth, he'd only ever cycled around it. The bluffer got bluffed. Then he went out and qualified seventh on debut, ahead of world champions and seasoned veterans. The paddock was stunned. A clutch failure ended his race before the first lap, but the message was clear: a generational talent had arrived.

Eddie had found him. And then – just as quickly – he lost him. What stung most wasn't the speed – it was the speed of betrayal. Eddie believed he had the young German secured under a watertight agreement. But behind the scenes, Schumacher's management – led by Willi Weber and supported by Mercedes – were already manoeuvring. In a crucial document, the wording had been quietly altered from "the contract" to "a contract" – a subtle shift that turned an exclusive deal into a loophole. Just enough for Benetton to make their move.

By the time Eddie realized what had happened, it was too late. No formal breach. No grounds to block the switch. Just a brutal lesson in how sharp Formula 1 politics could cut.

Eddie was furious. Betrayed. And aware that he'd just lit a fuse that would reshape the sport. As he stood reeling, Ron Dennis offered a quiet, pointed statement:

"Welcome to the Piranha Club."

It was a lesson learned – painfully, but permanently. Classic

Eddie: bold, instinctive, courageous. But that day, he got out-bluffed. And he never forgot it.

After the legal dust-up over Schumacher, Bernie Ecclestone pulled him aside. Bernie had stolen Michael from Eddie – and wanted to make it right. Eddie needed money, so Bernie made sure he got paid as part of the deal. And that was that. Everyone moved on.

It wasn't warm, but it was wise. A veteran's reminder that in Formula 1, winning the war often means walking away from the battle.

It hurt. Deeply. Eddie had taken the risk. He had opened the door. And he watched someone else walk through it. It stung not merely financially or politically – it stung personally. But Eddie never let bitterness define the story.

Over the years, despite the drama of that early departure, Eddie and Michael maintained a mutual respect. Schumacher never forgot who gave him his first real chance. In interviews and biographies, he credited Eddie for seeing something in him others hadn't – and for giving him a stage at the perfect time.

The "Schumacher Bet" was more than talent spotting – it was a way of life. It was about Eddie's ethos: trust your gut, act fast, and give people the moment that can change everything. Take the risk before it's obvious. Do what others are afraid to.

Even though he didn't get to keep Schumacher, Eddie's legend as a talent spotter was sealed. In that moment, in that bet, the world saw exactly what made Eddie Jordan special.

> *"One lap. That's all it took. He had that look – the stillness, the steel. I knew he was going to be great."*
> – **Eddie Jordan**

Ayrton Senna –
The Spark That Lit the Fire

Before Formula 1. Before Monaco glories, world championships, and the reverent whispers of "the greatest ever". Before all that, there was just Ayrton – a quiet, intense, wildly gifted young man from São Paulo, Brazil, who landed in England with a helmet, a purpose, and a presence that couldn't be ignored.

Eddie Jordan met him before the world did.

It was 1983 when Ayrton Senna arrived in the UK's fiercely competitive British Formula 3 series, and it was Eddie Jordan Racing that gave him one of his earliest drives. Senna had already gained a reputation from karting and Formula Ford, but he wasn't yet a household name. That would come later. What mattered in that moment was what Eddie saw – or *felt* – in him.

Eddie didn't just see speed, he saw *focus*. A strange kind of stillness. The type of intense concentration that separates the truly great from the merely good. "He didn't walk into a garage," Eddie said. "He entered it like it was a cockpit. Like he was already part of the machinery. Even at that age, he carried himself like destiny was on a stopwatch."

Senna was different. Methodical. Spiritual. Relentless. He treated driving as a craft – almost a form of prayer. Mechanics would whisper that he could *feel* grip before the car told him. Engineers were stunned by his feedback. Rivals respected him, but didn't understand him. There was something mythic, even then.

And Eddie – a man who trusted his gut more than anyone else's spreadsheets – gave him the space he needed. He didn't over-coach or micromanage, he let Senna race. Let him discover his edges. Let him lead with instinct.

It paid off. Senna dominated the British Formula 3 Championship, delivering stunning drives in difficult conditions. His control in the wet was already legendary, and his qualifying pace was telepathic. Eddie's team gave him the chassis and freedom; Senna gave them victory – and validation.

Their relationship wasn't built on long conversations – Senna wasn't chatty – but there was deep mutual respect. Eddie never tried to tame the tiger – just let him roam, trusted him fully, and made sure the team revolved around delivering performance for this young prodigy.

And then, as Eddie always knew he would, Senna left. First to Toleman. Then to Lotus. Then to McLaren, where he would duel Prost and win titles. Eventually to Williams, where tragedy would strike. But no matter how high he soared, Ayrton never forgot where the platform first stood.

In several interviews, Senna referenced Eddie Jordan as one of the few who "just got it" – who understood him as both a driver and a person when few did. "He let me be who I was," Senna said. "He didn't ask me to smile or sell. He just let me *drive*."

Eddie never claimed credit for Senna's rise. But he was proud – proud to have played a part in the journey of someone who would redefine greatness. "Ayrton made every lap feel like a life lesson," Eddie once said. "And when he was in the car, he wasn't trying to win – he was trying to find something *beyond* the win."

When Senna was tragically killed at Imola in 1994, Eddie felt the loss deeply. It hit him hard. He felt lucky to have witnessed such a divine spark – and watched it burn, then vanish, too soon.

In the years that followed, Eddie often referenced Senna when discussing young drivers. "If I see even a flicker of that kind of intensity," he'd say, "I pay attention. You don't ignore that. Ever."

Senna wasn't just one of Eddie's drivers. He was the ignition point – the first great fire that taught Eddie how to see what others missed, how to believe before there was proof, and how to *feel* greatness long before the world did.

> *"Ayrton was different. He didn't just want to win –*
> *he wanted to transcend. And even as a young man,*
> *you could feel it."*
> – Eddie Jordan

> *"I was lucky enough in 1983 finding a guy called da Silva.*
> *_Gave him his first drive in Silverstone in a Formula 3*
> *car. Then with Dickey Bennetts and myself, and Martin*
> *Brundle as well, and Roberto Guerrero, we went to*
> *Macau in '83 and this guy, da Silva, won the race, and*
> *he changed his name to Senna. He was electric from the*
> *start – calm, focused, almost mythical in how he con-*
> *nected with the car. That was the spark that lit it all."*
> – Eddie Jordan

Damon Hill –
From Overlooked to World Champion

Some talents burn bright from day one. Others take longer to spark. Damon Hill was one of the latter – a man whose legacy was shaped not by inherited glory, but by grit, patience, and the belief of mentors like Eddie Jordan.

As the son of double world champion Graham Hill, Damon was born into the paddock. But lineage only takes you so far. By the time Damon was carving his own path, he was already considered a late bloomer in the racing world. Many teams overlooked him. He lacked the brash confidence of youth. He didn't arrive with a suitcase full of sponsor money. He didn't set the junior categories on fire.

But Eddie saw something deeper: maturity, discipline, and an undercurrent of strength forged through adversity.

When Hill tested with Jordan, Eddie wasn't watching the stopwatch – he was watching the man. Damon asked smart questions. He debriefed with clarity. He treated mechanics with respect and absorbed data like a sponge. More than that, he radiated quiet hunger – the kind that doesn't shout, but endures.

Eddie gave him time, space, and trust. He introduced Hill to circles where he'd be seen for his potential, not only his surname. Even when Hill moved beyond Jordan's immediate reach, the mentorship stayed. Eddie continued to speak up for him, to champion him in a sport that often prizes flash over substance.

In 1996, Damon Hill became Formula 1 world champion with Williams – a moment that was about more than a trophy. It was validation for every doubter who thought he wasn't "the real deal". For Eddie, it was a triumph of belief.

"Damon taught the paddock a lesson," Eddie later said. "That humility and brains can beat arrogance and noise. That quiet people can roar too."

Their friendship continued off the track. Damon often credited

Eddie with helping him navigate the politics of Formula 1 and for reminding him, during dark moments, that legacy isn't something you inherit, it's something you *earn*.

For Eddie Jordan, backing Damon wasn't about pedigree. It was about principle. It was about spotting a man who had the heart to fight, the mind to learn, and the strength to outlast.

And as it turned out, that was exactly what a world champion needed.

> *"Everyone was busy comparing Damon to his father. I was watching Damon become his own man. And that man was a champion."*
> – Eddie Jordan

Eddie Irvine – Swagger and Speed

If Damon Hill was the gentleman racer, Eddie Irvine was the rockstar. Sharp-tongued, self-assured, and always dressed to stand out, Irvine was never short on confidence – or talent. And Eddie Jordan loved him for it.

Eddie first spotted Irvine's potential in Formula 3000. While some were put off by his cocky charm, Eddie recognized something else: composure under pressure and pure race craft. He wasn't trying to impress anyone – he was trying to win.

When Irvine joined Jordan in 1993, he brought energy, edge, and a flair for the unpredictable. He made headlines, on and off the track. In his very first Formula 1 race in Japan, he scored a point – and managed to enrage Ayrton Senna in the process by unlapping himself against the triple world champion. It was bold, maybe reckless. But it was pure Irvine.

Eddie defended him. He always did. Because he understood that behind the bravado was a razor-sharp mind and relentless determination. Irvine knew what he wanted, and Eddie respected that. He let him be himself – wild when needed, focused when it mattered.

Their partnership was never dull. Press conferences with the two were masterclasses in wit and provocation. Eddie once joked, "With Irvine, you get a driver, a fashion model, and a scandal magnet – all for the price of one."

But Eddie also knew that Irvine had the goods. When Ferrari came calling, Eddie didn't block the move – he helped it happen. He understood that mentorship meant opening doors, not holding people back.

Irvine would go on to finish runner-up in the 1999 World Championship with Ferrari, proving that Eddie's faith had always been well placed. Their relationship remained strong long after the racing stopped.

In many ways, Irvine was the perfect Jordan driver: unapologetic, fast, full of personality, and completely unwilling to conform.

And that's exactly why Eddie believed in him.

> *"Eddie Irvine was a handful – and I wouldn't have had him any other way. He was the chaos we needed, and the courage we admired."*
> – Eddie Jordan

Martin Brundle –
Racer Turned Commentator

If ever there was a driver who embodied grit, versatility, and intellect, it was Martin Brundle. Eddie Jordan had long respected Martin – not just for his skill behind the wheel, but for his enduring presence in the sport, his adaptability, and his sharp racing mind.

Brundle was a fierce competitor in British Formula 3, going toe-to-toe with Ayrton Senna in what many consider one of the greatest junior championship battles. Eddie saw close-up the steel that made Brundle stand out – his never-give-in attitude and sheer race craft. He may not have had the best machinery but always extracted the most from what he was given.

While Brundle's Formula 1 career didn't deliver the victories his talent deserved, Eddie saw him as world-class. His work ethic, professionalism, and ability to galvanize a team made him the kind of driver every boss wanted – especially one like Eddie, who valued character as much as lap times.

Their paths crossed many times – on track, in commentary boxes, and behind the scenes in team negotiations. Eddie admired how Brundle evolved after driving, becoming a trusted voice of the sport. His insight, humour, and candour won him global respect – and Eddie remained one of his biggest supporters.

Martin often credited Eddie for being one of the few who never let politics dilute passion: "Eddie was always straight with me. He had mischief in his heart, but fairness in his actions. That mattered."

To Eddie, Brundle represented a breed who raced for the love of it, analyzed it for the truth in it, and told its story with integrity. He was more than a great driver. He was – and still is – a great ambassador of the sport.

Martin: "Eddie, why are your cars so fast this weekend?"

Eddie: "Because, Martin, maybe you're not driving them anymore, I suppose."

Martin: "Thank you, mate, thank you very much – you've been saving that up for a long time!"

Giancarlo Fisichella – Loyalty in Every Lap

If ever there was a driver who embodied understated excellence, it was Giancarlo Fisichella. Talented, consistent, and incredibly loyal, Fisichella became one of the most trusted and respected drivers to ever race for Eddie Jordan.

He made his Formula 1 debut with the Jordan team in 1997 and immediately impressed with his poise and pace. While other rookies might crumble under the spotlight, Fisichella seemed born for it. He had a smooth, flowing style – less aggressive than some, but no less effective.

Eddie admired Fisi's technical precision and his calm head under pressure. But more than that, he valued his quiet loyalty. Fisichella was never one to play politics or chase headlines. He turned up, did the work, and delivered performances that often outpaced the car beneath him.

In a time when drivers often bounced between teams in search of better deals, Giancarlo remained deeply respectful of the chance Eddie had given him. Even after moving on to teams like Benetton and Renault, where he would become a race winner, he always spoke warmly of his time with Jordan.

Perhaps Fisi's most iconic moment in yellow came in Brazil, 2003. Driving once again for Jordan, he took the lead in a chaotic, rain-soaked Grand Prix. The win wasn't initially awarded to him due to a timing confusion, but days later, it was rightly handed back. Jordan and Fisichella had done it – a fairytale win.

The image of Fisi, tears in his eyes as he stood on the podium with Eddie, is one of the sport's most emotional moments. Two men, bonded by belief and persistence, finally getting their shared reward.

> *"Fisi never shouted for attention. He just delivered. He gave everything – and that win in Brazil proved it. He earned it the hard way, the right way."*
> – Eddie Jordan

Ralf Schumacher – The Next Chapter in the Family Legacy

When Ralf Schumacher joined Jordan Grand Prix in 1997, he did so carrying a heavy name and high expectations. As the younger brother of Michael Schumacher, the comparisons were inevitable and relentless. But Eddie Jordan never saw Ralf as a shadow of anyone – he saw him as a talent in his own right, with sharp instincts and a will to write his own story.

Eddie gave Ralf the room to grow. He understood that pressure can crush potential if not handled with care. Ralf responded with impressive performances, including a podium in just his third race in Argentina. He showed confidence, speed, and a deep desire to forge his own identity.

There was, however, one painful moment – Spa-Francorchamps in 1998. Ralf was chasing victory when the team issued orders not to overtake his teammate Damon Hill, securing a famous 1–2 for Jordan's first-ever Formula 1 win. Ralf obeyed, but it hurt. He believed he had the pace to win, and the moment left a scar. Despite the disappointment, the respect between Ralf and Eddie remained unshaken.

Off the track, Eddie and Ralf developed a genuine friendship. They spent time together in Monaco and Cape Town, and Eddie became an enthusiastic backer of Ralf's post-racing passion project – Schumacher Wines. Ralf owns an expansive vineyard in Slovenia, producing some truly excellent wines. Whether entertaining guests on his boat or hosting one of his famously wild parties, Eddie always made sure Schumacher's bottles were front and centre.

To Eddie, Ralf wasn't just a driver – he was a friend, a thinker, and a man determined to live his own truth in a world that too often demanded comparison.

> *"Managing Ralf was a full-time job in itself –*
> *but when it clicked, he was seriously fast.*
> *He had all the talent."*
> – Eddie Jordan

Jean Alesi –
Fire, Passion, and Loyalty

Jean Alesi was the embodiment of raw Mediterranean spirit – emotional, expressive, and utterly fearless. When he and Eddie Jordan worked together in Formula 3000 in 1989, the chemistry was immediate. Jean drove with instinct and fire, and he didn't just compete – he won. He took the 1989 Formula 3000 Championship under Eddie's banner, a victory that sealed his reputation as one of the brightest emerging stars in European motorsport.

Their bond deepened off the track too. Alesi even stayed with the Jordan family as a lodger during those early years – a living arrangement that brought trust, warmth, and plenty of laughter into the household. Jean became part of the family long before he became a household name.

Though their paths diverged in Formula 1, they would reunite over a decade later when Alesi drove for Jordan Grand Prix in the 2001 season. It was a full-circle moment – a nod to loyalty, friendship, and a shared history. Even if the results didn't reflect their earlier glory, the partnership meant something profound to both men.

Eddie often said that if you gave Jean a car with even a sniff of performance, he'd give you every ounce of his soul in return. In a sport that often polishes off the edges, Alesi stayed raw. And Eddie loved that.

Their friendship endured for decades. Every year, without fail, Jean would send Eddie wine from his vineyard – a small but heartfelt reminder of the deep bond they shared, forged in fire and friendship.

"Jean raced with his heart. That's why fans loved
him. That's why I did too."
– Eddie Jordan

Mentoring the Unsung Heroes –
Engineers, Mechanics, and the Quiet Stars

Behind every Jordan car that made it to the grid – and every surprise victory that lit up the paddock – was a team of unsung heroes: engineers, mechanics, designers, truck drivers, data analysts, kitchen staff, and admin teams who made the impossible possible. Eddie Jordan didn't see them as background figures, he saw them as the foundation.

One name that stands out is Andy Stevenson, Jordan's longtime team manager and later, sporting director. Stevenson became the steady hand, guiding the ship through countless storms, and Eddie often credited him with holding the team together through highs and lows. There was also Gary Anderson, the genius behind many of Jordan's best cars – a man whose technical brain was matched by his calm, candid demeanour. Dr Ian Thompson, the team doctor and trusted voice of reason, was another crucial figure behind the scenes. Then there was the tireless energy of press officer and media fixer Mark Gallagher, whose sharp wit and commitment to storytelling gave Jordan a voice off-track as distinctive as its cars.

In an industry where drivers and CEOs hog the spotlight, Eddie made sure the spotlight rotated. He walked through the garage with a personal greeting for every engineer, a story for every mechanic, and often a joke or a jab to lift the spirits of the youngest crew members. He paid attention. He noticed when someone hadn't been themselves or when someone had gone the extra mile, even if it meant getting grease on their suit or bloodied knuckles from a stubborn bolt.

Eddie's garage was a workshop of ideas, where hierarchy bent to innovation and job titles came second to contribution. He gave interns opportunities usually reserved for senior staff, pushed engineers to pitch directly into strategy discussions, and rewarded boldness even when it wasn't perfect. If someone made a mistake, Eddie didn't humiliate them – he turned it into a teaching moment.

He built the Jordan team like a band of rebels with a cause. People came to Jordan for more than a job, they wanted to be part of something bigger – a culture of belief, belonging, and boldness. Engineers could debate drivers. Admin staff could suggest tweaks to the workflow. Hospitality crew became emotional anchors during gruelling triple-headers. Everyone mattered.

There are now championship-winning team principals, legendary designers, and senior Formula 1 executives who began life in the yellow of Jordan. People who shaped the modern sport with the lessons they learned in Eddie's camp. They took with them the spirit of camaraderie and creative risk that made Jordan Grand Prix more than a team – it was a launchpad.

At post-race debriefs, Eddie would sometimes invite the garage crew to speak first. He celebrated mechanics on team radio. He sent flowers to partners who sacrificed weekends and holidays to let their loved ones chase motorsport dreams. And every

Christmas, he'd raise a toast not to results, but to resilience – to the unseen warriors who made the impossible feel inevitable.

When Jordan left the grid, it wasn't merely the end of a team – it marked the end of a people-first era. But its echoes remain in the paddock – in the humour of engineers, in the courage of race strategists, and in the values of every former Jordan team member.

Eddie's gift was vision – for speed and for soul. And his greatest legacy might just be the countless men and women who walk the paddock with pride, because once upon a time, Eddie Jordan believed in them.

> *"Behind every great driver is a dozen unsung heroes. And I wanted those heroes to feel like champions too."*
> – Eddie Jordan

> *"Eddie Jordan used to say I was only still there because no one else would f**king have me: Formula 1 mechanic set for 600th straight race."*
> – Andy Stevenson

Giving Media Voices a Platform

In a world where every driver wants the spotlight, Eddie Jordan made sure the spotlight also shone on the people telling the stories – the journalists, broadcasters, photographers, documentary makers, and digital storytellers who captured the heart of Formula 1.

Eddie understood early on that sport is only half spectacle – the rest is storytelling. He knew that if no one tells the tale, the magic fades. So, he took a proactive role in mentoring voices in the media. Whether it was a rookie Formula 1 journalist awkwardly holding a mic for the first time in the pit lane or a nervous PR assistant trying to keep a press conference together, Eddie offered encouragement, advice, and (more often than not) a great quote.

He believed the media mattered. It was more than to promote the team, it was to build the allure of motorsport. He made time for interviews. He helped translate complex race strategies into thrilling narratives. And when a journalist was bold enough to ask a difficult question, Eddie respected it – even if he didn't always answer directly.

He gave early opportunities to people who would later become household names. The likes of Louise Goodman, who worked with Jordan before becoming a popular face on ITV's Formula 1 coverage, and Mark Gallagher, whose role in media and communications grew into a respected career as a speaker and author. Eddie also championed the voices of broadcasters such as James Allen and Tom Clarkson, not because they flattered him, but because they were good at their craft.

He opened doors at Jordan for documentary crews and photographers when other teams shut them out. The result was that Jordan became the most media-friendly and, arguably, the most charismatic team on the grid – not just because of Eddie's antics, but because everyone had access to the behind-the-scenes truth.

He once told a young intern, "Tell it straight, but make it sing. If you do that, people will care."

Media professionals from Sky Sports to BBC Sport still credit Eddie Jordan with helping them gain access, confidence, and momentum at critical early stages in their careers. He even encouraged the humorous, offbeat angles – understanding that personality and perspective created fans beyond hardcore racing aficionados.

Eddie Jordan, Jake Humphrey, and David Coulthard were the irrepressible trio who redefined Formula 1 broadcasting for a new generation. With Eddie's mischief, Jake's polish, and David's sharp insight, they brought edge, humour, and heart to every race weekend. Together, they weren't just pundits – they were the three amigos who made Formula 1 feel like family.

At a time when Formula 1 was becoming more corporate, Eddie's open-door policy let the culture breathe. Fans weren't just shown results – they were invited inside. They saw the emotion, the arguments, the celebration, the chaos. And many of those moments only lived on because someone had a pen, a lens, or a mic – and Eddie let them use it.

> *"If a race happens and no one tells the story well, did it really happen? That's why I backed the voices – not only the engines."*
> – Eddie Jordan

Betting on Mavericks –
Cultivating Character Over Conformity

Eddie Jordan wanted talent, but that wasn't enough. He wanted character. He wanted people who coloured outside the lines and didn't apologize for it. Whether it was a driver with flair, a designer with wild ideas, or a team member with a rebellious streak, Eddie believed that individuality was an asset, not a liability.

In a sport that was becoming increasingly corporatized, Eddie carved out a space for mavericks – people who didn't fit the mould but brought fire, creativity, and boldness to everything they did. He welcomed strong opinions. He encouraged banter. He hired people who challenged him. And he defended them fiercely when the establishment raised eyebrows.

Eddie knew that teams succeed not just because of discipline and precision, but because of belief, passion, and a touch of madness. He brought in artists, musicians, and storytellers alongside strategists and engineers. He hosted wild afterparties that became legendary in the paddock. He let emotion fuel expression, knowing that joy, laughter, and the occasional heated argument were all part of what makes a team feel alive.

He cultivated an environment where people felt safe to be fully themselves. Where eccentricity was embraced, not hidden. Where ambition wasn't smoothed out by bureaucracy but sharpened by shared chaos.

Jordan Grand Prix was a force of nature. And behind it all stood Eddie, conductor of the beautiful noise.

> *"You can't win in this sport by following the rules of the room. Sometimes you have to kick the door off its hinges."*
> – Eddie Jordan

Bahrain – When the Gulf Came Calling

It wasn't just people he mentored and helped. Eddie Jordan played a pivotal role in bringing Formula 1 to Bahrain. In the early 2000s, as Bahrain aspired to host a Grand Prix, Eddie got a call: "Someone in Bahrain wants to borrow your car for a photoshoot". He said no problem. "How much?" He said there was no need to charge, he knew that goodwill always comes back tenfold. Shortly afterwards he received a set of pictures of his car in the middle of the desert, promoting Bahrain as the next Formula 1 member city.

This initiative helped generate excitement and visual appeal for the prospective race. The Bahrain International Circuit was constructed in Sakhir, with the inaugural Bahrain Grand Prix taking place in 2004, marking the first Formula 1 race in the Middle East. Over the years, the Bahrain Grand Prix has become a staple on the Formula 1 calendar, known for its night races and challenging desert conditions. The event has witnessed memorable moments, including Lewis Hamilton's multiple victories and the dramatic 2020 Sakhir Grand Prix. The circuit continues to host annual races, contributing to Bahrain's reputation as a key player in international motorsport. Eddie built deep friendships and relationships with people in Bahrain and nurtured them throughout his life even after Formula 1.

The Chinese Grand Prix –
The Early Scouting Mission

In the early 2000s, when Formula 1 was actively exploring its next frontier, Bernie Ecclestone had his eyes firmly on the East. China – with its population, economy, and rising global influence – was the ultimate opportunity. But it was unfamiliar territory for most of the Formula 1 establishment.

Bernie, ever the strategist, didn't want to send a corporate delegation, he wanted someone with feel. With charm. With rhythm. Someone who could read the room, shake the hands, have a drink, sense the politics, and tell it straight when he came back.

So, he sent Eddie Jordan.

Yes, he ran a team. But to Bernie, Eddie was the guy who got things done. Sharp, sociable, instinctive, and impossible to ignore. He could speak to ministers in the morning and musicians in the evening. He could close a deal in a bar and start a movement from a handshake. He knew when to talk – and more importantly, when to *listen*.

He travelled to China ahead of the official Formula 1 announcement to help scope out the appetite, the people, the practicalities. His role wasn't to negotiate the deal – it was to get a feel for whether this place could truly host the world's most-watched motorsport series. And whether the people behind it had the spark and vision to make it work.

He returned to Bernie and said what mattered most: "They're ready. And they want it."

Eddie's trip, and his informal endorsement, helped give the green light for what would become the Shanghai Grand Prix – first held in 2004 at the then-new $240 million circuit, built in just 18 months. Today, it's a core part of Formula 1's global presence, and a major commercial touchpoint for teams, sponsors, and fans alike.

His contribution wasn't documented in a press release. It wasn't shouted from a podium. But behind the scenes, Eddie Jordan's feel for people and places played a part – just as it did in Bahrain – in helping Formula 1 go truly global.

The Puma Deal

Eddie Jordan wasn't only known for being fast – he was known for being first. In the late 1990s, while most team bosses were preoccupied with tyre temperatures and lap times, Eddie was thinking ahead. He wasn't just building a team – he was building a brand. And when he looked across the paddock, he saw a gap. A brand that should be in Formula 1 – but wasn't yet: Puma.

At the time, Puma was big in football and streetwear. Cool, young, global – but nowhere near motorsport. Eddie saw the fit. Jordan GP wasn't your standard Formula 1 team. It was loud, colourful, unapologetic, fast, fun – exactly the kind of partner a brand like Puma needed to enter the grid. So, Eddie made the call. He pitched it. The vibe. The energy. The colour. The visibility. The rebel culture of Jordan. And Puma saw it immediately. They said yes – and Formula 1 changed.

But there was a catch. Puma didn't yet have FIA-approved racewear. No fireproof suits. No motorsport credentials.

So, Eddie, in true Jordan fashion, fused function with flair. He brought Sparco in behind the scenes – the trusted Italian motorsport safety brand – to deliver the compliance and safety gear. Suits, gloves, boots – all built to spec. Meanwhile, Puma fronted the brand, designed the style, and stamped their mark on the paddock.

It was bold. It was brilliant. It was pure Eddie. Jordan became the first-ever Formula 1 team to carry Puma branding. And it worked.

The Puma Speedcats – those sleek, low-profile shoes Eddie wore all over the grid – became instantly iconic. The Jordan team stood out even more. Puma got their global motorsport breakthrough. And Eddie proved once again that instinct beats committee.

Since then, Puma has become *the* brand in Formula 1 – supplying apparel, footwear, and merchandise to Mercedes-AMG Petronas, Scuderia Ferrari, Alfa Romeo, and more. But Eddie? He was first. And in his heart, he was always an ambassador.

Even after he left Formula 1, Puma didn't forget how it started – and neither did Eddie. Puma sent him a giant box of trainers every year, right up to 2025. And he wore them everywhere – on stage, on the bike, on boats, at gigs, in the paddock. The louder, the better. Bright yellows. Punchy reds. Signature blues. He wore them not to be noticed – but because they were him. Fun. Sharp. Unmissable. Full throttle.

And Puma noticed, too. At their headquarters in Herzogenaurach, Germany, there's a wall of legends. Framed photos of the icons who shaped the brand. Pelé. Maradona. Usain Bolt. Lewis Hamilton. Eddie Jordan.

No asterisk. No footnote. Because they knew. He wore the brand – and gave it a story. Puma got into Formula 1 through Eddie – and their first lap was his.

To show the impact of this deal for Puma, the company sold 28 million pairs of Speedcats over 25 years – all inspired by its origins with Jordan.

So just like Eddie did for drivers, engineers, and outsiders who deserved a shot – he saw something early, and made it move. Because Eddie didn't wait for the world to catch up. He picked up the phone. Told the story. Closed the deal. And brought the beat with him.

A little footnote to the deal: once the £1 million fee was agreed for the sponsorship, Eddie turned around and said, "I want free Pumas for my family." They were shocked – until Puma realized he was deadly serious. They said yes and walked away, shaking their heads. Eddie walked away thinking again, *"There's nothing nicer than the bit you steal."*

Making Room for the Next Act – The Legacy in Motion

When Jordan Grand Prix left the grid, Eddie Jordan didn't retire. He just took the same energy and pointed it somewhere new.

He didn't sit around thinking about legacy. That wasn't his style. He was too busy helping someone else get theirs off the ground. One day it was a startup pitch. The next it was a rugby club. Or a boat. Or a podcast. If it looked like fun, or like someone needed a nudge, he was in.

He didn't do it for credit. He didn't need his name on the front. He just liked the feeling of seeing something move. That's how you knew he still cared.

Eddie the Mentor (Talent, Loyalty, Mischief)

He worked with people younger than him, sharper than him, totally outside his world – and he never made them feel like they owed him anything. If he liked your idea, he'd back it. If he didn't, he'd tell you straight. But he'd still ask how your mum was and send you a playlist.

And while most people were slowing down, Eddie was speeding up in different ways. He wasn't chasing lap times anymore – he was chasing energy. Movement. Something interesting. If a room was too quiet, he'd find a way to turn it up.

He backed people because he believed in potential more than polish. Always had. He didn't care what your CV said – he cared if you had rhythm, guts, a bit of bite.

People talk about legacy like it's a statue. Eddie didn't want a statue. He wanted momentum. If something he did helped someone else go faster, further, louder – that was enough. That was the win.

And if you were lucky enough to get that nod from Eddie? You knew exactly what it meant:

"Go on then. Your turn. Full throttle. Go!"

> *"Legacy isn't what you leave behind.*
> *It's what you set in motion."*
> – Eddie Jordan

6

The Elder of the Paddock – Wisdom That Endures

The Unofficial Ambassador of Chaos.

Even after Jordan Grand Prix left the grid, Eddie didn't fade out. He just showed up in new ways – louder shirts, sharper lines, more time to say what others wouldn't.

He wasn't trying to be the wise old man of Formula 1. That's not who he was. But he'd seen more, done more, and been burned more than most – and people knew it. Drivers, bosses, broadcasters – they all wanted his take. Because it was never sugar-coated, it was useful.

On TV, he didn't play the game. He played Eddie. No notes. No script. One minute he'd be breaking down a pit strategy, the next he'd be telling someone to stop being an idiot and get on with it. And it worked. Because under the mischief was real substance.

He didn't do polished soundbites. He gave you truth, humour, and instinct in equal measure. He'd interrupt live coverage with a hunch, call out deals before they were announced, and somehow still manage to make the crew laugh in the ad break.

Young drivers looked up to him – not because he talked like a mentor, but because he acted like one. If he gave you a nod, a word, a phone number, it meant something. He didn't waste time, and he didn't give it lightly.

What made it matter wasn't the volume – it was the value. When Eddie said "you've got something", people believed him. Because he'd seen it before. And he knew what it looked like when it counted.

He wasn't looking for attention. He was looking for movement. For people with a bit of bite. People who needed a spark. That's what he gave. And if you really listened between the lines, it was always the same message:

Back yourself. Trust your gut. Don't wait, go full throttle.

> *"They call me the madman in the paddock,*
> *but I say what people are thinking. The sport*
> *needs more madness – and more truth."*
> – Eddie Jordan

Advice for the Next Generation

Eddie Jordan never claimed to have all the answers, but what he did have was experience – hard-earned, bruised, and brilliant. And he shared it with anyone brave enough to ask.

Young drivers, entrepreneurs, musicians, and engineers all came to him over the years, seeking wisdom. Some wanted tips on making it in Formula 1. Others wanted advice on leading teams, building brands, or navigating fame. Eddie's answer was rarely a list or a lecture. Instead, it came as a story – raw, hilarious, human, and unforgettable.

He'd tell the tale of backing a driver no one else would touch – and watching them become a world champion. He'd recount the time he lost millions on a deal, only to discover that the relationships built during the failure became more valuable than the money ever was. He'd share the quiet moments too – the heartbreak of losing friends, the loneliness of leadership, the beauty of a risk taken for the right reason.

His advice always circled back to a few key truths:

1. Trust your gut, even when others laugh. Eddie's greatest decisions came from instinct, not spreadsheets. He believed data was a tool, not a god.
2. Be fiercely loyal to your people. Eddie backed his team like family, and they gave him everything in return.
3. Don't hide your personality. Whether in a boardroom or a garage, authenticity always won over polish.
4. Make it fun. Joy was never a by-product – it was the strategy.
5. Bounce back fast. Mistakes weren't signs of failure. They were signs you were moving.

He'd sit with a young person and say, "You're going to get it wrong. That's the deal. But if you get it wrong with courage, you're still ahead of most."

What made Eddie different wasn't just what he said, but how deeply he cared. He didn't mentor for prestige – he did it because he believed in passing the baton. He saw greatness not as some-thing to hoard, but as something to ignite in others.

In the end, Eddie's real gift was making people believe in themselves. He didn't offer guarantees – he offered belief. And for many, that was enough to change everything.

"B-E-L-I-E-V-E. Because if you don't believe in yourself, how do you expect anyone else to?" – Eddie Jordan

Eddie Jordan's life was never built around rules – but around principles. He didn't teach them in classrooms or write them down in boardrooms. Instead, he lived them, breathed them, fought for them, and embodied them in moments large and small. Over time, those watching began to recognize a pattern – a rhythm to how Eddie moved through the world.

His principles weren't born from theory. They came from risks taken, backs against the wall, and an unshakable belief in people. What emerged is less a doctrine and more a way of life – one shaped by instinct, loyalty, creativity, and chaos. These ideas formed the backbone of how he built a racing team, mentored talent, and led a life that defied convention.

At the core of Eddie's philosophy is a simple truth: people come first. Whether it was a rising star in Formula 3, a young mechanic with ideas, or a business partner with a dream, Eddie believed in backing the person – not only the pitch. He saw raw-ness as potential, and imperfection as authenticity.

Eddie built cultures before he built companies. He was never the man obsessed with titles or spreadsheets – he was the one watching the energy in a room, the loyalty in a glance, the hunger behind a quiet idea. For him, strategy meant nothing without belief, and belief meant everything when times became hard.

He taught that you didn't need to be ready – you just needed to begin. Most of his boldest moves came before he had the money, the plan, or the approval. Jordan Grand Prix launched not because the stars aligned, but because Eddie refused to wait. Momentum was his magic.

He reminded people to be the fool first – to disarm rooms with humour and humility, to make space for surprise, to break down the walls others built too high. It was how he turned negotiation into performance, and boardrooms into dancefloors.

He believed in love as a leadership tool – love for the craft, for the people, for the journey. He knew that talent without care burned out, and that management without emotion was empty. His kind of leadership wasn't scalable, but it was unforgettable.

Eddie also understood the value of being unforgettable. He lived by the rule: "Never apologize for being interesting." Whether it was a paisley shirt on race day or a poetic rant on live TV, he knew that the world remembered colour, not compliance.

And most of all, he believed in celebration – not as reward, but as ritual. At Jordan, even small victories were amplified with music, dancing, champagne, and laughter. Celebration wasn't just for the winners. It was for the fighters, the dreamers, the risk-takers who made the grid.

These weren't corporate commandments. They were lived values, stitched into every risk he took and every person he backed. They were stories, moments, lessons whispered over drinks or shouted in the rain.

The Jordan Code is less a list than a lens. A way of looking at the world with curiosity, courage, and care. A reminder that success without soul is hollow – and that legacy, if it means anything, is the wake you leave when you've moved people forward.

"The goal isn't to be remembered. The goal is to be useful – so someone else can go even further."
– Eddie Jordan

The Final Turn – Eddie in Reflection

Eddie never parked the car and looked in the rear-view mirror, but every now and then – usually when the music softened, or the room got quiet for a second – he'd pause. Just briefly.

He didn't reflect the way most people do. No long monologues, no spreadsheet of achievements. If you asked what mattered most, he'd say: the laughs, the loyalty, the late nights. The people who stayed. The ones he backed. And the ones who backed him.

Even in his later years, when the paddock appearances slowed and the calls were more about mentoring than mayhem, he kept the same fire. He was still doing deals, still jamming on the drums, still making mischief in rooms where most people just nodded politely.

Legacy? He'd brush it off. "What legacy? I had a great time." But everyone knew he cared. He just didn't want it to get too serious, too clean, too tidy. That wasn't his way.

What he really left behind wasn't a list of wins – it was a way of being. Loud, loyal, fast, fearless. People didn't follow Eddie because he was polished. They followed him because he was real. Because when he walked in the room, the energy lifted. Because when he believed in you, you started to believe in yourself.

He didn't teach through lectures. He taught by momentum. And in doing so, he passed on something more lasting than a podium: the courage to go your own way, and go full throttle.

He often said he was trying to fit three lives into one. And looking back, maybe he did. Racer, rebel, rocker. Mentor, mischief-maker, mate. The man who could close a deal in the morning and kick off a jam session that night. He didn't compartmentalize. He didn't pace himself. He just lived – full tilt.

What defined him most wasn't the titles or the trophies. It was how many people called him a friend. How many stories he featured in. How many phones still ring because of introductions he made, careers he backed, or laughter he sparked.

He showed that you could lead without being cold. That you could be sharp without losing your soul. That a bit of chaos – if it comes with heart – can build something unforgettable.

People still tell the stories. They remember the shirts. The rhythm. The spoons. The way he never quite did things the way you were "supposed" to – and how that always turned out to be the magic.

He didn't slow down. He didn't tidy things up for anyone. He kept moving, kept giving, kept turning up the volume – right to the end.

And if there's one thing he'd want this book – and this reflection – to leave behind, it's this:

Don't copy him. Don't play it safe. Just live your life wide open. Loud. Loyal. And full throttle.

> *"Don't wait for the green light. Be the signal.*
> *Full throttle, always."*
> **– Eddie Jordan**

PART II

The Jordan Code:
25 Principles to Live and Lead

The Jordan Code

*How grit, instinct, and full-throttle living
built more than just a Formula 1 team.*

Eddie didn't write rules. He lived by rhythm – fast, loud, instinctive – and people paid attention. What started in racing spread into boardrooms, bands, boats, deals, dinners, and chaos. It was never just about Formula 1. It was about edge. About energy. About backing people and making things move.

He didn't care for perfect plans. He cared about feel. Sharp instincts. Movement. Make the call, take the corner, see what happens. That was the playbook.

These 25 principles aren't a framework. They're Eddie's way of operating – how he led, how he hired, how he built trust, closed deals, spotted talent, and made things happen. It's not theory. It's lived truth – messy, fast, sometimes contradictory, always useful.

Don't treat them like commandments. Think of them as conversations – the kind you have with someone who's done the laps and isn't afraid to tell you what matters. Take what sticks. Leave what doesn't. But whatever you do, don't sit still.

Eddie's approach was simple: be present, be bold, and keep moving.

Welcome to The Jordan Code

Section One: Vision, Belief, and Conviction

1. Think Big
2. One Goal, One Mission
3. Back Yourself
4. All or Nothing
5. Pull the Same Way

Section Two: Execution, Hustle, and Strategic Edge

6. Show Up, No Matter What
7. Sweat the Assets
8. Act with Urgency
9. Focus Improves Performance
10. Steal the Deal, Keep Your Honour
11. Find Your Edge

Section Three: Leadership, Trust, and Relationships

12. Lead with Trust
13. Ask, Listen, Learn
14. Respect Time
15. Be Present
16. Carry Cash and Share It
17. Spot Talent Early

Section Four: Authenticity, Energy, and Character

18. Show Up with a Smile
19. No Dimmer Switch
20. Stay Humble
21. Be Yourself and Inspire
22. Move Your Ass
23. Don't Carry Baggage

Final Lap – The Eddie Code Wrapped Up

24. Keep Attacking
25. Think Outside the Box

Section One:
Vision, Belief, and Conviction

1. Think Big

The Eddie Story

In the late 1980s, Formula 1 was an exclusive club of racing royalty. The paddock was filled with colossal names – McLaren with Senna and Prost, Ferrari with their scarlet dynasty, Williams with engineering genius. To even exist in that world was an act of bravery. To enter it as a complete outsider, with no factory team heritage, no big corporate backer, and no previous Formula 1 experience, bordered on insanity. But that's exactly what Eddie Jordan set out to do.

At the time, Eddie had already proven himself in the feeder series. Jordan Formula 3000 wasn't just competitive, it was a winner. In 1989, Jean Alesi had captured the Formula 3000 Championship under Eddie's stewardship, catching the attention of Formula 1 bosses. Eddie's knack for spotting and developing talent had become legendary in paddocks across Europe. But while others might have used that success to secure a safe job inside an existing Formula 1 team, his mind was elsewhere. He wasn't interested in climbing someone else's ladder – he wanted to build the whole house.

Friends, colleagues, and critics all warned him. The numbers didn't add up. The logistics were overwhelming. The politics were brutal. But Eddie wasn't reading from their script. He had what some call vision, what others call delusion – and what he himself called belief. He believed in himself, his people, and his ability to outwork, out-charm, and out-surprise the old guard. He loved it when people said, "It can't be done". As George Bernard Shaw said, "People who say it cannot be done should not interrupt those who are doing it."

The journey to the grid was a lesson in audacity. Without a car, without a base, and without confirmed funding, Eddie moved ahead as if all of it were already done. He found partners and persuaded sponsors with stories, sketches, and belief. He negotiated an engine deal with Cosworth for the Ford HB V8 – a serious piece of kit for a newcomer. He convinced designer Gary Anderson to build the car from scratch, out of an industrial unit in Silverstone with more character than comfort. And crucially, he created a brand – Jordan – that felt like it belonged in Formula 1 from day one. The team had energy. Swagger. Purpose.

That first car, the Jordan 191, would go on to become one of the most celebrated debut cars in Formula 1 history – though its birth was anything but glamorous. Money was tight. Timelines were ridiculous. The design process ran day and night. Anderson worked miracles with limited resources. Staff pulled all-nighters with no guarantee the car would ever turn a wheel in anger. But Eddie kept going. He kept believing. When obstacles came, he didn't scale them – he sprinted through them, talking his way past closed doors and doubters with that signature mix of charm, grit, and gall.

And then – in 1991, in the searing heat of Phoenix, Arizona – Jordan Grand Prix rolled out onto the track for its first-ever Grand Prix. The world blinked. The car looked stunning – sleek, aggressive, painted in 7UP green with purple and blue accents. But more than the looks, it had speed. Jordan wasn't there to make up numbers – they were in the midfield fight from race one. Against all expectations, the team scored points in its very first season, finishing fifth in the constructors' standings – ahead of established teams like Tyrrell and Lotus.

One of the most defining moments of Jordan's debut year – his discovery of Michael Schumacher at Spa – has already been told. But its legacy echoed far beyond 1991, forever marking the team as a launchpad for greatness.

There are few stories in Formula 1 that match the sheer audacity of Jordan's arrival. What made it even more special was that it wasn't done with unlimited funding or corporate muscle – it was built with instinct, charisma, and risk. It was built because Eddie Jordan thought big when others thought cautiously. He didn't wait for conditions to be perfect. He didn't seek permission. He just acted – boldly, unapologetically – and dragged reality along with him.

From that moment on, thinking big wasn't a choice for Eddie – it was who he was. It's how he made decisions in business. It's how he built a music career on the side of racing. It's how he lived always – taking life at full tilt, believing in magic even when the maths doesn't check out.

*"Turning up on the grid that first time –
with our own car, our own team – was like walking
onto the stage at Glastonbury. No one believed
we'd make it, but there we were."*
– Eddie Jordan

*"If you're going to risk everything, then you may as well
go all in. You've got to think big, or what's the point?"*
– Eddie Jordan

*"You don't get anywhere in this world by
thinking small. I didn't get into Formula 1
to finish last – I got in to shake things up."*
– Eddie Jordan

The Principle as Philosophy

Eddie Jordan never played small – because small thinking doesn't build teams, close deals, or change lives. He didn't tiptoe into conversations or wait to be asked. He moved early, fast, and with intent. Behind that energy was a belief: if you're going to do something, make it matter. Think bigger than what's in front of you.

To Eddie, thinking big wasn't about ego – it was about urgency. He knew life doesn't hand out permission. You either take the shot or spend your life watching others take it. You get on the grid or stay in the paddock, talking about what might have been.

Jordan Grand Prix wasn't born from neat business plans. It was born from instinct, clarity, and motion. Eddie didn't wait for all the answers – he started, then pulled the plan in behind him.

That was the point: start before you're ready. Move like it's already real. Back it with everything you've got.

Eddie didn't need the full roadmap. He needed a spark, a reason, a story worth building. Once he had that, he went all in. Not limited to race teams – to music, business, and people. Every time, he showed up with belief and made others believe too.

Most people never achieve big because they never think big. They limit themselves before the world ever does.

So, the lesson isn't just to think big on one project. The lesson is to think big everywhere. In how you work, how you lead, how you live. Make it a way of life – not a one-off tactic.

If you don't think big, you won't achieve big. It's that simple. Think as big as you can – because even if you fall short, you'll land further than most people ever start.

Make bold your default setting.

Because small thinking never lit a fire under anyone.

Practical Translation

Not everyone will start a Formula 1 team, jam onstage with musicians, or mentor future champions, but the principle of *thinking big* can apply to anyone. It's not about scale – it's about mindset. It's the refusal to let doubt dictate decisions. It's choosing imagination over hesitation. It's acting from belief, even when the path ahead isn't yet clear.

Eddie Jordan thought big not because he had all the answers, but because he knew the power of intent. When you show up with a vision, when you move before the conditions are perfect, when you bring energy and conviction to what you do – you shift the world around you.

Here's how to bring this mindset into your own work, life, and leadership:

1. Set a vision, not just a goal

Most people set goals based on what feels doable. But Eddie never asked, "What's realistic?" He asked, "What would be *remarkable*?" The goal was never to survive in Formula 1 – it was to create a team that mattered. To do something that left a mark.

Start with the bigger picture. Don't limit yourself to the version that fits neatly in a spreadsheet. Stretch it until it feels uncomfortable. That's where real possibility begins.

> **Ask yourself:** *What's the story I want to be part of? What's the scale of ambition that would excite, not simply satisfy, me?*

2. Act before you're ready

Eddie didn't wait for every piece to be in place before making his move. He started building before the blueprint was even finished. He knew that waiting breeds hesitation – and that movement creates momentum.

The same applies everywhere. Start with what you have. Take the next step before you think you're "qualified". If it matters, begin now – and let the plan evolve as you go.

> **Ask yourself:** *What am I waiting on that I could begin today? Where am I using preparation as a mask for fear?*

3. Believe in people and back them!

One of Eddie's superpowers was his ability to see potential in others before they saw it in themselves. He gave people chances – big chances. Not because they were proven, but because they were promising.

Thinking big isn't just about what you build – it's about who you bring with you. The boldest thing you can do is trust someone early. Push them forward. Give them the space to rise.

See the potential in people. Back them and help them be their best.

> **Ask yourself:** *Who in your world is capable of more than they believe? What happens if you tell them that?*

4. Use what you have

When Eddie launched Jordan Grand Prix, he didn't have the biggest budget or the most high-tech facilities, but he had something that counted more – belief, vision, and relentless energy.

You don't need perfect conditions, you need resourcefulness. Most people wait until everything's lined up. Eddie built while moving. He made calls, traded favours, borrowed confidence. He made the assets sweat. So can you.

> **Ask yourself:** *What am I underestimating that's already in my hands? What doors could open if I acted like what I have is already enough?*

5. Show up with energy

People followed Eddie not because of spreadsheets or job titles, but because he brought energy. He walked into rooms like something exciting was already happening – and suddenly, it was.

When you bring presence, intensity, and belief, people lean in. They listen more. They say yes. And that yes is what creates momentum.

> **Ask yourself:** *How do I carry myself when I'm at my boldest? What would happen if I showed up like that every day?*

Summary: Thinking Big in Practice

Start with vision, practicality can follow.
- Move before you're ready.
- Bet on people, not only the plan.
- Use what you have. Make it work.
- Show up with energy – it's contagious.

Thinking big isn't about ego, it's about generosity. It's about giving the world your full imagination, not being limited by your fears. And most importantly, it's about doing things that matter – even if they scare you.

As Eddie proved time and time again: it's better to go too far than not far enough. You can adjust the course – but only once you're moving.

Reflection

Eddie Jordan's biggest achievements didn't begin with certainty – they began with boldness. He didn't have a budget, a plan, or a safety net. He had belief, speed, and a story worth following.

Starting Jordan Grand Prix wasn't logical – it was outrageous. No factory backing. No guarantees. But he made it happen – and not just to race. The team scored points, launched careers, and made the grid feel more alive.

And he didn't stop at motorsport. Eddie blurred the lines between racing and music, business and storytelling. If something had energy, he went towards it. He didn't see walls – he saw doors to be kicked open.

More importantly, he lit a path for others. His boldness gave permission. His story gave belief. His momentum pulled others forward.

That's the quiet truth about thinking big: it spreads. Eddie didn't wait to be ready. He went big – and made room for everyone else to follow.

> *"I'm thinking about the bigger picture, further on down the road, or the next different plan of attack or the next opportunity, whether it's business or it's family or it's home."*
> – Eddie Jordan

> *"If you tell your dreams to someone and they don't laugh out loud at you, you are not thinking big enough."*
> – Eddie Jordan

2. One Goal, One Mission

The Eddie Story

At Jordan Grand Prix, there were no laminated mission statements, no management buzzwords, no PowerPoints. Just one line, passed from by word of mouth in the garage, on the pit wall, and in the boardroom:

"Make the car faster."

It wasn't a slogan, it was the heartbeat. A compass that cut through fog, politics, and noise. Everyone – from senior engineers to the newest intern – knew exactly what the mission was. And they didn't need reminding, because Eddie Jordan repeated it like a drumbeat.

Not because it sounded clever – but because it worked. And because it gave the team an edge money couldn't buy.

Eddie understood something most leaders forget: when people are clear on the mission, they don't need micromanaging. They start managing themselves.

From the very beginning, when Jordan was just an idea, he hammered home one truth: everything – engineering, logistics, strategy, sponsorships, ideas – had to serve one outcome. Make the car faster. If it didn't, bin it.

And he meant it.

Early on, the team drifted. Performance dipped. Sponsors started making demands. Internal teams pushed for shiny distractions – new hospitality programmes, rebrands, merchandising tweaks.

Eddie listened. Nodded. And then one Friday afternoon at the Silverstone factory, he climbed up on a packing crate and said:

"Right – this is getting silly. If it doesn't make the car faster, stop. Don't propose it. Don't work on it. Don't even talk about it. We're not a brand, we're a race team. Make the car faster, and the rest will follow."

The room stilled. People laughed, nodded – and something lifted. That moment became a legend inside Jordan – known simply as "the reset".

From that day on, the energy changed. Designers simplified. Engineers focused. Admins cleared clutter. A tighter, faster, hungrier team emerged.

And it didn't stop in racing. When Eddie played music with V10 or Eddie and The Robbers, the same rule applied: if a song didn't land live, cut it. Tighten the set. Stay on the groove.

When Eddie appeared on TV, he held the same filter: if a point didn't add clarity or energy, he didn't waste airspace.

In business – whether bidding for Playtech or closing sponsorships – it was the same: what's the core deal? What's the real mission? What gets us there faster? Bin the rest.

There was something almost musical about it – quick beats, clear tempo, no wasted motion. If you went off track, he didn't snap. He just smiled and said, "Sounds good – but doesn't feel right."

That clarity didn't suffocate people. It freed them. Because when people know the goal, they can improvise, innovate, and take risks – without ever losing their way.

That's what Eddie gave his teams: a simple line to follow, and the freedom to run.

And the impact? It went far beyond racing. People who worked with Eddie learned to think clearer, act sharper, move faster – and carried that clarity into boardrooms, startups, studios, and stages.

All from one principle: make the car faster. Simple. Unbreakable. Transformational.

The Principle as Philosophy

In the chaos of high performance – in racing, business, life – clarity isn't a luxury, it's oxygen.

Eddie Jordan understood that better than anyone.

In a world spinning at 200mph, where deadlines collide with emotion and decisions come faster than you can catch them, you need one thing to anchor it all.

One mission. One line. One filter.

At Jordan Grand Prix, that filter was simple:

"Make the car faster."

It wasn't a motto, it was the pulse of the team. It gave meaning to every task, every decision, every sacrifice.

Because without one clear goal, teams drift. Priorities blur. Energy scatters. Culture fractures.

But with it? They align. They accelerate. They become dangerous – to their competitors and to the limits people assume they have.

Eddie wasn't chasing complexity, he was building coherence.

And that coherence made Jordan Grand Prix – pound for pound – one of the most remarkable teams in motorsport history.

The principle doesn't just belong on the racetrack. It belongs wherever momentum matters:

- In boardrooms.
- In startups.
- In classrooms.
- In any project, anywhere.

Find your mission. Make it brutally simple. Protect it like hell.

Because clarity doesn't just remove distractions. It creates speed. It builds trust. It frees people to act boldly – because they know exactly what they're chasing.

Practical Translation

A clear mission isn't a leadership tool – it's a competitive advantage. Eddie knew that when people understand the goal, they don't need rules, layers, or pep talks. They start making sharper decisions, faster. They take ownership. They cut the fluff. One clear goal creates cohesion, urgency, and momentum. And when that goal is simple enough to be repeated at every level of the organization? That's when culture gets dangerous – in the best way:

1. Get brutally clear on the mission

If your team can't repeat the goal in one sentence, you don't have a mission – you have confusion. Clarity builds trust, speed, and results.

> **Ask yourself:** *If I asked everyone on my team what we're trying to achieve, would I get the same answer?*

2. Make it simple, make it stick

Eddie's mantra was "Make the car faster." It was short, sharp, and easy to follow. Simplicity cuts through complexity and gives people direction.

> **Ask yourself:** *Can I say our goal in five words or less?*

3. Repeat the mission until it becomes culture

Don't write it in a deck and hope it lands. Say it. Live it. Enforce it. Make it the lens through which decisions are made.

> **Ask yourself:** *When's the last time I reminded the team what really matters?*

4. Cut anything that doesn't serve the goal

Distraction is expensive. Projects, meetings, "nice to haves" – if they don't support the mission, scrap them.

> **Ask yourself:** *What are we doing right now that's not moving the mission forward?*

5. Trust your team once the goal is clear

With clarity, people don't need permission – they need space. Let go of micromanagement and give them the room to own results.

> **Ask yourself:** *Have I been clear enough to confidently step back?*

When Eddie said, "Make the car faster," it wasn't just a performance target – it was a code for how the whole team showed up. They didn't get distracted, they got aligned. That's the power of one clear goal. It simplifies, unifies, and amplifies. So, if you want to go fast – and far – say the mission out loud, say it often, and make sure everyone pulls in the same direction.

Reflection

The most powerful thing Eddie Jordan ever gave his team wasn't a budget – it was clarity. One line, one mission: make the car faster. That phrase united mechanics, drivers, designers, interns – everyone. It simplified choices, killed distractions, and gave people a reason to push. Because when a team knows what matters, they start to move faster, decide sharper, and believe harder. That's what clarity does. It doesn't just organize effort – it multiplies it.

Clarity isn't soft. It's a force. Use it.

"If it doesn't make the car faster, we are not doing it."
– Eddie Jordan

3. Back Yourself

The Eddie Story

Eddie Jordan never waited to be told he could do something. He just *did it*. And if you asked him how he knew it would work, he'd probably grin and say, "I didn't. But I knew I could handle it if it didn't."

That was Eddie's way – trust your instincts, move with speed, and back yourself before the world catches up. It wasn't a slogan, it was a strategy.

In 1991, with almost no money, no engine manufacturer deal, and no safety net, Eddie put a brand-new Formula 1 team on the grid. It was audacious. Some said reckless. But to Eddie, it was *obvious*. He didn't see barriers, he saw openings. He didn't see a lack of budget. He saw a surplus of hunger.

And crucially – he trusted *himself.*

Launching Jordan Grand Prix was a masterclass in guts over guarantees. Eddie leased engines from Ford. Pulled together sponsors through charm, hustle, and relentless belief. Convinced the likes of Gary Anderson to build a car from scratch. And then – with the world watching – rolled that car out on the grid in Phoenix.

He called his first car the Jordan 91.1. Launched in 1991, it was the first car – hence 91.1. He knew it would annoy Porsche, and it did. They wrote a cease and desist letter to him. He backed himself and wrote back, telling them where they could shove it.

The negotiations started, and when Eddie took possession of a brand-new Porsche 911, he happily changed the car's name to be the Jordan 191. Classic Eddie stunt.

But Eddie's "back yourself" philosophy didn't stop at the team. It showed up in the people he chose to bet on. The clearest example? Michael Schumacher. Eddie saw something others hadn't yet. A confidence. A posture. It was a risk. The team was under pressure. The sponsors were nervous. But Eddie trusted his gut – and Schumacher qualified seventh on debut. The rest is history.

"If you don't believe in yourself, why should anyone else?" he said later. "I wasn't the best engineer, the best strategist, or the richest team owner – but I had belief. And belief gets you on the grid."

That mindset extended far beyond the grid.

In business, Eddie repeatedly backed himself into projects others considered too risky – a bid for Playtech, investing in businesses outside motorsport, even launching a TV career with no formal training. But every time, he trusted one thing: *he'd find the way.*

In music, when The Robbers took the stage – whether in Monaco, a corporate party in Dublin, or playing to thousands of people at Silverstone on the GP weekend, Eddie didn't shy away. He wasn't worried about being the best drummer in the world, he focused on bringing energy, joy, and commitment. That's what people responded to. Not polish – *presence.*

In television, Eddie arrived as the wildcard voice. He didn't have a polished presenter background or media training, but what he *did* have was insight, humour, and the courage to say what others wouldn't. He backed his authenticity – and it paid off.

This kind of belief doesn't mean ego. In fact, Eddie often checked himself more than most.

Throughout this book you will see a lot of colour, swagger, and dealmaking that can seem somewhat unorthodox, but it's very important to note that this didn't happen by chance.

Eddie once said in a BBC interview:

"I needed to check myself every day to see that I had performed. Otherwise, I could be lazy."

That line tells you everything. Belief wasn't an excuse for comfort. It was a tool for action. A driver for progress.

Even in moments of failure – and there were many – Eddie never blamed the world. He owned it, learned from it, and moved forward. That's the second half of backing yourself: *you take the consequences too.*

And that's what made people follow him. Drivers trusted him. Staff stayed loyal. Partners leaned in. Because Eddie wasn't bluffing. He was *committed*. And when someone backs themselves with that kind of energy, you can't help but believe a little more in yourself, too.

He gave others permission to bet on themselves, simply by the way he lived. Because backing yourself doesn't mean you'll always win.

It means you'll *always move.*

The Principle as Philosophy

Before anyone else can believe in you, you have to believe in yourself. It sounds simple – obvious, even – but most people hesitate. They wait to feel ready. Wait for permission. Wait for validation. Eddie Jordan didn't.

He trusted his instincts long before the world confirmed he was right. He said yes while others were still making lists. He moved fast – because he believed fast.

Backing yourself, for Eddie, wasn't about ego. It was about

energy. Momentum. That unshakable internal signal that says, "I'll figure this out. I can handle it."

And that belief was contagious. It made investors lean in. It made drivers trust him. It made sponsors bet on a dream that wasn't fully built yet – but felt inevitable.

But it wasn't blind optimism. Eddie held himself to standards. Every day, he'd ask himself: *"Did I perform? Did I deliver today? Or did I get lazy?"*

That's the quiet discipline behind real self-belief. It's not loud. It's not performative. It's showing up like it matters – before anyone's watching.

Eddie didn't wait for someone else to back the driver, the business, the band. He put his name on the line first. His energy. His belief.

Because confidence isn't charisma – it's commitment. To the risk. To the room. To the rhythm of something that hasn't happened yet – but could, if someone just dared to start.

That was Eddie. And that's the invitation.

If you won't bet on yourself, why should anyone else?

Practical Translation

Eddie Jordan didn't wait for certainty. He moved when he had belief – and built everything else around it.

Backing yourself isn't about pretending to be fearless. It's about acting even when the fear is still there. It's not cockiness – it's clarity. It's about trusting your instincts, honouring your experience, and committing fully to what you know you can become.

It only works when you leave both ego and insecurity at the door.

That was Eddie's magic: he didn't posture. He didn't perform. He just showed up – with energy, intent, and momentum. Again and again. He believed in what he brought. And because he did, others believed too.

Here's how to practise that belief in your own life:

1. Decide first, then declare it

Eddie didn't wait for everything to line up. He said yes before the money arrived, before the risk was low, before the world was ready. That's how momentum begins – not with guarantees, but with declarations.

> **Ask yourself:** *What decision am I waiting to validate – when I could just claim it?*

2. Be confident, not cocky

Confidence is quiet. It's earned through action. Cockiness is a mask for doubt. Eddie didn't need noise – he trusted his record.

> **Ask yourself:** *Where can I turn down the volume and turn up the presence?*

3. Move before you're ready

Perfection kills momentum. Eddie started before it all made sense – and refined it in motion.

Ask yourself: *What if I took the first step, and trusted I'd grow into it?*

4. Leave your ego – and insecurity – at the door

Eddie didn't need to be the smartest in the room. But he didn't shrink either. He arrived ready, prepared, and present.

Ask yourself: *What part of me is holding back – and what if I let it go?*

5. Hold yourself to the standard you expect

Confidence without standards is just noise. Eddie backed himself, but he also held himself accountable – every day.

Ask yourself: *Am I matching my belief with consistent action?*

6. Know the difference between trust and arrogance

Eddie trusted his gut – but he also listened, adjusted, and learned. That's real confidence: less to prove, more to deliver.

Ask yourself: *Am I acting from experience – or from ego?*

7. Build the muscle — one risk at a time

Self-belief is earned. Every risk you take makes you stronger. Confidence grows by doing, especially when it's uncomfortable.

> **Ask yourself:** *What risk this week could stretch my self-belief?*

Backing yourself isn't about being the loudest. It's about being the most present. It's about knowing who you are – and showing up without apology or excuse. Because when you do that – clearly, quietly, consistently – the world doesn't need convincing. It just starts paying attention.

Reflection

There's a different kind of energy in someone who truly backs themselves. It's not loud or flashy – it's calm, clear, and steady. No flinch in their posture. No panic in their decision-making. They don't dominate the room – they just fully occupy their space.

That was Eddie Jordan. He didn't bluff for the sake of it (well, maybe sometimes). He moved with conviction – in boardrooms, paddocks, and big decisions – with a presence that said, "I know what I bring. Let's get to work." That kind of self-belief doesn't come from hype. It comes from action. From showing up when it's hard. From moving forward, even when the path isn't clear.

Of course he had doubts, but he didn't let them drive. He moved anyway. That movement built momentum. The momentum built reputation. And the reputation built trust – not just from others, but from himself.

Because backing yourself isn't a performance – it's a posture. And that posture invites the world to treat you differently.

The world backs those who back themselves first.

> *"I always felt that I could get the money. I always felt that I had the inner belief in my own self."*
> – Eddie Jordan

4. All or Nothing

The Eddie Story

Eddie Jordan didn't believe in dipping a toe. If he was in, he was *all in* – head, heart, wallet, rhythm, reputation. That commitment didn't come from strategy books or motivational quotes. It came from somewhere deeper – a refusal to live halfway.

That spirit of commitment showed up early. Eddie first got behind the wheel in karting – and once he caught the bug, there was no shaking it. In 1974, he had a serious crash at Mallory Park. It shook him. One of the knock-on effects was alopecia, and he lost all his hair – a reminder, as he'd later say, that the road is never without its costs. But rather than retreat, Eddie doubled down. He left the bank job behind, packed up for England, and threw himself into racing full time. Marlboro sponsored him and paid in cartons of cigarettes, which he swapped at the local shop for groceries on credit. That was Eddie. He didn't wait for the perfect conditions. He committed, fully – with grit, with nerve, with nothing held back.

That's why, when he launched Jordan Grand Prix, he built

more than a team – he sparked a movement. He committed every ounce of himself – financially, emotionally, physically – to making the grid. He mortgaged properties, borrowed money, sweet-talked suppliers, and brought in 7UP as title sponsor with nothing more than charm and vision. The people around him knew this wasn't a project. This was a *mission*.

It was never just about money – energy powered it all. Eddie showed up every day like everything was on the line – because it was. He answered his phone at midnight. He flew across Europe to make a deal in a pub. He put his name, his brand, his shirts, his voice, and his soul on the table. Not because he was reckless. Because he *cared*. Deeply. And when people saw that level of commitment, they couldn't help but match it.

That's what made Jordan different. The team wasn't built by corporates – it was built by believers. By people who saw Eddie throwing himself into the fire and decided to throw themselves in too.

He didn't ask for perfection. He asked for presence. He challenged you to show up.

When you work for someone who shows up like that, it changes your posture. You stop hedging. You start committing. That's why Jordan had loyalty other teams could only dream of. That's why engineers pulled triple shifts without complaint. Why drivers trusted him when every spreadsheet said not to. Because when Eddie backed something, he *backed it*. Fully. And it made others feel safe enough – and fired up enough – to do the same.

The Business Bets That Weren't "Just Business"

Eddie brought that same energy into business after racing – and it never softened. When he partnered with Keith O'Loughlin to bid for Playtech, a £3 billion global gambling technology group, most observers thought he was mad. It was high stakes, corporate warzone stuff. The kind of thing "former team bosses" were supposed to politely avoid.

Not Eddie.

He didn't walk into that deal thinking, *"Let's see what happens."* He walked in thinking, *"We are doing this deal. Period."* He studied the structure. Took meetings day and night. Flew back and forth across Europe. Took calls on boats, at airports, mid-ride on a bike. He put his brand and his credibility on the line – not for ego, but because he believed in the people and the purpose. Even when the deal didn't land, he didn't regret the commitment.

"If you're not all in," he said, "you don't get the good stuff. You don't get the luck. You don't get the loyalty. And you don't get remembered."

That's the thing. Eddie never half-lived anything. Whether he was launching a team, making a business play, mentoring a musician, or hosting a dinner in Monaco – he was *present*. Fully. You could feel it in the room. His energy wasn't casual. It was *involved*. And that changed things.

You saw it again in the London Irish rugby story. A club on its knees. A sport he didn't need to touch. But his son Kyle had a vision, and Eddie believed in it. So, he threw his weight behind it. Not cautiously – *committed*. Meetings. Capital. Calls.

Conversations with league officials, stakeholders, players, the press. No one told him to do it. No one paid him to do it. But that was Eddie – if he cared, he was *in*. All the way.

The Jordan 191 is generally accepted to be one of the most beautiful Formula 1 cars in history, but it took a little work to make that so. Eddie decided he wanted a green car with a nod to Ireland, and then he backed himself to get sponsors who had a dark shade of green as their primary colour – quite a niche market! PepsiCo's 7UP brand was one of the first targets, but they 'only' had $2 million in their budget because they had committed to sponsor Michael Jackson's upcoming *Dangerous* world tour.

Eddie took the cash and then looked for his next "victim". He called Fujifilm and couldn't get through to talk to anyone. He tried every way and came up short. "F**k it, I'm going." Eddie then jumped on a flight to Japan and parked himself in the Fujifilm offices, pretty much refusing to leave until they saw him. When he finally got to discuss his proposition, he suggested that he was about to sign a deal with their key rival, Kodak. "In the end, they actually gave me a deal just to get me to leave. They couldn't take any more!" That was Eddie, backing himself and not leaving until he got his result.

In Music, Media, and Mentorship

Racing. Business. And a lot more besides. Eddie's commitment stretched to the places most people would treat as hobbies. To him, music wasn't a distraction – it was another stage where commitment counted.

He didn't play drums like a man doing a side hustle. He played like a man headlining the main tent and as though he owned the crowd. V10, Eddie and The Robbers – they weren't just pub bands. They toured. They rehearsed. They played with legends. Because Eddie gave the same commitment to music as he did to a pit wall.

Same in TV. When he started appearing on the BBC and Channel 4 coverage, he wasn't just a pundit. He was a *presence*. Full throttle. Sometimes messy. Often loud. Always honest. Loud shirts. Colourful language. Cheeky grin. He didn't phone it in. He didn't cruise. He treated every live broadcast like a qualifying lap – show up sharp, speak with truth, leave a mark.

And in mentoring, he never half-listened. When a young entrepreneur or driver came to him, he leaned in. Gave them time. Made calls. Opened doors. Connected them with others. Even when he had nothing to gain. Because once he said yes, he he was in. That was the deal.

And the people he mentored? They never forgot it. Because they knew the truth:

He cared. Eddie didn't do anything by halves.

Not a deal. Not a dinner. Not a friendship. Not a risk. Not a race. Nothing.

The Principle as Philosophy

In a world that celebrates flexibility, Eddie Jordan lived by a different code: commitment is the edge.

He didn't flirt with ideas. He didn't "try things out". He said yes – and meant it. That kind of energy is rare. It draws people in. Because when a leader is all in, the team follows – not by instruction, but by instinct.

Eddie understood what most don't: partial commitment is invisible. It doesn't inspire. It doesn't move people. But full commitment? That's magnetic. It creates momentum.

When he launched Jordan Grand Prix, there was no Plan B. No cushion. Just belief. He committed fully, and that rhythm carried the whole team – from mechanics to marketers. It wasn't about being the smartest, it was about being the most in.

That carried through to everything he did – music, business, media, mentoring. If he said yes, he brought 100 per cent. No dimmer switch. No hesitation.

And when things didn't work out? He didn't disappear. He owned it, learned, and moved on again. That's what made his commitment powerful: not that it always worked, but that he always stayed in the fight.

Most people aren't short on ideas. They're short on commitment. They want certainty first – Eddie moved first. He backed people before the numbers lined up. He stood up when others were still working out the odds.

Because to Eddie, commitment wasn't a feeling. It was a decision: "I'm in. All in. No matter what."

And in a world where most people show up at 70 per cent, Eddie's 100 per cent made all the difference.

Practical Translation

Eddie's commitment wasn't loud for show – it was loud because it was total. You don't need a race team or a spotlight to show that kind of energy. You need a decision: to stop sitting on the fence and get fully in the game.

Whether you're building a business, learning a skill, raising a family or chasing a dream – the rule holds:

Partial effort produces partial results. In a winner-takes-all world, being 10 per cent behind usually means losing everything. Being just slightly ahead? You win it all. So, if you're not giving 100 per cent, don't be surprised when you come away empty-handed.

Full commitment creates momentum.

Here's how to live this principle – Eddie-style:

1. Say yes like you mean it

Don't nod vaguely. Don't "kind of try". If it matters, say yes – then act like it. Commitment shows up when it's hard.

> **Ask yourself:** *Am I really committed to this – or just interested?*

2. Burn the escape route

Eddie didn't carry a parachute. If things went sideways, he didn't bail – he adapted. If you're always ready to quit, you'll never push far enough to break through.

> **Ask yourself:** *Have I built a backup plan just in case I don't believe?*

3. Show up like it's everything

Commitment isn't just effort – it's presence. Energy on. Eyes up. Phone down. People feel the difference when you're fully there.

> **Ask yourself:** *Am I showing up like someone who's all in?*

4. Let people see your investment

Eddie never hid his belief. He said, "We're doing this," and then threw everything into it. That visible energy pulls others forward.

> **Ask yourself:** *Am I modelling commitment – or waiting for others to go first?*

5. Review yourself, every day

Eddie's mantra: "I needed to check myself every day to see that I had performed. Otherwise, I could be lazy." That's not perfectionism – it's honesty.

> **Ask yourself:** *What's one commitment I can check in on daily?*

6. Commitment is greater than certainty

Most people wait for all the green lights. Eddie moved first and figured it out later. You don't get clarity before you act – you get it by acting.

> **Ask yourself:** *Am I using uncertainty to delay a decision I've already made in my gut?*

7. Build a culture around commitment

People don't copy what you say – they copy how you show up. Eddie's teams didn't lean in because of speeches, they leaned in because he did.

> **Ask yourself:** *Would someone watching me today believe I'm fully committed?*

Bottom Line: Don't flirt with your future. Don't "try" your dream. Commit. Loudly. Visibly. Relentlessly. Because when others see your full commitment – they move. And when *you* feel it? You stop waiting. You start building. You win.

Reflection

Eddie Jordan's life was full of wins – but just as full of moments when things nearly fell apart. Sponsorships that vanished. Drivers that walked. Deals that didn't land. He didn't always know how it would work out, but he committed anyway.

That commitment – raw, visible, and total – was the difference.

From day one, he walked into rooms with nothing but a sketch and a story and said, "We're doing this." Not asking for permission. Declaring intent. He didn't have the biggest budget or the longest CV – but he had belief. And belief moves people.

It made engineers stay late. Made mechanics care more. Made

drivers put their futures in his hands. Because commitment has a frequency – and Eddie broadcasted it constantly.

Even when things failed – and they did – he didn't turn on others. He stayed in the room. Owned the outcome. Learned the lesson. That kind of follow-through builds more respect than any podium.

That's the power of real commitment. You won't always win – but you'll always be in the race. You'll move faster, build trust deeper, and become the kind of person others lean on when it gets hard.

Eddie didn't win despite going all in. He won because he did. Over and over again.

When the car broke down, he committed again. When the bid collapsed, he committed again. When the story got messy, Eddie stayed in it.

Because commitment doesn't wait for the weather to improve. It's the engine that pulls you through the storm.

Commitment is an internal decision – quiet, personal, and unshakable. It comes from your gut, not your mood. It's the promise you make to yourself to keep showing up, no matter how hard it gets. And when that promise holds, everything else follows.

"Once you decide to go for it, you commit. No half-measures. That's how we got on the grid – total commitment."
– Eddie Jordan

5. Pull the Same Way

The Eddie Story

The Belgian Grand Prix. Spa-Francorchamps, 1998. Chaos in the air. Weather all over the place. Everyone tense.

The Jordan team had never won a race. The car was good. The drivers – Damon Hill and Ralf Schumacher – were sharp. But no one really expected them to beat the Ferraris, the McLarens. Not without luck. Not without something special.

But what happened that day wasn't luck.

It was *teamwork* – down to the very last man.

His name was Dave. He drove one of the Jordan trucks. Not an engineer. Not a strategist. Not a pit crew specialist. Just Dave – the guy who got the lorries in and out, early and late, week after week.

On that Sunday, just before the race, Dave had finished his duties early. The grid was buzzing. Everyone was in race mode.

Dave wasn't the kind of guy to stand around doing nothing. So, he walked up to Eddie.

"Eddie, what can I do to help?"

Eddie – focused, under pressure – replied quickly: "Dave, I'm busy."

Twenty minutes later, Dave came back.

"Anything I can do?"

"Still busy."

Another 20 minutes passed.

"Eddie . . . anything?"

This time, Eddie paused. Looked at him. "Actually, Dave, yeah – I've no idea what the weather's doing. It's all over the place. Do me a favour – get in the car, drive about 3km out that way, and if you see rain coming in, give me a call."

Dave didn't blink. He got in the car. Drove off.

Halfway through the race, Eddie was standing at the pit wall. Focused. Fully in it.

Suddenly, his assistant tapped him on the shoulder.

"Eddie – Dave wants to talk to you."

Eddie, still locked in, said: "Tell him I'm busy."

A few seconds later, the assistant returned.

"Eddie, he says it's urgent."

Eddie took the call.

"Rain's coming in. Heavy. Very soon."

Eddie didn't wait. He made the call. Brought both cars in. Switched them to wet tyres.

It was a gamble. The rest of the grid stayed out.

And then – boom. The heavens opened.

Rain lashed down. Chaos unfolded. Cars skidded, teams panicked, tyres failed.

But the Jordans? They were already out there – *ready*.

They flew past.

And when the chequered flag dropped, it was *Damon Hill, P1. Ralf Schumacher, P2*. Jordan's first-ever win. A legendary one-two finish. Headlines around the world.

Most people gave the credit to Damon. Some to strategy. Some to the weather gods.

But if you asked Eddie?

He'd tell you about *Dave*. The truck driver who kept asking how he could help. Who saw a gap. Who made a call. Who *changed the course of history* – not by being a hero, but by being *part of a team* that trusted *everyone* to make a difference.

Because at Jordan, you didn't need a title to matter.

You didn't need to be on the pit wall to have an impact.

You just needed to *care*. Everyone was invested. Jordan was "their" team.

And if you cared – Eddie listened.

That was the spirit of the place.

Everyone bought into the vision. They weren't just engineers or drivers or crew. They were *rock 'n' roll*. They had their own band. Literally. The team partied together, laughed together, cried together. They were the underdogs, but never no-hopers. They didn't sulk about the big teams having more money. They kept *knocking on the door*, looking for an edge, waiting for an opening – just like their leader.

They were *Jordan*.

They came, they challenged, they shook things up – and did it *as a team*.

They gave people chances. Gave outsiders a shot. Took risks on raw talent. They believed. All of them. From the mechanics to the cooks to the drivers to the truck driver parked on the edge of the forest, calling in the rain.

And when they won?

They all won.

Not because they got lucky.

But because *everyone* had a part to play – and *everyone* played it. Together.

The Principle as Philosophy

Eddie Jordan knew that stars don't win alone.

It's easy to put a driver on the podium and think that's where the win happened. But Eddie had seen enough of life – and racing – to know that what *actually* gets someone to the top step is the team *behind* them. The ones who carry, push, build, repair, believe.

He never pretended otherwise.

He knew that teamwork wasn't simply about collaboration – it was about culture and shared commitment. The belief that no role is small. That every voice matters. That effort counts, even when no one is watching. That the guy cleaning the garage floor might be the reason you finish the race.

At Jordan, everyone was in. No passengers. No egos. No layers of power that left people waiting for permission to step up.

If you were part of the team, you mattered. And if you had something to offer, Eddie wanted to hear it.

That's what made Jordan GP special. And it's what made so many people stay – long after they could have gone elsewhere for more money or more prestige.

Because it wasn't just a job.

It was *a band*. A tribe. A movement.

And the reason it worked wasn't simply because they were talented – it was because they were *together*.

That's what real teams are: places where people believe in *something bigger than themselves* and are brave enough to show up for each other over and over again.

Practical Translation

Great teams don't happen by accident. They're built – through trust, rhythm, and belief.

Here's how to build them the Eddie way:

1. Involve everyone, not just the obvious players

Your "Dave" might have the next big idea. Give everyone a chance to contribute, not only those with fancy titles.

> **Ask yourself:** *Who in my team has insight I haven't heard yet?*

2. Celebrate the small roles loudly

It's not only about the goal-scorer, it's the assist. The setup. The person who stayed late. Make people feel seen. The person who washed the kit.

> **Ask yourself:** *Who helped quietly this week – and have I recognized them?*

3. Build culture around trust, not fear

People will give more when they feel safe to speak, safe to try, safe to fail. Build that.

> **Ask yourself:** *What am I doing to make people feel they belong? Allow people to make mistakes.*

4. Let ideas come from anywhere

Eddie never cared where a good call came from – only that it came. Leave space for unexpected genius.

> **Ask yourself:** *Am I letting people speak – or just letting them nod?*

5. Make it fun

Teams don't just need structure. They need joy. Laughter. Music. Eddie had a *band*, for God's sake!

> **Ask yourself:** *Is my team having fun together – or just working? Everyone knew it was serious business, but it's got to be a fun on the ride.*

6. Model what you want to see

Work hard. Take feedback. Share credit. Apologize when you screw up. That's what real leaders do.

> **Ask yourself:** *What am I showing people about how to be part of this team?*

Reflection

Jordan Grand Prix didn't just beat the odds – they rewrote them. They proved you don't need to be the biggest. You need to be the most connected. The most committed. The most together. Because when belief runs through a team – from the pit wall to the paddock to the back of the truck – extraordinary things happen.

At Spa in 1998, it wasn't one person who won. It was everyone. Dave, the truck driver, spotted the rain. Damon Hill drove the car. Eddie made the call. The engineers guessed. The crew gambled. The whole team worked, worried, hoped – and pulled the same way.

That's what made it work. Not money. Not miracles. Trust. Momentum. Total buy-in.

That kind of team? You don't forget it. You carry it with you – into the next project, the next partnership, the next leap. Because Eddie built more than a race team: he built a way of working. A way of believing. A way of showing up. That's why the team he created still exists on the grid today – racing as Aston Martin.

He showed people what it feels like to be all in – and to matter. You don't need a hero. You need a band. A group of people who show up, back each other, and bring their best – not for credit, but because it matters.

When everyone pulls the same way, you stop working harder – and start moving faster.

> *"It wasn't about one of us.*
> *It was all of us – flat out, no passengers."*
> – **Eddie Jordan**

Section Two
Execution, Hustle, and Strategic Edge

6. Show Up, No Matter What

The Eddie Story

Formula 1 doesn't wait. It doesn't stop for illness, delay for indecision, or bend to circumstance. There's a race every other weekend. The trucks roll, the gates open, the lights go out – ready or not. And the unforgiving nature of that rhythm was something Eddie Jordan both respected and thrived on.

To survive in that world, you had to build a team that treated turning up as non-negotiable. Not only in the literal sense of arriving at the paddock with cars and tools-but in the deeper sense. Jordan Grand Prix showed up with intent, spirit, and performance, even when the odds were stacked against them. Especially then.

In the early 1990s, there were dozens of times when it would have been easier not to show up. Funding that didn't land in time. Cars still being assembled on the freight plane. Engineers burning out. Eddie himself juggling lawsuits, debts, and driver drama. But when the grid formed on Sunday, Jordan was there. Against the odds. On the limit. Proud.

One particularly brutal stretch came in 1992. The team was struggling with sponsorship after a tough second season. Performance had dipped and so had the cash flow. With backers pulling out and suppliers unpaid, the Hungarian Grand Prix looked impossible. The staff were exhausted, the freight was delayed, and even the tyres were in question.

People around Eddie told him to skip it. One race wouldn't end the world. Better to regroup for Spa, they said. But that wasn't in his vocabulary. Instead, he sold a personal asset to cover the freight costs. He called in favours from his deep phone book-suppliers, former partners, even rival teams. He negotiated a delayed payment plan with Goodyear over dinner and a handshake. Then he rallied his crew – not with corporate pep talks, but with raw, unfiltered fire: "We're racers. Racers show up."

That weekend, the car didn't finish in the points, but something far more valuable happened. The team had shown the world – and themselves – that no matter what happened in the background, they could be counted on. That reputation would serve them again and again in the years ahead.

Eddie lived this mindset well beyond racing. Racing was just a way for him to compete and win. He did the same in business. He turned up to meetings after red-eye flights and all-nighters. When deals fell apart or press turned against him, he still arrived with a handshake and a grin. He didn't vanish when it was hard – he leaned in.

Even in his personal life, this was true. Friends going through a difficult time knew Eddie would be there. Whether it was a dinner, a flight, or just a call at 2 a.m., he answered. Not always perfectly.

Sometimes clumsily. But always fully. He showed up with the same rhythm he brought to the pit wall: animated, loyal, alert.

He once said, "The reason most people lose is that they simply don't turn up when it matters. You don't have to be brilliant. You just have to be there – with heart."

For Eddie, consistency was power. Presence was commitment. And showing up was more than a personal virtue – it was a cultural commandment. It became the heartbeat of Jordan Grand Prix and the people who moved with him from venture to venture, city to city, challenge to challenge.

And it's no coincidence that the people he mentored – drivers, engineers, executives – carried that same principle with them long after Jordan Formula 1 was gone. Because showing up builds something more than a reputation: it builds trust.

The Principle as Philosophy

Showing up isn't about waiting for the right mood or the right conditions. It's about being fully there – especially when it's hardest.

Presence signals belief: in the team, in the mission, in yourself. It builds trust when words aren't enough. It creates momentum when everything else stalls.

People don't remember who looked perfect. They remember who stood steady. Who stayed present when things got messy.

That's why Eddie's teams pulled harder. Why his business and sponsorship partners stayed longer. Why his friendships lasted decades. Because when Eddie showed up, he brought energy, loyalty, and life – and made others want to do the same.

Presence isn't a tactic, it's a choice. A daily decision to be real, to be reliable, to be ready – whatever the circumstances. And over time, that choice becomes the difference between those who are forgotten, and those who are remembered.

Practical Translation

Eddie Jordan didn't wait until conditions were perfect to act. He understood that the simple act of showing up – consistently, reliably, and fully – is what separates professionals from pretenders.

Whether you're chasing a dream, building a business, leading a team, or just trying to be more present in your life – this principle works. Here's how to apply it:

1. Build the muscle of consistency

Showing up isn't about heroics, it's about habits. Don't wait to "feel" motivated – create rituals that make it easier to start. Set times. Block off time. Turn up, even when it's awkward or inconvenient. That's how trust – and momentum – are built.

> **Ask yourself:** *In what small ways can I be more consistent every day?*

2. Don't let mood dictate motion

If you only act when you're in the mood, your progress will be slow and scattered. Eddie showed up whether he felt amazing or not – because discipline beats motivation every time. Success is often about doing the thing, especially when you don't feel like it.

> **Ask yourself:** *Where am I letting my mood overrule my commitment?*

3. Be reliable, especially under pressure

Eddie showed up in chaos – delayed flights, bad results, public heat – it didn't matter. That reliability built loyalty. Your presence under pressure tells people they can trust you – and that's what builds real teams.

> **Ask yourself:** *How can I show deeper loyalty and reliability to those around me?*

4. Presence is more than just physical

Don't just show up to the room – be in the room. Put the phone down. Ask real questions. Listen fully. When people feel your full attention, they give you theirs.

> **Ask yourself:** *How can I be more present with every person I'm with?*

5. Honour your commitments like currency

Eddie was known for following through. If he said he'd be there, he was. Every commitment you honour builds credibility. Every time you flake, you lose it.

> **Ask yourself:** *Where have I let someone down – and how can I make it right?*

6. Find your non-negotiables and stick to them

What matters most to you – your health, your creative work, your family? Treat those things like a race day. Show up for them, no matter what.

> **Ask yourself:** *What are the non-negotiable principles I choose to live by?*

7. Let others see you turn up when it's hard

Eddie didn't hide on bad days. He leaned in. People don't need to see perfection, they need to see presence. Turning up when it's tough earns a different kind of respect.

> **Ask yourself:** *Where have I been hiding instead of showing up?*

Bottom Line: Success doesn't come from waiting for inspiration. It comes from being there, again and again.

Show up when it's hard. Show up when it's boring. Show up when you're tired. Because showing up changes everything.

Reflection

You can have the talent, the strategy, the ambition – but if you don't show up when it matters, none of it counts. Eddie Jordan understood that instinctively. More than any spreadsheet or plan, it was presence that made the difference.

He didn't only show up when things were going well. He showed up when the sponsors pulled out. When the car broke down. When the freight didn't arrive. When everyone else was tempted to step back, Eddie stepped forward – sometimes loud, sometimes scrappy, but always there.

And that mattered.

Because showing up is about more than being seen – it's about being counted. It tells your team, your partners, your people: "I'm in. Still. Especially now."

Eddie didn't wait for perfect conditions. He showed up tired, under pressure, in chaos – and still brought humour, belief, rhythm. In an increasingly polished world, he stayed raw and real. That's why people followed him. That's why they trusted him.

Over time, showing up – fully, consistently, even imperfectly – becomes identity. It becomes legacy.

So, wherever you are – in a tough season, in doubt, in the middle of a long climb – ask yourself the only question that really matters:

Will I show up anyway?

Because that's the moment everything starts to change.

> *"You don't have to be brilliant.*
> *You just have to be there – with heart."*
> – Eddie Jordan

7. Sweat the Assets

The Eddie Story

If there's one principle Eddie Jordan lived by every single day, it was this: nothing sits still. If it has potential, it has purpose. And if it has purpose, it has to be *used*.

At Jordan Grand Prix, this was never a formal policy. It didn't need to be. It was simply how Eddie operated. He didn't like waste – not financial, not creative. Idle ideas. Idle machines. Untapped talent. To him, these weren't just inefficiencies – they were missed opportunities.

Eddie came from a background where you *made do*. In his early years, he learned how to hustle – not in the dishonest sense, but in the inventive one. You fixed things. You reused things. You found the edge inside what you already owned. And when he entered Formula 1 – one of the most extravagant, high-burn industries on the planet – he brought that scrappy, industrious mindset with him.

The Jordan team didn't have the luxury of excess, but that became an advantage. They were lean, quick, and creative. The wind tunnel wasn't idle in the off-season – it was used to test third-party designs for revenue. The parts department didn't just churn out components for Jordan cars – they fabricated pieces for other teams on the grid. The engineering department took side commissions during the winter months, and Eddie encouraged this. He believed that unused capacity was *waste*. And waste, in a competitive environment, was a form of disrespect – to the team, to the mission, and to the opportunity in front of them.

One of the best examples was the team's decision to build

bikes in the winter. In between race seasons, when other teams went quiet, Eddie's factory kept buzzing. They designed and built high-performance bicycles using the same materials and techniques they'd perfected in motorsport – carbon fibre, wind-tunnel-tested aerodynamics, lightweight frames. It wasn't a money-spinner at first, it was a *mind-spinner*. It kept the team active. It sharpened their thinking. And eventually, it became a modest commercial success.

But it went deeper than equipment or inventory. Eddie applied the same principle to people. He believed every person on the payroll had more to give – not by overworking them, but by freeing them. He encouraged engineers to pitch new ideas, even if they weren't part of the car programme. He let marketing interns shadow strategy meetings. He pulled people into unexpected roles not to test them, but to *trust* them.

He did it with his own assets, too. Eddie owned boats – beautiful, big boats – and instead of letting them sit idle in harbours, he chartered them. Used them for client meetings. Filmed on them. Hosted events. He used his homes for production shoots, team gatherings, and more than a few serious business conversations over dinner. He didn't wall off the different parts of his life – he activated them.

Even his time was treated as an asset to be sweated. A morning bike ride meant much more than fitness – it was a chance to connect, coach, think, and build loyalty. A dinner wasn't just a meal – it was a chance to make someone feel included, respected, and part of something bigger. A moment backstage wasn't idle time – it was an opportunity to listen, mentor, or spark something unexpected.

This wasn't idle busyness, it was *intentionality*. Eddie saw opportunity everywhere, and he hated seeing anything – or anyone – left underutilized.

He once said to a young entrepreneur, "If you're not using every part of the thing you've built – space, time, people, momentum – then you're carrying dead weight. And you can't win races with dead weight."

And it wasn't about maximizing for money. It was about momentum. About keeping things moving. Keeping people engaged. Turning friction into flow.

In 1994, Eddie was approached by a major oil company looking to sponsor the team. The catch? He already had a title sponsor whose name was on the side of the car. But turning down sponsorship money was never an option. So, in classic EJ style, he found a workaround: he put one sponsor's name on the left side of the car and the other on the right. And at race weekends, he took it a step further – placing one sponsor's hospitality suite on the outside of the track and the other on the inside, so whichever side their car passed, their brand was always in view.

That mindset helped him survive – and win – in the most competitive environments on earth. Formula 1, finance, media, hospitality, and music. Wherever he went, Eddie asked the same question:

"How can we use what we already have to go further?"

And that question led to deals, ideas, breakthroughs, and moments that others never saw coming – because they were too busy waiting for the next big thing, while Eddie was squeezing magic from what was already in the room.

The Principle as Philosophy

Eddie Jordan hated wasting time, talent, or tools. If something existed, it had a purpose. A wind tunnel, a yacht, a connection, a moment – he found a way to use it.

This wasn't about money. It was about respect – for what you'd built, earned, and already had.

Where others saw downtime, Eddie saw opportunity. Where others saved things for later, he asked, "Why not now?" He looked at machines, people, and relationships and asked: Could this be doing more?

That mindset came from his roots. Nothing got thrown away. Even with success, he stayed scrappy. He treated every asset like it had to prove its worth – because it did.

At Jordan Grand Prix, the factory didn't sit idle in winter, it took outside work. Staff weren't boxed in – they spoke up, solved problems, crossed boundaries. If something wasn't pulling its weight, it was fixed – or left behind.

This principle shaped his life, too. Boats became meeting rooms. Gigs raised money. He didn't talk about potential – he activated it.

To Eddie, letting anything sit idle was wasteful. Worse – it was disrespectful.

Why wait for more when you can use what's already there?

That's not a tactic – it's a mindset. One that creates momentum. One that wins.

Practical Translation

Eddie Jordan didn't waste things.

Not food. Not fuel. Not time. Not talent. Not money. Not energy. And never – ever – *the moment*.

He came from a home in Dublin where waste wasn't an option. If you left the lights on, you got told. If you wasted bread, it wasn't just waste – it was *disrespectful*. And that mindset stayed with him for life. He turned off all the lights in his house every night. Period.

He used everything. And he expected others to do the same.

Whether it was a wind tunnel in winter, a yacht sitting in port, a bike in the garage, or a contact on speed dial – if something could be activated, Eddie would find a way. Not to hoard value, but to *honour it*.

This wasn't about being cheap. He was generous, deeply so – with friends, with time, with loyalty. But he never confused generosity with waste. In fact, he believed they were opposites. He was tough in deals because he respected money. He bartered with what he had. He negotiated hard, not out of greed, but out of *discipline*. Because if you waste the small things, you'll waste the big ones too.

He didn't own things just to own them. He made them *work*.

A yacht broker once said, "Eddie's the only person I know who made his boat pay for itself in charters every year." But that didn't happen by accident. It happened because he hustled. He marketed. He watched the calendar. He treated every asset like it had a job to do.

And that mindset can be yours – whether you run a race team or just want to be more deliberate with your life. Here's where to start:

The Jordan Code

1. Respect what you already have

Make a list – not only of possessions, but of people, ideas, space, and experience. Ask what each of these could do *if activated with intent*. If you don't respect what's already in your world, why should more come to you?

> **Ask yourself:** *What am I sitting on that I'm not using – or appreciating – enough?*

2. Make your stuff work for you

Eddie never worked just to afford more things. He worked to make his life *move*. That meant making sure his assets pulled their weight – whether it was his boat, his brand, or his network.

Let your tools earn. Let your spaces earn. Let your past experiences earn. Flip the equation.

> **Ask yourself:** *Am I spending my life maintaining things – or letting them support my momentum?*

3. Use discipline in the small things

Turn off the lights. Pay attention to the details. Fix what's broken. If you're careless with the little things, how can you be trusted with the big ones?

Eddie believed in discipline. Quiet, consistent discipline – the kind that builds trust, sharpens leadership, and earns respect.

> **Ask yourself:** *Where have I become casual with things I should be careful with?*

4. Barter before you buy

Eddie was a master of leverage. If he could trade value – a favour, a connection, a shared resource – he would. Not to get away with less, but to *make the most of more*.

Assets aren't just objects. They're stories. Relationships. Influence. Be creative.

> **Ask yourself:** *What do I already have that could open the next door – if I used it differently?*

5. Expect others to respect what's theirs

Eddie didn't just live this standard – he expected to see it in others. You didn't need to be rich, but you needed to care. To turn up on time. To treat equipment well. To finish what you started. To notice the small things.

He believed you could tell everything about someone by how they treat what's already in their hands.

> **Ask yourself:** *Am I surrounded by people who respect the tools, time, and trust they've been given?*

6. Move things that have gone still

Motion is the signal that something's alive. Eddie didn't let systems, ideas, or people stagnate. If something wasn't being used, he asked why. Then he moved it. Or moved on.

You don't need more. You need to get things flowing again.

> **Ask yourself:** *Where in my world has energy gone still – and how can I wake it up?*

Eddie's world worked because he *worked his world*.

He didn't waste things. He didn't chase more for the sake of more. He made use of what was already close, already earned, already paid for. To him, that wasn't efficiency. It was *respect*.

Respect for the home he came from. Respect for the time it takes to build anything real. Respect for the discipline it takes to lead something well.

So, whether it's a boat or a bicycle, a business card or a bold idea – don't leave it sitting in the dark.

Switch it on. Let it earn. Let it move.

Sweat the asset.

Reflection

Eddie Jordan didn't waste things – not because he was frugal, but because he was sharp. He respected time, space, tools, and above all, people. He came from a household where nothing was thrown away without a reason, and that mindset never left him.

Unused potential wasn't neutral to Eddie – it was disrespect. If you'd earned it, built it, paid for it, then it had work to do.

Value to unlock. Movement to offer. That applied to machines, moments, factories, connections, even conversations.

At Jordan Grand Prix, this philosophy pulsed through everything. The factory didn't rest in winter, it made parts for other teams or pivoted to build carbon-fibre bikes. Staff weren't boxed in – they were encouraged to learn across roles and challenge norms. Off-seasons weren't quiet – they were launching pads.

Because when Eddie looked at what he had, he didn't see cost – he saw momentum. He saw what could be activated, not what should be preserved. He turned tools into opportunity, downtime into invention, and every corner of his world into something that moved.

It wasn't about grinding harder, it was about thinking sharper. About having the discipline to see what's in front of you – and use it. Eddie turned off every light before bed, not to save money, but because, in his words, "That's just respecting the house."

He even used his Formula 1 engineering team to build for others – not only for cash, but because if the capacity was there, why not put it to work?

That was Eddie. Always on. Always active. Always asking: what more can this do? He didn't wait for better conditions, he got the best out of what was already in his hands.

That's the legacy. Respect what you've got. Then make it move.

> *"They're not just assets.*
> *They're possibilities waiting to move."*
> – **Eddie Jordan**

8. Act with Urgency

The Eddie Story

Eddie Jordan didn't live life in neutral. He didn't stroll through days. He didn't believe in "getting around to it". He moved through the world like someone who knew – not feared, but *knew* – that the clock was always ticking. Not metaphorically. *Actually ticking.* Every second gone was gone forever, and Eddie wasn't about to waste it.

From the outside, he looked like a man in constant motion – and he was. But it wasn't chaos, it was choreography. There was a rhythm to his pace, a clarity to his direction, a kind of full-hearted commitment to *now*. Being around him meant learning to keep up. Physically. Mentally. Emotionally. Energetically. His presence made you more alert – not from pressure, but from proximity to someone who respected time in a way most people only claim to.

He used to say, almost casually, like it was obvious, "Time is the most valuable thing you have – so don't waste it." It sounded simple until you realized, he meant it. And not just in business meetings or on race day. He meant it when he showed up to a dinner on time. When he answered your call on the first ring. When he kept the promise he made in a passing conversation. He meant it every time he gave someone his attention – and every time he expected the same in return.

He lived by an internal clock that never reset. And the people who worked with him – and the people who loved him – knew it. If he said 9:00, he meant 8:55. If you missed a deadline, you got one chance to explain. Maybe two, if he liked you. But never three. And not because he was unkind – because he had *urgency.* Because he had a relationship with time that wasn't casual. Because he believed the fastest way to show someone you didn't care was to *waste their time.*

Formula 1 didn't just teach Eddie how to build a team or run a business, it taught him the sacredness of *timing.* In that world, everything is measured in milliseconds. You can lose a race with a perfect car and the perfect driver if a pit crew tightens a bolt a half-second too late. You can watch a podium disappear because someone hesitated on a strategy call. There's no room for "we'll get to it". You get to it now, or you don't get to it at all.

That mindset soaked into every corner of his life. Not only his work – but his presence. *All of it.* If you were spending a day with Eddie – even a social day, even on holiday – there was always a sense of structure. Of purpose. You might be heading to a gig on a yacht or planning a dinner with 20 people with no notice or flying to the other side of the world for something that looked like fun from the outside but was organized like a military operation underneath. But whatever the plan was, there was a *plan.* It had pace. And it had intention.

Eddie liked to say he was trying to pack three lives into one. It wasn't a metaphor, it was a manifesto. You saw it in his schedule. You felt it in his energy. Meetings in the morning. A call with a driver in the back of a taxi. A performance in the evening. Ideas in between. Messages answered. Problems fixed. And always – always – something on the move.

And yet, it never felt like he was in a panic. He wasn't chasing time. He was *using it.* That's the difference. Urgency, for Eddie, wasn't about pressure – it was about *presence.* It was about not letting the moment pass without taking it seriously. It was about making things happen instead of waiting for someone else to move first.

He had a phrase, "Time is the enemy of all deals." The longer it drifted, the more risk of things that could scupper the deal. "Close it or not. Just get it f**king done!" was his war cry.

As he got older, that urgency didn't fade – it intensified. Because with success came a new awareness: the more you have, the more clearly you can see what really matters. The money gets better. The deals get bigger. The stage gets louder. But time? That gets *shorter*. And Eddie saw that coming. And he said it, as only he could:

"Eventually, you realize you've got MMTT – more money than time."

And once that truth lands – once you see that time is the *only* thing that doesn't scale – you start to treat it differently. You start saying no faster. You stop indulging people who dance around decisions. You let go of meetings that could've been a call. You delete the calendar blocks you're not passionate about. And you hold close the people and the moments that *matter*.

Eddie lived like someone who had already learned that lesson. He lived like the clock wasn't just ticking – it was precious. He lived like *now* was all we really get. And when you watched him – *really* watched – you started to feel that urgency in yourself. You started to realize how much you'd let drift. How many things you'd parked. How many corners you coasted through, thinking you'd find your way later.

He didn't coast. Not ever. Not in a race. Not in life. He treated the first lap with the same seriousness as the final one. Because he knew the shake-up doesn't happen at the end unless you *show up at the start*.

That was Eddie.

He didn't make a fuss. He didn't talk about hustle. He just *moved*. And in doing so, he gave everyone around him a question that mattered more than any answer:

What are you waiting for?

The Principle as Philosophy

Urgency didn't mean rushing to Eddie. It meant respecting time – your own and everyone else's. It wasn't panic or pressure, it was presence.

To him, urgency was about showing up fully. Acting instead of hesitating. Deciding instead of drifting. Most people wait for perfect timing or a clearer signal. Eddie didn't wait – he moved.

He saw time for what it really is: not an endless resource, but a finite currency. You can earn more money, fix a mistake, rebuild trust, but you can't get back the hour you wasted doubting yourself – or the moment you let pass because you thought there'd be another.

That mindset shaped how he worked. He made quick decisions, gave straight answers, and didn't waste words. If something mattered, he acted on it. If it didn't, he moved on.

Time was, and is, the most valuable thing in the world. It doesn't wait. And if you don't use it . . . it's gone. It's more valuable than money. MMTT.

That's the heart of it. Urgency isn't about rushing, it's about being awake. Focused. Alive to the moment in front of you, and disciplined enough not to waste it.

That's how Eddie lived. And it's why people trusted him with their time, because he never took it for granted.

Practical Translation

Urgency doesn't mean chaos. It's not about rushing, panicking, or running on fumes. It's about treating time like it matters – because it does.

Eddie Jordan didn't move fast to impress anyone. He moved fast because he respected the day. He respected the people who gave him their time. And he respected himself enough not to drift through life waiting for "later".

He lived by a rhythm: if it matters, act now. If it doesn't, move on.

The beauty was in how he made it look simple. Because to him, it was.

So how do you live with that kind of urgency? You begin by seeing where your time really goes – where it leaks, where it stalls, where it's handed over to things that don't match what you value. Then you tighten the loop. Sharpen the decision. Speed up the moment of action.

This isn't about going faster. It's about becoming sharper. More awake. More deliberate.

Here's how to live it:

1. Finish what you've started

Most people aren't stuck for ideas, they're stuck with unfinished ones.

Ask yourself: *What unfinished project needs to be closed today?*

2. Clear the clutter

Don't let your calendar fill with noise. Guard your energy.

> **Ask yourself:** *What low-value things or people do I need to say no to?*

3. Prioritize what matters

Urgency doesn't mean saying yes to everything. It means doubling down on what counts.

> **Ask yourself:** *To what high-value things can I give a little more time?*

4. Be fully present

Real urgency isn't speed, it's depth. When you're with someone, really be there.

> **Ask yourself:** *What's the next question to ask here?*

5. Start before you feel ready

Clarity often comes *after* the first step, not before.

> **Ask yourself:** *What can I do to get started, to build momentum right now?*

6. Respect other people's clocks

Show up early. Keep your word. Finish on time.

> **Ask yourself:** *How can I be five minutes early for everything today?*

7. Say what needs to be said

The apology. The idea. The truth. If it's on your mind daily, it's time.

> **Ask yourself:** *What is the uncomfortable thing being left unsaid right now?*

8. Question your time habits

Time isn't just spent, it's invested. Spend it with intent.

> **Ask yourself:** *How long have I been carrying this unfinished task? Is this really how I want to spend my time? What am I actually waiting for?*

Eddie understood this deeply: time is the most expensive thing in the room.

You can recover from failure. You can earn back money. But you can't reclaim a week spent drifting. You can't un-spend the hours you gave to things you didn't believe in.

He didn't tell people to move faster – he just showed what life looks like when you do.

He lived with urgency. With clarity. With purpose. And when you were around him, you felt it: the energy, the decisiveness, the respect for the moment.

That's what made you want to live differently. Because when you treat time like it matters, you start doing things that matter.

> *"Time doesn't care who you are. It doesn't wait, it doesn't pause, and it sure as hell doesn't rewind. You either move with it – or you get left behind."*
> – Eddie Jordan

Reflection

There's comfort in believing we have time – that tomorrow will come, that the project can wait, the call can be made later, the moment will somehow be better someday.

But Eddie Jordan never lived like that.

He knew time was passing – not in theory, but in reality. That's why he moved when others stalled. He showed up early, made decisions quickly, and followed through. Not to rush, but because he respected the hour in front of him.

To be around Eddie wasn't to feel pressure, it was to feel presence. He gave his time generously – and he made it matter. He acted with urgency – he didn't hesitate. He activated. People. Projects. Rooms. Lives.

He made urgency feel like a gift – a chance to treat time as sacred and move towards what matters.

Eddie didn't chase time, he used it. He didn't wait for green lights. He became the signal:

"Time is money. But more than that – time is life. And you don't get it back."

Later, with success behind him, he'd put it even more simply:

"Races are won by milliseconds. If you don't value time, how can you even compete – never mind win?"

Time underscored everything at Jordan: capacity, resources, transport, logistics, performance. It was the one currency they couldn't afford to waste.

So take the turn. Make the call. Start the thing. Do it now. Don't wait.

Because that's what Eddie did.

And he made it count.

9. Focus Improves Performance

The Eddie Story

In the earliest days of Jordan Grand Prix, long before the champagne and the shock podiums, the team would rehearse pit stops late into the night under fluorescent lights in a cold factory garage. No cameras. No fanfare. Just mechanics sweating in silence, repeating the same motion over and over again. Jack up. Tyre off. Tyre on. Jack down. Reset.

Eddie would stay. He didn't need to. He wasn't checking their work – he was honouring it. Watching. Encouraging. Occasionally offering a cheeky joke or a rhythm cue like a drummer guiding a band. To him, this wasn't grunt work, it was choreography. And it mattered. He said, "They didn't even talk to one another. They all just knew what their role was."

In 1991, those stops took 12 seconds. By 1999, they were under six. That wasn't about technology, itt was about trust. Repetition. Focus. Teamwork so aligned it became instinct.

Eddie never viewed the pit crew as anonymous foot soldiers. He gave them respect – and with that, responsibility. He knew their names, their families, their strengths. They were the unsung athletes of the paddock, and he treated them accordingly. At Jordan, a great pit stop was celebrated with the same enthusiasm as a driver overtaking into Turn 1.

In the early days of Jordan Grand Prix, pit stops were a steep learning curve. At their 1991 debut in Phoenix, the crew had never rehearsed a live stop until the race itself. Andy Stevenson, now sporting director at Aston Martin, recalled, "We had never practised a live pit stop until the race and I don't recall it being particularly quick." But over time, what began with inexperience became a core strength. As the team matured, so too did their precision, speed, and ability to deliver under pressure.

By 1999, that evolution was clear. At the French Grand Prix, Jordan secured a stunning victory through strategic excellence and flawless execution. Heinz-Harald Frentzen's one-stop strategy, combined with a slick, perfectly timed pit stop, allowed him to leapfrog rivals and win the race outright. It was a masterclass in pit lane discipline and race-day focus – proof that sharpening the basics, like pit stop performance, could turn a midfield team into a race winner.

That attitude permeated every layer of his organization. Eddie believed the car could only be fast if *every* part of the system was tight. From the engineers designing new wings to the logistics crew loading the trucks, from the finance lead managing sponsor cash to the cleaner keeping the facility spotless – everyone's work *fed the lap time*. And if it didn't, it was a distraction.

There was no ambiguity in his team. No confusion about purpose. At Jordan, the mission was simple: "Make the car faster. Everything else is noise".

That focus created freedom. It meant you didn't need endless meetings. You didn't need job title hierarchies to determine importance. If your work contributed to performance, it was valuable. If it didn't, it didn't happen. It was ruthless in the best way – clear, honest, energizing.

The philosophy extended far beyond Formula 1.

When Eddie was touring with his band V10, the same logic applied. The drummer, the lighting tech, the sound engineer, the bus driver – everyone had to be on. Eddie used to say, "You can't have a singer waiting while the mic's buzzing. You've got to nail it – live. And if one person slips, the whole vibe goes." That's more than music – that's execution culture.

On television, it was even more intense. Live Formula 1 broadcasts are measured in seconds. A missed cue. A mistimed handover. A panel guest off-topic. It can spiral fast. But Eddie thrived in that space. Not because he was polished, but because he was *present*. Tuned in. Reading the flow of the room like a race strategist watching tyre degradation. When the camera light blinked on, he hit the beat – with colour, wit, and clarity.

Because he knew the truth: high performance isn't about solo brilliance – it's about collective sharpness.

And it wasn't ego-free because people didn't *have* egos. It was ego-free because they were aligned. When you're all locked onto the same mission, there's no time for politics.

Eddie used to call that "clearing the noise". Once the distraction drops, people rise.

And when it all came together – in the pit lane, in the garage, on a stage, or in a studio – Eddie would lean back, grin wide, and say:

"That's it. That's the magic."

Not luck. Not chaos. But rhythm. Unity. Precision.

Teamwork. Focus. Performance.

The Principle as Philosophy

Formula 1 is decided in split-seconds. One slow call, one fumble, and it's over. It's not just talent or tech that wins. It's rhythm. Precision. People moving as one, tuned to the same signal.

Eddie Jordan understood that. Performance doesn't come from chaos – it comes from clarity. At Jordan Grand Prix, everyone knew the goal. Everyone had a role. Everyone was trusted to deliver. Whether you were lead engineer or unloading tyres, you mattered.

Because when teams feel like teams, they move like one.

That unity came from culture, trust, and a simple rule: *If it doesn't make the car faster, don't do it.*

Eddie didn't micromanage. He cleared the noise, set the rhythm, and let people breathe. That freedom made them sharper.

No clutter. No hesitation. Just focus.

And with that focus, people stop playing it safe. They back each other. They move quicker – because they're not second-guessing. That's why Jordan's pit crew became great. Why their cars punched above their budget. Why people stayed.

Because in a real team – one that's clear, trusted, and fearless – you don't want to leave. You want to go again.

Eddie knew it from music too: it's not about the perfect solo, it's about the band being in sync.

Great teams don't just function.

They flow.

And when they flow – they're dangerous.

Practical Translation

High performance looks effortless from the outside – but underneath, it's made of *structure, rhythm, and trust.*

Eddie Jordan didn't lead with checklists, he led with clarity. He didn't obsess over control – he created *flow*. And that flow was only possible because his teams were aligned, focused, and deeply tuned into one another.

The mission was clear. The trust was real. The margin for error was tight. And somehow, in the middle of all that pressure, people still smiled.

That's what great teamwork looks like: Less friction. More feeling. Less permission-seeking. More *doing*.

Here's how to build it – whether you're leading a race crew, a business unit, a classroom, or a kitchen:

1. Start with a shared mission

Everything flows from this. At Jordan, the mantra was simple: "Make the car faster." Everyone, everywhere, understood it. That gave each person autonomy and alignment at once.

> **Ask yourself:** *Is our team truly working towards one thing – or are we pulling in slightly different directions?*

2. Name the critical few – and cut the rest

Too many priorities kill focus. Eddie cut through noise with ruthless simplicity. He asked, "Does this help us win? Does it make the car go faster?" If not, it was gone.

> **Ask yourself:** *Are we overcomplicating things? What could we remove that's actually in the way?*

3. Trust the people – or change the people

Eddie didn't second-guess his team every step of the way. He gave responsibility early and loudly. That trust created speed. Loyalty. Energy.

> **Ask yourself:** *Am I empowering people to lead – or waiting for them to prove they won't fail?*

4. Don't let ego get in the way of rhythm

Jordan wasn't about job titles. Ideas could come from anywhere – a mechanic, an intern, a chef. What mattered was contribution. Rhythm. Cohesion.

> **Ask yourself:** *Have we made space for the best ideas to rise, regardless of where they come from?*

5. Rehearse transitions, not only strategy

In Formula 1, it's often not the car or the driver that makes the difference – it's the *handoff.* The pit stop. The breakdown moment.

Eddie made his crew rehearse pit stops late into the night – not for perfection, but for *confidence under pressure.*

> **Ask yourself:** Where are we dropping the baton? Can we practise the messy moments, not just the ideal ones?

6. Celebrate tight execution, as well as big wins

At Jordan, a sub-seven-second pit stop was as celebrated as a Top 10 finish. Why? Because that's where real performance lives – in the micro-moments most people miss.

> **Ask yourself:** Are we recognizing the work behind the win – or just the headline outcome?

7. Tune the culture like a band

Eddie thought like a drummer. He wasn't after volume – he wanted *rhythm and flow.* He wanted timing. Feel. Attunement. And he led with that same musical instinct – give people the beat, then let them play.

> **Ask yourself:** Does our team feel locked in – or are we just playing our parts separately?

Great teams don't get there by accident.

They get there by aligning focus. Clearing noise. Removing friction. And by trusting each other enough to move *faster than logic should allow.*

That's what Eddie built. A group of people who worked like a crew – but moved like a band.

You can do the same.

Reflection

Strip away the speed, the pressure, the noise of Formula 1, and what wins races – what *always* wins – is focus.

Eddie Jordan understood that. He built a team that wasn't the richest or best resourced, but often the most focused. That's why Jordan Grand Prix could punch above its weight. That's why they finished fifth in their first season. That's why they won at Spa.

Because when a team knows what matters – and commits to it completely – they outperform expectation. Every time.

Focus sharpens. It turns effort into execution. Chaos into choreography. Individuals into a team.

At Jordan, focus wasn't spreadsheets or silence. It was shared intention. Everyone understood the mission. Everyone pulled in the same direction. That's why decisions came faster, energy hit harder, and results went deeper.

Focus removed the friction. It cut the noise. It stopped second-guessing, and let people deliver at their best.

And it didn't stop at the car. Focus deepened trust. It built rhythm. It allowed people to try, speak, fail – and go again. It turned a budget team into a real contender.

Jordan Grand Prix had flow. Not perfection, not polish-*pulse*.

That's what Eddie created. Not through control, but clarity. Not through pressure, but belief.

He didn't chase superstars. He built harmony. Not everyone playing the same note, but everyone playing the same song.

Formula 1 felt it. Jordan made the sport less predictable, more human. They added chaos, colour, personality – and made the giants sharper in the process.

They were the rock 'n' roll garage. The rebels with rhythm. The team with just enough budget and far too much belief.

And at the centre was Eddie – showman, hustler, heartbeat. To compete? Yes, but also to *change* the sport.

So whatever team you're a part of – a family, business, a startup, a band – the principle holds:

Set the mission. Clear the noise. Build the rhythm. Trust the people. And go. Because when focus becomes shared and trust becomes real, you don't just win races.

You change the game.

10. Steal the Deal, Keep Your Honour

The Eddie Story

Eddie Jordan was a deal junkie.

That was his phrase, and it was true. He didn't chase wealth for its own sake. He didn't collect cars, covet watches, or hoard assets. What got him moving was the *deal*. The duel. The negotiation. The theatre of it. The adrenaline. The moment when two people locked horns and something was on the line.

Whether it was for £10 or £10 million, Eddie brought the same energy. He didn't scale his intensity based on the stakes – because for him, the joy wasn't in the size of the deal, it was in the duel. The pressure. The way it all hinged on reading the room at the exact right second.

He lived for it. The battle. The play. The win. And when the deal came off – when he felt that shift, when the pen hit the page or the nod confirmed the agreement – he'd grin wide and throw his head back in delight: "We robbed that!"

It wasn't arrogance, it was celebration. He hadn't lied, bullied, or manipulated. He'd simply played it better. Faster. With feel. He'd spotted the crack in the wall and made his move. He saw what others didn't. He asked for what others wouldn't dare. He turned value others missed into momentum. And when it worked? He was buzzing.

He didn't need the whole thing, he just needed that one sliver. "There's nothing sweeter," he'd say, "than the bit you steal." That little edge. That margin. The thing you weren't quite supposed to get – but you found a way. That was the magic.

He read people like others read newspapers. The nerves, the bluster, the pride, the weakness. When to bluff. When to wait. When to ask for more. He played fast – but he played fair. He could win the deal and still leave you smiling. Still shake your hand. Still buy you a pint afterwards.

He respected people who came back hard. Who pushed him. Who didn't give in too soon. That's what he wanted – the contest. The stretch. The mutual recognition at the end that you both brought your A-game.

And he never played it down. Eddie loved the game so much, he couldn't hide it. He didn't want to win quietly, he wanted to feel it. Celebrate it. Own it. He once tried to sell back a giant Methuselah of rosé to his friend Nigel – the same bottle Nigel had gifted him the year before. "Doing you a favour," Eddie said, straight-faced. Nigel paused. "Eddie . . . I gave you that as a gift last year." One beat of silence. Then laughter. Pure mischief. Classic Eddie.

Because even when the punchline was on him, he loved the game too much to care.

But for all the speed and charm and cheek, Eddie never crossed the line.

He was a hustler – but he was honourable.

He didn't just make deals, he kept them.

If he said yes, he followed through. If he said no, he said it early. There were no games, no delays, no smoke and mirrors. If he gave his word, that was the deal.

"You can't cash promises," he'd say. It wasn't a deal until it moved. Until it happened. He didn't want talk, he wanted results. Action. Delivery.

He brought the same focus to every room – from pub back rooms with young startups to high-gloss boardrooms in Monaco. He didn't scale his respect based on status, he scaled it based on how people showed up.

He noticed everything. How people treated their staff. How they responded to pressure. Whether they flinched when the numbers got real. If the energy was off – if the intent wasn't clear – he'd walk. No matter how big the deal.

And he never forgot what it was like to be overlooked.

He didn't pull the ladder up behind him, he held it steady. He gave his time to people who hadn't yet "made it". Not to tick a box, but because he believed in them. If he saw hunger, and the beginnings of an idea, he leaned in. He didn't need polish, he wanted edge.

Jordan Grand Prix was an underdog team built on feel, not flash. His deal-making reflected that. He didn't chase the obvious. He didn't over-promise. He made it real, and he made it last.

He often said: "The best deals I ever did weren't the biggest. They were the ones that built trust. That's what lasts."

And that's what made Eddie different. He didn't treat deal-making as a transaction, he treated it as a relationship. As a test of who you are. As a chance to compete – and connect.

That's why people kept coming back.

That's why deals with Eddie stood out.

Because it was never just about the numbers.

Because there was always an edge.

Because every deal had colour, character, and something both sides walked away from having learned.

Because he understood that deals are human – not just trans-actions.

Because he respected every deal, whether it was £10 or £10 million.

Because he knew that how you handled the small ones shaped how you earned the big ones.

From selling cars out the back of a bank to brokering Adrian Newey's move nearly 50 years later – it was always about the deal.

Because he was real.

Sharp.

Present.

Honourable.

The Principle as Philosophy

Eddie Jordan wasn't just good at deals – he was world-class. A negotiator in the truest sense: instinctive, sharp, and fearless. He didn't hide behind silence or legal fog. He walked into the room with a story, a smile, and a scalpel. You didn't realize you were on the back foot until it was too late. And somehow, you didn't mind.

Because Eddie didn't bully. He didn't bluff to impress. He didn't play games for ego. He played for edge – and played to win.

And when he did win? He left people smiling. Because it wasn't just about closing the deal – it was about how you did it.

That was the code:

Be bold. Be brilliant. Be fair.

Eddie understood something most people miss: deals are never just about numbers. They're about energy. Feel. Trust. They reveal how someone behaves under pressure. How they treat people when there's no fanfare. Whether their word carries weight – or floats away in the silence.

That's why Eddie respected every deal – whether it was £10 or £10 million. He didn't scale his effort based on the cheque. He showed up properly, no matter what was at stake. Because in his world, reputation wasn't built in the spotlight – it was built in the repetition.

If you cut corners on the small ones, you're not ready for the big ones. If you're casual when no one's watching, you haven't earned the stage.

Eddie brought discipline to the art. Consistency. Commitment. A kind of unspoken precision. He believed that how you treat the earliest deals – the ones without the glamour – defines whether you'll ever be trusted with the big ones.

Respect wasn't soft, it was structure.

Presence wasn't performative, it was professional.

And trust wasn't a tactic. It was the whole point.

He didn't honour the deal for what it might lead to, he honoured it because that's what you do.

Whether it was a call returned, a favour followed through, or a handshake in a pub – if Eddie said he was in, he was in. Fully. That's what people remembered.

Because the truth is, the biggest deals rarely look like it at first. They grow from the small ones that were taken seriously. The ones where people showed up, stayed sharp, and gave their word – and meant it.

And it's telling that nearly everyone Eddie dealt with – across decades, industries, and continents – kept a connection with him. They stayed in touch. Stayed friends. They remembered the deal, yes. But more than that, they remembered how it was done. That, in the end, was the real testament.

That's how Eddie worked.

And that's how he won.

Practical Translation

Eddie Jordan didn't just do deals – he lived them. He made them sharp, fast, human, and unforgettable. He brought presence, nerve, instinct, and discipline. And he treated every deal like it mattered – because it did.

Here's how to bring that same energy and honour into your own way of dealing:

1. Show up the same, no matter the size

Don't save your best for the high-stakes rooms. Whether it's £10 or £10 million, bring the same presence, intent, and rhythm. That's where consistency becomes strength.

> **Ask yourself:** *Am I giving the small deals the same focus I give the big ones?*

2. Read the room – not just the numbers

Deals aren't spreadsheets. They're human. People reveal more in tone, posture, and pauses than in the figures. Pay attention. That's where the leverage lives.

> **Ask yourself:** *What is this person really trying to say – and not saying?*

3. Master the ask

This is where most people hesitate – Eddie never did. He asked clearly. Confidently. Without flinching. And without apology. If you believe in the deal, ask. If you don't ask, you definitely won't get.

> **Ask yourself:** *Am I asking boldly enough – or waiting to be offered?*

4. Make the ask worth saying yes to

Eddie didn't just push – he delivered value. He built clarity, energy, visibility, and momentum around every ask. That made people lean in.

> **Ask yourself:** *How can I make this easier to say yes to?*

5. Earn trust with your follow-through

It's not what you promise – it's what you do. Eddie was remembered because he delivered, and didn't just agree.

> **Ask yourself:** *Am I someone people trust to follow through without chasing?*

6. Don't judge deals by size – judge them by how you show up

A small deal done with full integrity builds the mindset that wins big ones. Eddie never switched off.

> **Ask yourself:** *Am I practising my standard – or saving it for later?*

7. Push hard – play fair

Eddie didn't negotiate to be liked. He negotiated to win – but always with respect.

Ask yourself: *Am I fighting for the deal – or just trying to win at any cost?*

8. Treat the conversation as the beginning, not the end

For Eddie, a deal was never just about closing – it was about starting something.

Ask yourself: *What kind of relationship am I building through this deal?*

9. Know when to walk

If the energy was wrong or the behaviour off, Eddie would walk – no matter the money.

Ask yourself: *Am I willing to walk away from a deal that doesn't feel right?*

10. Honour the deal once it's done

Winning means nothing if you don't deliver. Eddie didn't vanish after the handshake – he showed up.

Ask yourself: *Would I be proud to have my name on this – after it's signed?*

Reflection

For Eddie Jordan, deals weren't just business, they were performance. They were how he made his mark.

Every negotiation was pure Eddie: quick-thinking, charismatic, fiercely committed, and always a step ahead. He didn't just win deals, he made them unforgettable. A sponsor pitch, a merchandise push, a boat sale, even his party piece, which was a press-up challenge against athletes. The duel. The challenge. The win.

And when he landed it? You'd hear that laugh echo across the room. A laugh that said: *We pulled it off – and did it with style.*

He taught those around him that great deals aren't about trickery. They're about timing, feel, presence. He showed that negotiation isn't a dark art – it's a bright one. Full of energy, humour, and precision.

Eddie never bullied. Never bluffed without a reason. He read the room, played the rhythm, and trusted his instincts.

He didn't wear a mask. He didn't need to.

He walked in with eyes dancing, already reading the angles. The charm was the distraction. The deal was the mission. And when it clicked – when the papers were signed and the handshake sealed – it felt like the final beat of a perfect solo.

Because Eddie knew what most people forget: The win isn't in the volume. It's in the craft. The edge isn't in deception. It's in discipline. And the joy? It's in the feel.

He made deals fun. He made them fair. He made them matter. And in doing so, he left a lesson behind:

If you've got the nerve to see the angle, the feel to move at the right time, and the style to do it with soul – you don't need to wear a mask.

11. Find Your Edge

The Eddie Story

Eddie Jordan didn't play fair in the traditional sense. He played smart. He played fast. He played for the edge. Not by cutting corners, but by constantly asking: *Where's the angle no one else is seeing?*

Whether it was racing strategy, talent spotting, contract deals, or media attention, Eddie was always scanning, always moving. While others waited for green lights, he was already halfway down the road.

That mindset – seeing what others missed and acting before they hesitated – made him dangerous. Especially for a team like Jordan Grand Prix that didn't have the deepest pockets or biggest backers. They had hustle. And they had Eddie.

Chaos as Strategy

When Jordan entered Formula 1 in 1991, they were scrappy underdogs up against McLaren, Ferrari, and Williams. Eddie knew charm and a clever chassis weren't enough. So, he built something different: a team that moved fast, took risks, and thrived in chaos. They ran light, attacked qualifying, backed bold drivers, and made quick, clever calls. Where others waited for perfect conditions, Jordan made the most of imperfect ones.

They didn't outspend rivals, they outthought them.

The Personality Advantage

In a paddock full of corporate suits, Eddie stood out by design. The loud shirts, sunglasses, goatee, and rock 'n' roll energy weren't vanity, they were strategy. "I'm a small guy, so I knew I had to be different," he said.

He became the character Formula 1 didn't know it needed. Jordan GP wasn't just a team – it was a show. Fans loved it. Sponsors noticed. The brand had edge. And Eddie *was* the brand.

Spotting Talent Early

Eddie had a rare instinct for potential before proof. He gave Michael Schumacher his first race. Saw the spark in Ayrton Senna. Backed Hill, Barrichello, Alesi, Ralf Schumacher, Irvine – before they were names.

He didn't wait for CVs. He watched body language. Focus. Fire. He trusted feel. And when he felt it, he moved – fast.

Deals, Business, and Hidden Angles

Off-track, Eddie was just as sharp. He played chess behind the scenes – bidding on assets, flipping businesses, backing brands.

His £3 billion bid for Playtech surprised many – but not those who knew him. He'd seen timing, done the homework, built the team. Same with his move to back London Irish Rugby Football Club – a chance to combine heritage with structure. Smart play. Strategic heart.

And when he sold Jordan Grand Prix in 2005, most assumed he walked away. But he quietly kept the lease on part of the

Silverstone site. Classic Eddie: never just sell the car – keep the keys to the garage.

The Edge in Everyday Life

The edge was more than business – it was feel. It was how he lived. Eddie saw opportunity in jam sessions and dinner tables. He used his boat for business. Turned friends into partners. Ideas into assets. He was relentless.

He didn't wait to be the biggest. He just moved first – or moved differently.

Because that's the final lesson: The edge isn't something you steal, it's something you *spot*. It's something you *give yourself* by refusing to play the game the usual way. Eddie never chased the headlines – he chased the angle behind the deal. And more often than not, it paid off.

The Principle as Philosophy

In Eddie Jordan's world, advantage didn't appear – it was created.

He didn't wait for perfect timing or obvious opportunities. He trained himself to *see the edge* in places others ignored – and to move quickly, boldly, when it showed up.

Because that's the thing about edges: They don't arrive wrapped in certainty, they arrive disguised as something *a little mad*.

A driver no one's heard of. A sponsorship deal that's unconventional. A look that breaks every dress code. A business play that feels premature – until it's too late for anyone else to catch up.

Eddie didn't gamble recklessly, he calculated instinctively. He stayed sharp by staying curious. He didn't copy – he noticed. Didn't wait – he moved.

He wasn't just asking, "What are we doing today?" He was asking, "What's the hidden path? What's the thing no one else has thought of yet?" He tried not to limit his thinking ever.

That mindset is what made him dangerous. Not just in racing, but in business, in culture, in rooms where people underestimated him – and left regretting it.

And the beautiful part is this edge wasn't just about speed. It was about feel. It came from listening more closely. Watching the moment. Understanding rhythm. Knowing when to sit still, and when to strike.

Eddie styled himself deliberately for the same reason he styled his deals – to stand out, to gain ground, to express who he was without waiting for permission.

That's the deeper point: The edge isn't a tactic. It's a mindset. It's how you enter a room. How you ask a question. How you position yourself. How you choose to be remembered.

It's not always loud – but it's always intentional.

Because when the resources are limited and the playing field isn't level, the edge is what makes the difference.

And the best ones don't come from force, they come from feel.

Practical Translation

Finding the edge isn't about being clever, it's about being *awake*.

Eddie Jordan didn't always have the fastest car or the biggest wallet, but he *noticed things*. He looked for patterns. Loopholes.

Leverage. He listened when others were speaking. He watched the room when others were busy trying to dominate it.

And that gave him something few others had: a sixth sense for opportunity others hadn't seen yet.

You don't need to be in Formula 1 to build that skill, you just need to practice looking at your life with a little more *angle*.

Here's where to begin:

1. Zoom out and scan for hidden openings

Most people stay locked into the way things are. Eddie constantly asked: *What's not being used? What's being overlooked? What's just slightly off-centre from the obvious move?*

> **Ask yourself:** What's the opportunity hiding just outside the path I'm already walking?

2. Make surprise part of your strategy

Eddie wore wild shirts in boardrooms for a reason. He threw off expectations. Kept people guessing. Created space for negotiation, humour, pressure release – all while staying in control. Sometimes the edge is as simple as not being what people expect.

> **Ask yourself:** Where could I break the pattern – and change the energy in the room?

3. Use what you've got in unexpected ways

Eddie used his Formula 1 factory to build parts for other teams. Turned downtime into bike production. Used his boat to host meetings. Turned personality into presence.

You don't always need more, you need to *see more in what you already have.*

> **Ask yourself:** *What's underused in my world – and what would Eddie do with it?*

4. Look for people everyone else overlooks

Eddie found world champions before they were champions. He wasn't looking for polish – he was looking for fire. That same edge exists in business, in teams, in friends. Look for hunger. Look for spark.

> **Ask yourself:** *Who in my world has more to give than they've been allowed to show?*

5. Use chaos as a competitive advantage

Spa 1998 wasn't a perfect race. It was a *mess*. Rain. Crashes. Confusion. And Eddie won because he stayed calm and found clarity in the storm.

Edges often appear when others are distracted. If you can stay sharp when others are scrambling, you'll find your move.

> **Ask yourself:** *What's the next moment of chaos – and how can I be ready while others panic?*

6. Turn your personality into positioning

Eddie didn't tone himself down to fit the sport. He *turned himself up* to shift the energy.

You don't need to be the loudest – but you do need to show up *as something specific*. That's how you get remembered. That's how you create leverage.

> **Ask yourself:** *What if being myself – more clearly, more consistently – is actually the edge I've been holding back?*

7. Think like a storyteller, not just a strategist

The edge is often in how you frame the thing – more than in the thing itself. Eddie didn't pitch like a banker, he pitched like a showman. He made people feel the value, not merely hear it.

> **Ask yourself:** *Am I just delivering facts – or am I helping people believe?*

Edges aren't always about doing more, they're about seeing differently.

They're in the cracks. The corners. The rhythm. They're what happens when you stop playing the game exactly as written – and start playing *with feel*.

Eddie found the edge – then danced and played spoons on it.

Reflection

Eddie Jordan didn't wait for perfect conditions. He moved when others were still asking questions. That was the edge – not bravado, not luck, but the courage to see things sooner and act before the window closed.

He looked for advantages where others didn't look. He kept searching long after others had quit. He scanned for what others missed: the detail, the tone, the moment behind the moment. And when he found it, he didn't hesitate.

That mindset made him dangerous. It made him effective. And it made him unforgettable.

Because the edge isn't always dramatic. Sometimes it's quiet. Subtle. A decision to listen more carefully. To notice what others dismiss. To act before consensus forms.

Eddie thrived in chaos not because he craved it, but because he could *handle* it. He had a feel for timing, and he backed it. On the pit wall, in the boardroom, at the dinner table – it was the same principle: look closer, move faster, trust your instincts.

But what set him apart even more was this – he stayed *open*.

Not soft. Not indecisive. Open. He listened to ideas from people half his age. He asked honest questions and absorbed the answers. He wasn't afraid to hear 20 ideas and take only one. He had the clarity to choose, but the humility to keep learning.

Because confidence, to Eddie, wasn't about knowing everything. It was about *staying open to what you might not see yet.*

He knew power came not from control, but from perspective. And you only gain perspective when you're willing to shut up and listen. *Really* listen.

That's what made his teams loyal. That's why his deals surprised people. That's why young drivers, engineers, and business partners trusted him. Because he gave people space to be honest, and he used their input to make sharper moves.

He had the courage to be challenged. He invited it. He'd say: "Don't give me any bullshit. I asked you for a reason."

That's rare leadership. Leadership without pretence.

And in the end, that was Eddie's real edge.

He moved first, but stayed open until the moment to move came. He kept learning when he could have coasted. He trusted feel, but earned it through awareness. He never stopped scanning. Never stopped asking:

What don't I see yet?

So, if you're building something – or just trying to stay in the game – don't wait for the conditions to be perfect. Look for the edge no one else is seeing. Ask the question no one else is asking. And when the moment comes – move.

Because the edge is always there. You just have to be awake enough to see it – and brave enough to use it.

Section Three:
Leadership, Trust, and Relationships

12. Lead with Trust

The Eddie Story

Eddie Jordan never needed to explain what he stood for – he just lived it. He didn't carry around a personal manifesto. There were no lectures on values, no virtue-signalling, no need for applause. But anyone who knew him – *really* knew him – would tell you the same thing: you could trust him. And that trust was never part of a performance, it was part of his *presence*.

You felt it. In the way he looked you in the eye when he gave you his word. In the way he remembered what you said, even months later. In the way he followed through on a promise without needing to be chased.

Eddie's way of doing business – and life – wasn't complicated. It was simple, because it was *solid*.

He came from a background where your word mattered more than your wealth. Where reputation travelled ahead of you – not because you were trying to control it, but because the way you treated people *always got out*. He grew up around people who didn't have much, but who had each other – and that code stuck.

If he trusted you, you were in. Fully. No half-loyalty. No "wait and see". You got everything: belief, access, protection, his full weight behind you.

That loyalty extended beyond business – it applied everywhere.

If you were a friend of Eddie's – truly a friend – you knew something most people never get to feel in their life: *what it's like to be backed without condition.* If you called him at 3 a.m. and said you had a flat tyre and no clue what to do next, he'd answer. Not groggily. Not reluctantly. *Immediately.*

He'd show up. No questions. Well – not at first.

He'd fix the problem, get you safe, make sure you were ok. And then, once the dust settled, he'd let fly:

"What the f**k were you thinking? Why the hell didn't you call me sooner?" And then he'd smile. That unmistakable Eddie grin – part frustration, part affection, all loyalty.

That's how he loved. Loudly. Presently. With his sleeves rolled up and his phone always on.

And once you were inside that circle, it meant something. Because you were part of something real. But just as powerfully, when that trust was broken – it was gone. Quietly. Cleanly. Without a speech.

Eddie wouldn't storm out or burn bridges. He'd just vanish. Fully. The door closed without slamming. The conversation ended mid-sentence. And you never got another one.

Because trust, to him, wasn't a mood: it was a bond. And once that bond was gone, he didn't see the point in pretending it could be repaired.

You could make mistakes – he made plenty himself. But break

his trust? Show him you weren't who you said you were? You lost the thing that made any relationship worth having.

He didn't judge, he just decided. And once that decision was made – he never looked back.

It wasn't about being rigid, it was about being *clear*. There was a code Eddie lived by – not written, but deeply understood:

Be who you say you are. Keep your word. Don't disappear when things get hard. Stand by the people who've stood by you. Honour the room, even when you could get away with something else.

That was it.

He expected it in racing. He expected it in music. He expected it in friendship, business, and love. And he gave it back – not with ceremony, but with consistency. That's why people trusted him. And why, decades later, those same people still picked up the phone when his name appeared.

Eddie never believed that trust came from paperwork. It came from *character*. If you needed fine print, you were already in the wrong deal.

He often shared something Bernie Ecclestone told him – a line that became a kind of private philosophy:

"Shake my hand and look me in the eye, and we have a deal. Try get me to sign a contract, and I'll find a way to get out of it."

It was vintage Bernie – sharp, dangerous, unforgettable. And Eddie didn't just laugh – he *agreed*. Because he knew what Bernie meant: *If you don't trust me, why are we doing this at all?*

That was the world Eddie operated in. Where the deal wasn't on the page – it was in the *person*. And if he gave you his word, you didn't need anything else.

And if someone crossed the line – no matter how small the line looked on the surface – he let them go. Not as punishment. As principle.

He spoke often, too, about the weight of reputation.

"If you lose your reputation and integrity," he said, "you've got nothing left."

He meant it. It wasn't said to sound good, it was said to *remind himself.* Because he knew that the world moved fast, that people sometimes forgot what they stood for when the pressure came on. He'd seen deals fall apart over ego. Seen leaders unravel because they forgot what got them to the table in the first place.

Eddie never forgot.

Reputation, to him, wasn't about PR. It was about *who showed up when he wasn't in the room.* And the only way to protect that was to live in such a way that no one had to guess.

He didn't always get it right – he wasn't trying to. But he *tried to stay right with people.* To mean what he said. To back who he believed in. To keep his name clean – not only publicly, but privately too.

That's what people felt when they talked about Eddie. It wasn't only his ability to entertain – it was the steadiness he brought. It wasn't only his charisma – it was the depth of his character.

And when people trusted him, they never forgot what that felt like. And when they lost his trust, they never forgot *why.*

Because he didn't offer it lightly. But when he did – it was everything.

The Principle as Philosophy

Some people wear their values like a badge. Eddie Jordan carried his like a compass.

He didn't broadcast integrity. He didn't overuse the word "trust" in meetings. He simply lived his values – through how he led, how he negotiated, and how he handled relationships. If there was a line he wouldn't cross, you knew it. And if you crossed it, that was the end of the conversation.

To Eddie, trust wasn't a one-time achievement. It was something you maintained: moment by moment, choice by choice. A living thing. Integrity wasn't what you showed when the spotlight hit – it was what you held onto when no one was watching.

He saw trust, honour, and integrity not as abstract virtues but as real, working principles. They shaped deals, built friendships, protected reputations, and formed the invisible structure of a life that mattered.

For Eddie, this wasn't softness: it was strategy.

In a world full of people looking for the angle, he found his edge by being straight. Saying what he meant. Doing what he promised. Turning up, telling the truth, and standing by the deal – even when it hurt to do so.

That's why people trusted him. Why doors opened. Why he was welcomed back – not merely tolerated, but *wanted* in the room.

He didn't aim to win every deal. He aimed to win the relationship. In doing so, he built something more valuable than leverage: *reputation*.

Eddie knew that integrity rarely feels urgent – but it's always essential. Because trust isn't usually lost through loud betrayals.

It's chipped away by quiet compromises: the small lie, the silent omission, the easy excuse. That's why he stayed alert to his own standards – and built teams that aimed for more than results. They had purpose, and they protected what mattered most – far beyond performance.

He believed your name was your currency. Every time you honoured your word, especially when no one else was watching, you added to its value. You built something invisible – but indestructible.

Eddie wasn't perfect – he didn't need to be. But he was consistent. And in the long run, that's what people trust. Not image. Not charm. Not cleverness. *Consistency.* A quiet force that says: *You can rely on me.*

Eddie didn't want to be remembered as the most successful man in the room. He wanted to be remembered as someone you could trust. Someone who honoured the financial deal and the *human* one. The relational one. The one that says: *If I shake your hand and look you in the eye, I'm all in.*

And if you did the same? He gave you everything.

He didn't need it to be complicated, he just needed it to be true.

Because once the contracts are signed and the meetings end, all that's left is the reputation you carry – and the people who'll still answer your call when things get rough.

That's what Eddie built his life on. Not perfect results. But a name you could count on.

Practical Translation

Living with trust, honour, and integrity doesn't start in big moments. It starts in small ones – the kind most people think don't matter.

It's in whether you return the call you said you would. Whether you're honest when the truth costs you something. Whether you honour the commitments no one else remembered but you.

That's how Eddie did it. Not through grand gestures. Through consistency.

He didn't wake up trying to build a brand. He just tried to *be the same person in every room* – on and off the record, behind closed doors and out front. And over time, that way of living gave him something more powerful than leverage: it gave him *reputation*.

You can do the same. Here's how:

1. Start by looking at how you show up in the smallest agreements

How you handle the small things is exactly how you'll be trusted with the big ones.

> **Ask yourself:** *When I give my word, am I doing it to impress others – or to build a foundation of trust that will outlast the moment?*

2. Keep your word even when it's inconvenient

Follow up, even when the other person wouldn't chase you. Let people trust your presence more than your promises. Make your word mean something again – not for appearances, but to build invisible credibility that lasts longer than applause.

> **Ask yourself:** *How can I offer trust generously while staying attentive to whether others are meeting me with the same respect and energy?*

3. Give trust first – but not blindly

Be generous, but observant. Trust doesn't mean being naïve. It means giving people the chance to match your energy – and walking away cleanly if they can't.

> **Ask yourself:** *When someone breaks my trust, am I able to withdraw my belief with grace – without needing to make noise or seek validation?*

4. Hold your line – quietly

If someone breaks your trust, you don't need to shout. You don't need to punish. You just need to stop giving them access to your belief – and keep moving forward.

> **Ask yourself:** *In the moments when no one is watching, what do my actions say about the person I am becoming?*

5. Be reliable when no one's watching

When there's no one measuring you and no performance to keep up, that's when your integrity speaks the loudest. That's when people learn who you really are.

> **Ask yourself:** *When no one's watching, am I still showing up like it matters?*

6. Protect your name, not your ego

Let your name mean something – not because it's the loudest, but because it holds strong when it matters. Build a reputation that doesn't shout, but stands.

> **Ask yourself:** *Am I living in a way that, over time, makes my name quietly stand for something strong and true – beyond appearances or approval?*

Over time, you'll become known for more than what you do – you'll be seen for *how you do it*. And that's when people trust you deeply enough to build with you, follow you, and bet on you – again and again.

That's what Eddie earned. Not by being perfect. By being *reliable*. And by holding a line the world could feel – even when it wasn't written down.

Reflection

When people talk about leadership, they mention vision, ambition, presence. But beneath all that – beneath the headlines, the deals, the drama – there's a quieter test: *Can you be trusted?*

Will you show up when it's inconvenient? Will you protect the people beside you, not only the ones who benefit you?

Eddie Jordan understood this instinctively. He didn't perform trust when the cameras were on – he carried it when no one was watching. He spoke straight, even when it was hard. He honoured his word, even when it cost him. He backed his people, even when the scoreboard didn't.

That kind of consistency – steady, quiet, unshakable – is rare. It changes everything.

Trust is what made mechanics work through the night. It's what made drivers pick Jordan when they had other options. It's why sponsors came back, and why friendships lasted long after the podiums.

In a world obsessed with results, it's easy to forget: *trust is the infrastructure.* Without it, teams fracture, communication breaks, and people start playing small.

But when trust is high, people go further. They move faster. They fight harder – for themselves and for each other.

That's what Eddie built. Not just a team. A culture. A standard.

He didn't lead with rules. He led with rhythm. His values didn't need to be written down – you could feel them in how he showed up and see them in who showed up for him.

He didn't keep score, he just kept his word. Quietly. Consistently. Especially when it mattered most.

And people felt that. In the calls he answered at 3 a.m. In the times he appeared, fixed the thing, swore at you for being an idiot – and then never mentioned it again.

That was Eddie's style. Loud in loyalty. Soft in ego. Fierce in integrity.

But he didn't offer trust lightly. He gave it fully – but expected it back the same way. If you said one thing and did another, he saw it. And when trust broke, so did the foundation. Eddie never built on broken ground.

He could forgive mistakes. He could work through tension. But when it came to integrity, there were no grey areas. You either held the line, or you didn't. And if you didn't, he didn't come back. Not punishment. Principle.

That's why people trusted him. Why his reputation lasted. Yes, because he was bold or brilliant – but more because he was *reliable*. Because his word meant something.

And that's what built the legacy that still moves through rooms, still opens doors, still makes people proud to say, "I knew him."

So, if you want to build something that lasts – a team, a business, a name – start here:

Be the one people can count on. Show up when it's hard. Keep your word when no one's watching. Let your name mean something. Because in the end, people remember how you made them feel – safe, seen, and certain they could trust you.

Eddie did.

> *"I don't need to be the biggest in the room. I just need to be the one they can believe in."*
> – Eddie Jordan

13. Ask, Listen, Learn

The Eddie Story

If there was one thing Eddie Jordan lived by – something that powered his whole journey from the streets of Bray to the grid of Formula 1 – it was this: every day is a school day.

Growing up in Ireland, Eddie learned early on that education wasn't just important – it was revered. In his community, the headmaster of a school was spoken of alongside the town's surgeon or the parish priest. Teachers weren't just instructors. They were leaders. Guardians of possibility. And Eddie never forgot it.

He often said that the greatest fortune of his early life was the quality of his education. It wasn't flashy. It wasn't easy. But it instilled in him a deep respect for learning – and for those who taught. His time at Synge Street CBS was tough, disciplined, sometimes brutal. But it also gave him something that would shape every stage of his life: the understanding that learning is the difference between standing still and moving forward.

That attitude stayed with Eddie long after he swapped text-books for engines and boardrooms. To him, every day – every conversation, every mistake, every opportunity – was a class-room. And the moment you thought you had nothing left to learn was the moment you started losing ground.

Eddie never carried himself like someone who knew it all. Far from it. When he was facing a big decision – about a driver, a sponsor, a business deal, even a personal move – he didn't retreat into certainty. He opened up. He asked questions. He sought counsel. Sometimes it was formal, over a table with contracts and coffee. Sometimes it was quick, spontaneous – a question tossed over dinner, backstage at a gig, walking across a racetrack.

"Tell me what you'd do," he'd say. "Don't give me any bullshit – I asked you for a reason."

And when you answered, he listened properly. Full presence. Full focus. He wasn't looking for validation. He wasn't looking to be flattered. He was looking to learn – even if it meant hearing something he didn't want to hear.

Because Eddie knew: you can't see every angle on your own. You need the input. You need the friction. You need other people's experiences, instincts, and mistakes adding weight to your own. He didn't just listen to experts. He listened to engineers, truck drivers, young musicians, old friends. If you had something to say – if you had a lens he didn't have – he wanted to hear it.

Eddie didn't fear contradiction. He welcomed it. He didn't fear admitting he was still learning: he saw it as a strength. And that openness didn't make him soft. It made him sharp. It meant when he finally made a call – whether hiring a rookie, taking on a new business venture, switching a strategy mid-race, or backing a bold idea – he moved with full clarity. Because the decision had been tested. Strengthened by different views. Sharpened by questions.

That's why people trusted Eddie. Not because he always agreed. Not because he always knew. But because they knew he had truly listened. Respected their perspective. Measured it seriously before acting.

Even at the height of his success, Eddie kept learning. He studied Bernie Ecclestone – not by asking for lectures, but by watching. Observing. Picking up lessons from the silences, the sidesteps, the timing of a handshake. "Bernie never lectured anyone," Eddie would say. "He just did. And if you were smart, you paid attention."

And Eddie was smart enough – and humble enough – to keep paying attention, right to the end.

He didn't separate learning from leading. To him, they were the same thing. If you weren't learning, you weren't leading.

Whether it was picking up the latest trends in media, understanding a new business model, learning to sail across the Pacific, or just being humble enough to ask a younger colleague what they thought – Eddie stayed awake. He stayed a student.

Because he knew: if you think you know everything, you'll learn nothing. And if you stay open – even when it's uncomfortable, even when it stretches you – that's when the real breakthroughs happen.

That's when trust grows. That's when instincts sharpen. That's when you stay alive to possibility, even as others start to fade.

"Every day is a school day," Eddie would say with a grin, no matter where he was: a race, a regatta, a board meeting, or a bike ride through the hills.

Not as a joke. As a reminder.

A reminder that curiosity is the real competitive edge. A reminder that arrogance is the real enemy. And a reminder that the people who stay open, stay winning.

The Principle as Philosophy

In a world that often confuses knowledge with certainty, Eddie Jordan lived by a far sharper rule: *Stay open. Stay learning. Every day.*

He wasn't indecisive. He wasn't unsure of himself. But he understood something most leaders forget: true strength doesn't come from knowing everything. It comes from being willing to learn anything.

From his earliest days at Synge Street CBS, where teachers commanded respect alongside surgeons and bishops, Eddie knew that education wasn't just a phase of life. It was a lifelong posture. A way of being. A mindset that separated the stuck from the soaring.

And he never let it slip.

At every major decision point – launching Jordan Grand Prix, hiring new talent, navigating business negotiations, adapting to media and music – Eddie didn't assume he had all the answers. He asked. He listened. He learned.

He would seek out views from people who weren't just his closest advisors. Sometimes a mechanic would offer an insight that a CFO missed. Sometimes a musician would give him a better marketing idea than a consultant. Eddie didn't close the door to new input just because someone didn't fit a formal box. He stayed open to where the best idea might come from.

That openness wasn't weakness – it was discipline. He didn't flinch from difficult lessons. He didn't shut out uncomfortable advice. He leaned into it, processed it, and decided with a view sharpened by more than just his own instincts.

Because Eddie knew:

- If you think you already know, you stop learning.
- If you stop learning, you start declining.
- And if you start declining, you lose – slowly at first, then suddenly.

That's why he treated every conversation, every challenge, every new domain – from sailing to startup investing – like a classroom. It's why he was comfortable being the student when others expected him to act like the professor. It's why he kept adapting, kept growing, long after most people in his position would have drifted into comfort.

He stayed awake to what he didn't know yet – and he encouraged everyone around him to do the same.

"Every day is a school day, lads," he'd say – sometimes light-heartedly, but always seriously underneath.

And that belief made him dangerous – because it made him endlessly adaptable.

Where others closed off – hardened by ego, dulled by past success – Eddie kept moving. He stayed curious. He stayed sharp. He stayed relevant.

That's the real edge in leadership, in business, in life: Not just knowing what you know – but knowing how much more there is to see.

Eddie didn't need to perform certainty. He performed adaptability. He showed that leadership isn't about pretending you're finished. It's about being willing to learn faster, sharper, and deeper than anyone else – and then acting from that fresh place of clarity.

Learning wasn't a hobby for Eddie. It wasn't a chore. It was a way to stay alive to possibility – forever.

And it made him smarter, but more than that – it made him wiser.

It made him Eddie.

Practical Translation

Eddie Jordan didn't treat learning like a phase of life. He treated it like oxygen. Essential. Continuous. Non-negotiable.

He stayed curious even when he was winning. He stayed humble even when he was celebrated. And because of that, he stayed dangerous – always evolving while others stood still.

He didn't just ask questions for politeness. He asked because he wanted to stretch his own view, sharpen his own edge, and stay alive to what others missed. He knew that momentum comes not from being the loudest voice – but from being the sharpest learner.

Here's how you can live that principle the Eddie way – every day:

1. Start by asking – then actually listen

Most people ask for advice only to justify what they already plan to do. Eddie wasn't like that. When he asked someone for their view, he gave them real space to answer. He listened without rushing to correct them, defend himself, or polish his image.

Ask yourself: *Am I asking to learn – or asking to validate myself?*

2. Choose counsel over crowd noise

Eddie didn't take advice from everyone. He chose wisely – people with skin in the game, real perspective, sharp instincts. Not flatterers. Not spectators. He picked people who'd challenge him, not just comfort him.

> **Ask yourself:** *Who in my world has earned the right to challenge my thinking?*

3. Be ready for the hard lesson

Eddie leaned into learning, *especially* when it was uncomfortable – when someone spotted a weakness he didn't want to admit or pointed out a blind spot. He didn't shy from the hard feedback, he welcomed it.

> **Ask yourself:** *What feedback am I avoiding because it feels too raw?*

4. Lean into learning something new (especially when it's hard)

When Eddie learned music, sailing, digital media, and international business expansion, he didn't pretend to be an expert. He let himself be bad first – so he could get good later. He knew learning wasn't about looking clever, it was about building competence over time.

> **Ask yourself:** *Where am I holding back because I'm afraid to look like a beginner?*

5. Separate learning from pleasing

Eddie didn't listen to flatter people. He listened to learn. And sometimes, after listening carefully, he still made a decision that others disagreed with. Openness isn't about pleasing everyone – it's about sharpening your view.

Ask yourself: *Am I learning – or am I performing to be liked?*

6. Stay curious when others close off

The longer people stay in leadership, the more they tend to close doors – thinking they've seen it all. Eddie stayed open. He asked young drivers, old friends, rivals, and newcomers for their view. He never stopped gathering perspective.

Ask yourself: *What's a fresh voice I can seek out this week to widen my perspective?*

7. Make "every day is a school day" a personal standard

For Eddie, curiosity wasn't occasional, it was daily. Every project. Every challenge. Every failure. Every unexpected moment was an invitation to learn faster than yesterday.

Ask yourself: *If I treated today like a school day, what lesson is here for me to learn?*

Learning is not a sign you're falling behind. It's proof that you're staying sharp – staying dangerous – staying alive to possibility. That's what kept Eddie ahead. And it's what can keep you ahead too.

Reflection

In a world that rewards fast answers and loud certainty, it's easy to overlook the quiet strength of staying open. But Eddie Jordan knew better.

He built everything – teams, deals, businesses, friendships – on a deeper foundation: *learning is leadership*. Learning isn't what you do before the action – it *is* the action. The edge doesn't come from knowing it all, it comes from staying awake to what you don't know yet.

Eddie never let confidence harden into stubbornness. He never let early success close his mind. Instead, he stayed curious, sharp, and fully engaged-with every room, every person, every conversation. That's why people trusted him. Not just because he made smart moves, but because he *listened*. Fully. Actively. With no agenda other than to understand. Even when he was the most powerful person in the room, he still made space for other perspectives. And people could feel that.

His openness didn't slow him down – it made him faster, better, bolder. It sharpened his decisions, attracted sharper people, and created cultures where honesty thrived. Where challenging the norm wasn't punished, it was *expected*.

He welcomed friction – the good kind. The kind that rubs off

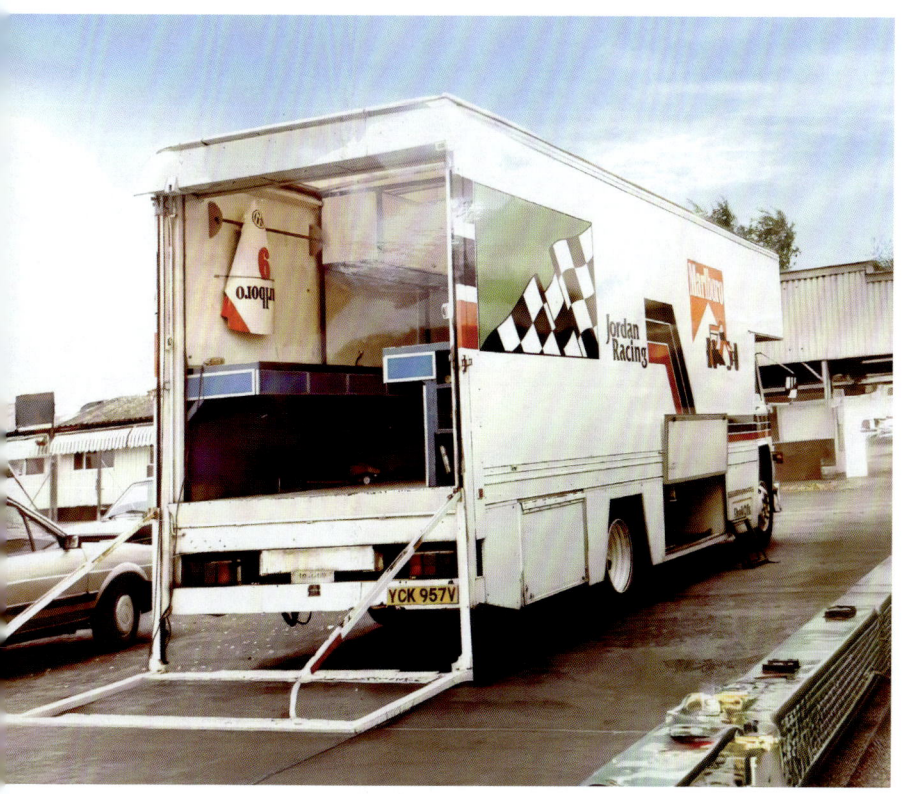

The original Jordan Racing transporter – old, battered, and full of dreams.

A 1980s classified advert in an Oxford newspaper: "I dare you to bid me for the lot!" (Even the ads had Eddie's trademark cheek.)

Eddie Jordan with his Marlboro Team Ireland March 803 Toyota, in the pit lane at Silverstone during the 1980 British F3 season.

Michael Schumacher making his F1 debut in the Jordan 191 at Spa, 25 August 1991. Still regarded as one of the most beautiful F1 cars of all time.

Above: Eddie Jordan and Martin Brundle. Martin drove for Eddie Jordan Racing and famously battled Ayrton Senna for the British F3 championship in 1983.

Right: In 1982, Ayrton Senna tested an Eddie Jordan Racing F3 car at Silverstone – his first time behind the wheel of an F3 machine.

Above: Michael Schumacher always gave Eddie great credit for giving him his F1 debut.

Right: Eddie with Damon Hill and Ralf Schumacher after they finished first and second, delivering Jordan's first ever victory – seven years after entering F1.

Eddie with HSH Prince Albert II and David Coulthard, photographed at the Prince's Palace in Monaco, 2022.

Eddie with Bernie Ecclestone, his long-time mentor and friend.

Eddie in his happy place – behind the drums. He started playing in his teens and performed in several bands. In 1994, he launched the F1 after-race gig – a tradition that still goes strong today.

Eddie sailed around the world on his Oyster 885, a boat he named *Lush*.

Cycling was one of Eddie's great passions. Pictured here with Keith O'Loughlin, chatting away, while former world champion Thor Hushovd rides behind.

Eddie, Keith, and Nigel Northridge sharing a moment during a party in Sotogrande, Spain.

Eddie, Keith, and Spencer Matthews at their White Party in Castellar de la Frontera, Spain. The T-shirt was for Eddie's band on the night – "The Castellar Robbers".

Eddie and Marie, surrounded by the four children, their partners, and a growing gang of grandchildren.

Eddie lit up the stage, but Marie was the steady beat behind it all.
Together nearly 50 years – the heart and soul of every room they walked into.

assumptions and exposes sharper truth. He didn't need to be right first, he needed to get it right.

And because he stayed open, he kept evolving. While others settled, he kept shifting gears. Still moving. Still learning. Still mattering.

That was Eddie's real edge. Not just his energy or charisma. His willingness to stay a student – every day, in every room, with every opportunity. He never graduated from growth. Never stopped sharpening the lens. And that's why he remained relevant – long after many had faded.

If you ever asked him how he kept going, how he kept winning, how he kept surprising people, he'd just smile and say: "Every day is a school day."

It wasn't a motto, it was a mindset.

So, if you're stuck, coasting, or too sure of your own answers – remember Eddie. Remember that staying open isn't weakness. It's strength. It's movement. It's the kind of leadership that lasts.

Keep asking. Keep learning. Keep showing up like the next insight is just around the corner.

Because the real race doesn't go to the one who knows the most.

It goes to the one who *never stops learning.*

14. Respect Time

The Eddie Story

If you ever worked with Eddie Jordan, you learned one thing fast: *don't be late.* Eddie wasn't uptight. He wasn't formal. He didn't run on spreadsheets or wear a watch just to check it. But if you made a plan with him – you'd better be on time. Because to Eddie, punctuality wasn't about being organized. It was about *respect*. He wouldn't be late to meet you so why would it be ok for you to be late for him and disrespect him?

He believed time was the most valuable thing you could give someone. More than money. More than words. More than promises. If someone gave you their time, you honoured it. If you said you'd be somewhere – you were there. No drama. No delay.

"If you show up late," he'd say, "you're telling the other person their time matters less than yours. And that's bullshit."

He lived it.

One morning, we were due to cycle at 7:30 a.m. sharp and I was cycling down to the meeting point. Right on the dot – not a second late – my phone rang. "Where are you?"

"Eddie, it's just turned 7:30. I'll be there in 30 seconds – it will still be 7:30."

"Hurry up, FFS!", he said, urgency and humour wrapped into one.

Sure enough, 30 seconds later I pulled up at the meeting spot – and there he was. Helmet on. Bike ready. Big grin on his face. He was already on the phone. Bored waiting even those few seconds.

I had a similar experience with him more recently in Spain.

We were due to go to lunch at 1 p.m. I had a conference call that was finishing at 12:45 p.m. – enough time, I thought, to get us to the restaurant. At 12:40 p.m., I heard Eddie shouting up the stairs, "I'm going!"

I wrapped up, headed down – only to see that he'd *already taken my car* and was sitting behind the wheel, ready to roll.

I jumped in. He looked at me and said, "Where's Marie? Is she coming?"

A calm voice piped up from the back seat: "I'm here, Eddie."

The whole car burst out laughing.

That was the thing about Eddie – his respect for time wasn't rigid, it was *relational*. It wasn't about being controlling, it was about making the most of the moment. Keeping things moving. Living *fully on the beat*.

In the paddock, in business, in life – Eddie lived by rhythm. And that rhythm always started on time.

He never rushed the moment. But he never wasted it either. He showed up. Fully. On time. And expected the same in return.

Because for Eddie, being on time wasn't just about being prompt.

It was about showing you care.

The Principle as Philosophy

To Eddie Jordan, time wasn't just a resource – it was the most important one. And it was never to be wasted.

He treated time like others treated money – carefully, intentionally, and always with a sense of urgency. He knew that while fortunes could be won and lost, you can only use time once. And once it's gone, it's gone. So, you'd better use it well.

Eddie didn't believe in drifting through life. He didn't believe in waiting for the "right moment". He believed in moving. In showing up. In staying sharp. He saw time as a finite, one-way ticket – and he lived accordingly.

He'd say it often: "Eventually, you realize you've got

MMTT – more money than time. And then it hits you. Time's the only thing you can't earn back."

That clarity shaped everything. Whether it was a team briefing at Jordan Grand Prix, a business meeting in London, or a lunch ride in the hills above Monaco – he showed up early, present, ready. Not out of routine, but out of respect. Because for Eddie, time was more than how you measured your day – it was how you measured your values.

If you showed up late, you were disrespecting someone else's hour. If you cancelled last-minute, you were wasting energy that had already been spent. If you didn't deliver when you said you would, you weren't just delaying progress – you were betraying trust.

This mindset didn't make Eddie rigid – it made him *real*. He wasn't obsessed with schedules, he was obsessed with momentum. He understood that life moves. And if you're not moving with it, you're missing it.

And more than anything, he lived by a personal rule: "I'm trying to fit three times more into every day than anyone else." That wasn't bravado. It was a mindset. A way of squeezing every drop from every day. Whether it was a bike ride, a business call, a band rehearsal, or a birthday dinner – he made time count. Always.

Because he knew: you can't bank time. You can't save it for later. And you can't get a refund. So, you show up. You start now. You act with care, with presence, and with clarity.

Eddie's whole life was a masterclass in momentum. Because he never treated time casually. He treated it like the most valuable thing in the room.

Because it was.

Practical Translation

Eddie Jordan didn't just talk about respecting time – he modelled it. Every single day.

He understood that time is a mirror: how you treat it reflects how seriously you treat your life, your work, and the people around you.

And here's the thing – it's not difficult. It takes some planning, sure – but not much. Being on time isn't hard, it's just a choice.

It's as easy to be on time as it is to be late. But the difference in how it feels – and how it's received – is massive.

Here's how to bring Eddie's approach into your own life:

1. Be early — not to impress, but to prepare

Eddie didn't show up early because he was obsessive. He did it to be ready, not rushed. Arriving early sharpens focus, creates calm, and shows others you care.

> **Ask yourself:** *Am I arriving early to create calm and readiness – or am I still letting myself be ruled by last-minute rush?*

2. Respecting time reduces stress

Being late creates stress – you're anxious, apologizing, catching up. Being on time brings confidence, clarity, and respect. It changes the tone for you and everyone around you.

> **Ask yourself:** *How much unnecessary stress in my life could I eliminate simply by choosing to honour time better?*

3. Trust is built — or broken — by time

If you can't be trusted to show up on time, people quietly wonder what else they can't trust you with. Respecting time builds trust. Disrespecting it erodes it.

> **Ask yourself:** *What message am I sending about my trustworthiness through the way I show up for others' time?*

4. Finish what you start

Respecting time isn't just about punctuality – it's about integrity. Don't over-promise. But if you commit, deliver. Fully.

> **Ask yourself:** *Where in my life do I need to close a loop I opened – to honour my word and strengthen my integrity?*

5. Say "no" faster

Dragging out decisions wastes everyone's time. Say yes when you mean it – and say no, kindly but clearly, when you don't.

> **Ask yourself:** *Where am I dragging my feet with a "maybe" – when a clear and honest "no" would be kinder and more powerful?*

6. Cut the drift

Scrolling, stalling, overthinking – all time-killers. Eddie spotted drift quickly and re-centred. You can too: take one clear action now to move things forward.

> **Ask yourself:** *Right now, what one clear action could I take to shift from drifting into momentum?*

7. Build your rhythm, then protect it

Eddie lived by rhythm, not rigidity – stacking energy, meetings, rides, music, deals into flow. Find your natural rhythm – and defend it.

> **Ask yourself:** *What rhythm of work, rest, and flow feels most natural to me – and what boundaries do I need to protect it?*

8. Fit more in – with joy, not stress

Eddie aimed to fit three times more into a day than most – not through rushing, but through choosing. Fill your time with meaning, not busyness.

> **Ask yourself:** *Am I filling my days with tasks that drain me – or with meaningful choices that expand my joy and presence?*

Respecting time doesn't mean rushing, it means caring. Caring enough to be prepared. Caring enough to show up. Caring enough to be trusted.

And it's not complicated.

You don't need an app. You don't need a spreadsheet. You just need a decision. Respect time – it changes everything.

Reflection

If you spent any real time with Eddie Jordan, something subtle became clear: he didn't waste time. Not his. Not yours. Not anyone's. He made moments count – not by rushing, but by being fully present. He respected time as something valuable, finite, and revealing. And if you paid attention, it made you reflect on your own pace – how often you drift, delay, or tell yourself "just five more minutes" when you know better.

Eddie didn't need to talk about discipline. He lived it. He didn't call you out for being late. You felt it. Because when someone treats time with care, you either rise to match them – or fall behind.

His respect for time wasn't about control – it was about clarity. He kept his word, met his deadlines, honoured every minute he gave. And that created trust. In racing. In business. In friendship.

Because time is the first test of reliability. If someone can't manage time, what else might they let slip?

Eddie understood that. He didn't just keep time, he *set* it.

His teams moved faster. His deals closed sharper. His people leaned in. Because his rhythm created confidence. You always knew where you stood with Eddie – because you could measure it in minutes.

He didn't treat time like a clock to chase, he treated it like a statement:

This matters. You matter. Let's move.

He built teams, trust, and culture around it. And most of all, he showed that when you honour time, you start honouring everything else.

So yes – it's just a schedule. Yes – it's just a watch.

But it's also a signal. That you care. That you're here. That you mean it.

That's the rhythm Eddie moved to. Not frantic. Just focused.

He didn't worship time. He *used* it – with intent.

Because he knew: time is the most honest currency there is. You can't fake it. You can't pause it. You can't earn more of it. Once it's gone, it's gone.

So, he spent it well. And when you were with him, you felt it too.

That's the principle: Respect time. Be present. Show up. Move like it matters – because it *does*.

And as Eddie said, again and again:

> *"Eventually, you realize you've got more money than time. And when that happens, you learn very quickly how to spend the day properly."*
> – Eddie Jordan

15. Be Present

The Eddie Story

Eddie Jordan didn't just show up to a moment – he *landed* in it. Fully.

He wasn't a man of half-measures, and that included his attention. When he was with you, he was with *you* – undistracted, unhurried, and completely tuned in. Not scanning for the next conversation. Not nodding while checking his phone. Not waiting to speak. He listened. Properly. Deeply. Quietly.

He made you feel like, in that moment, there was *nowhere else he'd rather be.*

It didn't matter who you were – a driver, a chef, a sponsor, a stranger – if Eddie locked onto you, you felt it. The eye contact. The slight lean-in. The quiet, mischievous grin that said, "I'm here. I'm listening. And I care."

But Eddie wasn't just being polite.

He was actually *interested.*

That was the key.

He didn't ask questions to fill the silence – he asked them because he wanted to *know*. And if you answered with something bland or surface-level, he'd raise an eyebrow, give you that Dublin glint, and say: "Ok, now tell me the truth."

And you would. Because somehow, with Eddie, it was easier to drop the act. He made space for that.

And the reason he could do that – the reason people opened up to him so instinctively – was because he wasn't just hearing what they *said.*

He was *watching.*

He was *reading.*

Because when you're truly present – not distracted, not planning your response – you *notice everything.* The hesitation before someone answers. The small shift in their eyes. The drop in their voice. The way they glance at the door or hold their hands. And Eddie *noticed.*

He was brilliant at seeing people for who they really were – not because he had some special gift, but because he paid attention. He blocked out the noise. He concentrated. And in doing so, he caught the cues that most people miss.

I saw it again and again. He'd meet someone, talk to them for five minutes, and later turn to me and say, "That guy's a bluffer," or "She's the one to back – she's got something." And 99 times out of 100, he was *right*.

Because he wasn't distracted by what people were trying to *present*.

He was tuned into who they actually *were*.

And the more present he was, the clearer it became.

It was the same whether he was listening to someone pitch a business, or watching a Formula 1 race, or sitting at a rugby match. You could speak to him mid-race, mid-match – but you'd be talking to yourself. Because Eddie, in those moments, was *locked in*. Focused. Still. Absorbing everything.

And later, he'd break it down for you – every nuance, every tactic, every beat of the game or race that most people had missed entirely.

Because when you concentrate, *really concentrate*, you don't just watch. You *see*. You don't just hear. You *understand*.

And that's how Eddie lived.

With his eyes open. His mind tuned. His presence fully on.

Even near the end – even when he had every reason to withdraw – he didn't.

He still asked questions. Still leaned in. Still wanted to know what was going on with *you*.

Even when he was very ill towards the end of his life, when someone would walk in, no matter how he was feeling he would look up, smile softly, and say, "Right, sit down. Tell me what's happening."

And he *meant it.*

He wasn't being polite. He wasn't making small talk. He was making *connection.* He was saying, "You have my full attention. Let's make this moment real."

That was Eddie.

No performance. No politics. No pretending to listen while thinking about the next thing.

When he was with you – he was *with you.*

Fully.

Because he understood the rarest truth:

That attention is love. That presence is respect. And that being in the moment . . . is where life actually happens.

> *"People talk about intuition. But intuition is really just memory + attention. You see things others miss when you're really paying attention."*
> – **Eddie Jordan**

The Principle as Philosophy

In a world built for distraction, presence is a radical act.

Most people think generosity is about time, or money, or giving advice. But Eddie Jordan knew the truth: the rarest, most powerful thing you can give someone . . . is your *attention.*

To look them in the eye. To listen to what they're really saying. To care enough to *concentrate.*

He didn't treat presence as a personality trait, he treated it as a discipline. Something you choose – moment to moment, person to person. You let go of whatever noise you're carrying. You stop trying to be interesting. You *become interested.*

Eddie understood that presence isn't just politeness, it's perception. When you're truly present, you *see more.* You read between the lines. You notice what's not being said. You feel the beat of the room, not just the sound of the words.

That's why he was such a good judge of people. He didn't get fooled by flash. He watched how people moved, how they hesitated, how they talked about others. And because he was paying attention, he rarely missed.

He wasn't trying to read people like a trick. He was *honouring them* by giving them his focus.

That's what this principle is really about.

Don't skim your life. Don't just show up with your body.

Show up with your *presence.* Because the people who master that?

They don't just have better conversations. They have *better relationships.* Better judgement. Better impact.

And the people around them?

They never forget how it felt to be seen.

Practical Translation

Being present isn't about being quiet or zen. It's about being *available.* Open. Focused. With yourself, with your work, with the people in front of you.

Here's how to live this principle the Eddie way:

1. Make eye contact and mean it

It sounds simple, but it's not. Most people don't really look. Eddie did – try it.

> **Ask yourself:** *When I speak to someone, am I actually seeing them?*

2. Ask better questions – and wait for the answers

Eddie didn't rush, he let the moment breathe. Ask. Then *listen* – not to reply, but to understand.

> **Ask yourself:** *Am I present enough to hear what's not being said?*

3. Put the phone away – properly

You can't fake presence. Phones kill focus. Give people your eyes – and your ears.

> **Ask yourself:** *Would I feel heard if someone gave me the attention I'm giving now?*

4. Be where your feet are

Don't run ahead. Don't rehash what just happened. Be *here*. In this room. This chair. This conversation.

Ask yourself: *What's one thing I'm missing right now because I'm not really here?*

5. Concentrate on people, not just performance

Whether watching a race or meeting someone new, notice the small signals. Presence reveals more than preparation.

Ask yourself: *What could I learn right now, if I slowed down and paid attention?*

6. Give presence to the people who matter most

Clients, crowds, or colleagues – and your friends. Your partner. Your family. The ones who often get the *leftovers* of your attention.

Ask yourself: *Who have I been half-listening to lately – and when will I give them my full self?*

Reflection

Eddie Jordan didn't need to command the room to be remembered. He didn't need to shout to be heard or dominate to be respected. He simply *paid* attention – and people felt it.

That's why so many walked away from a chat with him feeling lighter, seen, more certain of themselves. Because when someone truly listens – when they really *see* you – it restores something in you.

Presence, at its core, is about making space for someone else to be real. And Eddie gave that gift. Again and again. In garages. On boats. In boardrooms and restaurants. In joy. In stress. In grief. In life.

He didn't just show up – he *arrived*. Fully. Quietly. Intentionally.

Yes, he moved fast. Lived loud. Beat the drum. Filled the room.

But underneath the rhythm and stories was something deeper: stillness.

A focus so steady that when he turned it towards you, it felt like a beam of light.

He wasn't thinking about the next thing, he was *here*. With you.

He didn't just look at you – he *saw* you. Didn't just ask questions – he *listened* for the truth.

That's what made his conversations matter. That's what made people open up. That's what made his presence unforgettable.

And that's what we need more of.

So put down the noise. Drop the act. Close the tabs in your mind.

Be where you are. Be with who you're with. Pay attention. And be present.

Because when you are, you don't just connect more deeply. You *live* more fully.

Just like Eddie did.

16. Carry Cash and Share It

The Eddie Story

Eddie Jordan believed in carrying cash.

Not because he didn't have cards. Not because he didn't like banks. And not because he didn't trust the system. He carried cash because he believed – *deeply* – in being ready.

Ready to help. Ready to tip. Ready to say, "Thanks," or "I got you," or, simply, "Here, let me."

He wasn't one for waiting on formalities. He wasn't interested in bureaucracy. He liked to move fast, act in the moment, and fix the thing that needed fixing. And for that, cash was king.

He'd say, "Always carry a few quid. You never know when you might need it – or when someone else might need it more."

It was a quiet code he lived by. Not showy. Not staged. Just folded notes tucked into a pocket, ready for the moment. A tool, not a trophy.

And Eddie didn't just carry cash – he *used* it.

Not to accumulate. Not to collect. But to *give*. To keep money in flow. In momentum.

At dinners, he always made sure the staff were looked after – before things even started. He'd slip the waiter a tip before the food had even arrived. Just a quick handshake, a quiet gesture, a folded note passed like a secret.

If you asked him why, he'd grin and say, "Give it early, and the night goes better. Everyone relaxes. Everyone's seen. Everyone's happy."

It wasn't about service, it was about *setting a tone*. About acknowledging someone's work before they had to earn it. About saying, "I see what you're about to do, and I respect it."

It was old-school generosity. Done with modern soul.

And he didn't stop at restaurants. He noticed the people most others walked past. The man sweeping the pavement. The back-stage crew packing up the gear. The car park guy doing a double shift in the cold. The kid standing at the back of the room, holding a clipboard and trying not to be in the way.

Eddie would spot them.

He'd make a joke. Ask a question. Share a moment.

And often – he'd hand them something.

Not out of pity. Out of *recognition*. Out of *rhythm*.

That was Eddie's currency: human connection. And a few notes passed quietly in the right moment could turn a whole day around.

One story still stays with me.

In Cape Town, about a mile from Eddie's house, there was a man in a wheelchair. He had one leg. Always sat in the same place. Quiet. Still. Watching the world go by.

Whenever Eddie cycled past – which was often – he stopped.

It wasn't a big gesture. Just a word, a nod, and a few folded notes.

And if you were cycling with him, he'd always say the same thing: "Do me a favour – never pass that man without giving him a few quid."

And later – in true Eddie fashion, quietly, without asking for any credit – he arranged for the man to get a new wheelchair. Just like that. No post. No plaque. No story. Just a solution.

Because that was Eddie. He didn't need attention, he just needed *action*.

And he *loved* the feel of cash. Not in a greedy way – in a *practical* way. He liked the speed of it. The decisiveness of it. The fact that he could fix something *now*. No receipts. No forms. Just *sorted*.

That's why he always knew what was in his pocket. He wasn't careless, he was *sharp*. And he didn't like to be overcharged – not by a euro, not by ten.

Like that time at his 75th birthday ski trip in Courchevel.

He'd bought a three-day ski pass the day *before* his birthday. All good. On day two, one of the instructors made a casual comment: "Pity you didn't buy it today. You'd have got the discount for over-75s."

Eddie didn't say much at the time. Just raised an eyebrow.

Two days later, I was driving back to Monaco with him and we were just leaving the ski resort when he suddenly tapped me and said, "Stop the car. There – on the left."

We pulled over near the ski pass office. He got out. Walked in.

Ten minutes later, he came out holding €120 in crisp notes.

Grinning. Eyes sparkling.

"F**kers overcharged me," he said. "I turned 75. Two days! That's my money, not theirs."

That was Eddie. A man who loved the thrill of a deal, the logic of a ledger, the sharpness of the transaction – but who gave away more than he ever kept.

Especially in Monaco. During the Formula 1 Grand Prix each year, he became a kind of mythical figure – hopping from one yacht to another, performing, storytelling, sometimes drumming, sometimes just lighting the space.

In 2024, while battling serious illness, he did *20 gigs* in just four days. Twenty.

He'd go boat to boat on Friday night, running on tight slots, pre-arranged times, his name pencilled in like a jazz act doing back-to-back sets across town.

He'd show up, perform, smile, share a drink, crack a line, pose for a photo, maybe play a tune or tell a story he'd told a hundred times but somehow always made it sound new. "Who was your favourite driver, Eddie?" "I went to the Macau Formula 3 in 1983 with a driver called da Silva. He won it hands down and I represented him. I came away with a bag of cash, and he went straight to Formula 1 . . . and changed his name to Senna." Every time he told the story, it had the same passion as the first time he told it.

And after each gig?

He'd leave with a little bundle of cash.

An envelope. A handshake. A thank-you. A quiet grin.

I was with him one year, going boat to boat, having the craic and helping him set up. My phone buzzed with a message: "Just saw you on Sky Sports at the Formula 1 – what's that random-looking rucksack on your back?". It was the bag of cash that I was carrying for Eddie. After every boat gig, he would come over and throw another wad of cash at me and give me his trademark grin. "Come on. We have another gig in 15 mins."

He loved those "deals" as much as the huge deals he also did. The challenge. The handshake. The exchange. The rhythm of it.

Because Eddie loved cash not for what it was worth – but for what it *meant*.

It meant freedom. It meant action. It meant you could *do something good* and not wait to be told how.

He believed that if you had something in your hand, and someone else needed it more – you passed it on. No questions. No strings.

Eddie's toughness in business was about doing the best deal. He would not give in. It was a battle. Like hand to hand combat. But it was never about the cash – it was about the challenge and the duel. Once he got the cash, he could use it and share it if it was needed.

Because generosity, like rhythm, should *move*.

And Eddie? He never stopped moving.

> *"If you've got a few quid in your pocket, don't hang onto it too tight. Someone else might need it more than you – and you'll never miss it."*
> – Eddie Jordan

The Principle as Philosophy

"Always carry cash," Eddie used to say. But what he really meant was: *be ready to give.*

He carried money – yes. But he also carried rhythm, mischief, generosity, presence, and the kind of instinct that doesn't wait to be told what the right thing is – it just *does it*.

Eddie knew that generosity isn't about grand gestures, it's about small, quiet decisions. A note in the hand before dinner. A folded bill at the door. A bundle of cash passed back down the line to someone who deserved it and probably didn't expect it.

And more than that – he understood something most people miss:

Cash moves fastest when it's not held too tightly.

He believed that wealth wasn't measured by what you kept, but by what you *could pass on*.

Eddie's version of carrying cash was never about showing status, it was about *carrying readiness*. Carrying responsibility. Carrying *respect* for the people around you.

When you walked with Eddie, you saw how lightly he held the world – but how firmly he held onto *principle*. He wasn't careless. He wasn't wasteful. But he *noticed*. And when he saw something he could do, he *did it*. Right there. No drama. No delay.

Because the truth is, you don't have to be wealthy to be generous.

You just have to *decide* that when something is in your hands – and someone else needs it more – you'll let it go.

Practical Translation

This principle isn't about carrying €50 in your wallet just in case. It's about living in a way that's *alert to need*, and *eager to act*.

Here's how to bring it into your world:

1. Keep a note for a moment that matters

Not every act of generosity needs a plan. Sometimes it needs a note in your back pocket and the decision to notice someone.

> **Ask yourself:** *Do I have something in my hand right now that could change someone else's day?*

2. Give before you're asked

Don't wait for the tip jar. Don't wait for the bill. Don't wait for a GoFundMe. Give *because you can* – not because someone asked.

> **Ask yourself:** *Where in my day can I be proactive, not reactive, in kindness?*

3. Start with a gesture, not an outcome

You don't have to fix someone's life, you just have to lift the moment. One sandwich. One note. One cab fare.

> **Ask yourself:** *Am I holding back because I think it's "not enough"?*

4. Be generous without needing credit

Eddie never did it for thanks, he did it because it was *right*. The best kind of giving is the kind that disappears once it's done.

> **Ask yourself:** *Would I still give this if no one ever knew I did?*

5. Respect the value of things — even the small things

Like getting €120 back on a ski pass. Like topping up your stash after a small win. It's not about hoarding, it's about *respecting the rhythm of what's yours*.

> **Ask yourself:** *Am I honouring the value of what I earn – and sharing what I don't need?*

6. Teach others by example, not instruction

Slip someone a note. Show your kids how to tip early. Help quietly. Don't talk about generosity. *Model it.*

> **Ask yourself:** *Who's watching how I give – and what might they learn from it?*

Reflection

There are people who walk through the world collecting things – and then there are people who walk through the world distributing them. Eddie Jordan was the latter.

He didn't carry cash to show off. He carried it to be ready – to notice a moment, to shift a mood, to sort a problem fast. A folded note passed with a nod. A quiet gesture that said: "I've got you."

He loved to see the face on a waiter when he slipped them a £50 note before the meal even began – not as a bribe, but as a tone-setter. "You're seen. You matter. Let's have a good night." It lifted the whole room. It changed the rhythm. That's what Eddie did.

He didn't need to hold on tight. Because he knew that the real power of money – and time, and energy – isn't in how long you can keep it. It's in how quickly and cleanly you can move it towards someone who needs it more.

That's impact.

It's not about the size of the tip, it's about the spirit behind it. The decision to look up. To look around. To connect. Not with performance, but with presence. A way of saying – with or without words – "I see you."

And the truth is, you don't have to wait for the right moment to do it. Eddie never did. He made the moment. Over and over again.

Because in a world that waits for approval, receipts, or perfect timing – Eddie just acted. Quickly. Generously. With rhythm and with heart.

He taught us that generosity isn't about having loads. It's about recognizing when you have enough. And when the moment comes? You don't hesitate, you give.

So yes – carry cash. But carry more than that.

Carry awareness. Carry readiness. Carry rhythm.

And above all – carry a willingness to act.

Not for credit. Not for show.

But because, like Eddie, you've decided to make the world just a little lighter for someone else.

17. Spot Talent Early

The Eddie Story

Eddie Jordan never waited for someone to be finished before believing in them. He wasn't drawn to polish or titles or perfection. He was drawn to potential – the kind of rawness most people overlooked because they didn't know how to handle it.

But Eddie knew.

He could feel it. Sometimes it was a posture. Sometimes it was a silence. Sometimes it was the way someone looked up at the right moment and didn't blink.

That was often all he needed. He'd seen enough.

Because Eddie had this instinct. A human radar. A way of tuning into people quickly and deeply. When he asked questions, he listened closely – not just to the words, but to what was beneath them. The tone. The hesitation. The energy. The eyes.

He had this thing he'd say when he was trying to get to the bottom of someone:

"Tell me what you'd do. And don't give me any bullshit. I asked you for a reason."

He didn't want a polished answer, he wanted the truth. The real take. The moment someone dropped the performance and just spoke. And when they did, Eddie was fully there. Reading their expression. Their rhythm. The way they sat. He noticed it all.

That's how he saw talent – not in the results, but in the feel of the person in front of him.

It's how he found Luca.

Just a busker on the streets of Dublin. Guitar in hand. Singing to whoever would listen. No spotlight. No audience beyond the passersby. But Eddie stopped. Listened. Noticed the way the guy held himself. Heard something in the phrasing, the control, the heart. And when the song finished, he stepped forward, handed Luca a card, and said:

"Call me."

That was it. No performance. No hype. Just a moment that turned into something lifelong.

Luca didn't live on the second floor – but he did go on to live in Eddie's world. They became friends. Played together. Travelled.

You could find them in Monaco during Grand Prix week, hopping from yacht to yacht, guitar in hand, Eddie on drums, jamming between champagne toasts and race briefings. They weren't doing it for attention. They were doing it because the connection was real – and because Eddie had recognized something in that young man on the street that deserved a bigger stage.

And he gave him one.

That's what Eddie did – again and again. In motorsport. In music. In life.

He saw what others couldn't. And more importantly, he acted on it.

One of the best examples? Andy Stevenson.

In 1987, Eddie was running his Formula 3 team and a young mechanic named Andy came for a job. At first glance, Eddie wasn't sold.

"Don't hire him," Eddie said. "I don't like the look of him."

But Andy was given a task anyway – something Eddie was sure he wouldn't be able to do. It was a kind of test, maybe even a brush-off.

Thirty minutes later, the job was done – perfectly.

Eddie was surprised. He changed his mind on the spot. Andy got the job.

And he didn't just stay for a season. He stayed for a lifetime.

Thirty-eight years later, Andy Stevenson is now the sporting director of Aston Martin Formula 1, one of the most respected and enduring figures in the paddock. He's survived multiple ownership changes – Jordan, Midland, Spyker, Force India, Racing Point, and now Aston Martin – and outlasted countless team bosses and senior figures.

That's what Eddie could do: spot someone, test them, and if they rose to it, back them all the way.

But spotting talent was only part of the story.

Eddie didn't just want to find potential – he wanted to surround himself with it. He believed the people around you define your direction, your energy, your edge.

"You are the sum of the people closest to you," he'd say. "So make sure they're go-getters. Progressive. Brave. People who move things forward, not hold things back."

Eddie built his world around builders. Around people who had fire in their belly, but humility in their heart. People who didn't need hand-holding – they just needed someone to believe in them.

And when he hired? He was crystal clear:

Hire people smarter than you – and get out of their way.

No micromanagement. No ego. Just clarity, trust, and belief.

He gave people room to lead – not just to deliver, but to own their space and thrive. He didn't want to be the smartest person in the room, he wanted to build a room full of the sharpest minds, the biggest thinkers, the most committed teammates.

And he believed deeply in showing up for those people. In investing in relationships, not just using them.

Because people who only take – who only show up when it serves them – never win in the long run.

"You always get back what you invest in people. Tenfold."

Eddie's loyalty to his people was real. Fierce. Often unspoken, but deeply felt.

He remembered birthdays. Called when someone was going through a tough time. Checked in after a bad weekend. If someone was out of work, he asked, "What do you need?" If someone had a spark, he asked, "Who do you need to meet?" He cared.

Because Eddie didn't just believe in people – he connected them.

He connected with people. He connected people to each other.

"My net worth is my network," he'd often say – and he meant it.

He didn't build his reputation in a boardroom. He built it in conversations, coffees, backroom deals, backstage moments, and late-night calls. He knew that success wasn't about holding power. It was about sharing it. Moving it. Multiplying it.

He didn't hoard his contacts. He activated them.

He didn't gatekeep his relationships. He opened doors – fast.

If he believed in you, he didn't wait for the perfect moment. He picked up the phone.

"You need to talk to my friend," he'd say.

And suddenly, you were talking to someone who changed your life.

That was the Eddie effect.

Potential, connected. Talent, lifted. Energy, multiplied.

Too often, people get obsessed with short-term goals and instant results.

Eddie played a longer game. He understood that developing talent, building relationships, and growing a network doesn't happen overnight – but when you do it right, it pays back for years. It's one of the highest-return investments you can make with your time – as long as you pick the right people.

You don't just build momentum.

You build a legacy that keeps building itself.

He gave Michael Schumacher his first Formula 1 race after a single test session. Just one. That was all he needed.

"He had that stillness," Eddie said later.

"That look. That menace. You just knew."

He then gave Michael's brother Ralf a drive at Jordan and was a good customer of Schumacher wine (at mates' rates) for many years.

He didn't call ten people to confirm it. He didn't check in with the rest of the paddock. He just made the call.

The same with Ayrton Senna in Formula 3. He gave him the seat before the world was paying attention. Because he saw the hunger. The restraint. The edge.

Eddie and Ayrton Senna shared such deep mutual respect that, at one point, Eddie even explored bringing Senna into Jordan Grand Prix as a part-owner – a bold move that might have rewritten the future of the team, and of Formula 1 itself.

He backed Damon Hill when others said no. He bet on Jean Alesi. On Rubens Barrichello. On Eddie Irvine. On Ralf Schumacher. On Giancarlo Fisichella. On a dozen names people forget started with Jordan. He didn't just recruit them. He supported them. Gave them room. Let them drive. Let them crash. Let them grow.

That's the part people miss. Eddie wasn't trying to control them. He wasn't moulding them into something they weren't. He was removing the fear. He was making space for them to find their rhythm – without having to look over their shoulder every lap.

And they paid him back. In performances. In podiums. In loyalty.

Even those who became world champions – even those who left him too soon – most never forgot what Eddie gave them. It wasn't really about the seat. It was the first time someone truly believed in them. And it wasn't only about drivers.

There are hundreds of stories – across the sport, across industries – where Eddie saw something in someone and said:

"You've got it. Let's go."

He didn't wait to be asked. If he saw something, he acted. If you needed a meeting, he made it. If you needed a shot, he opened the door. No fanfare. No power play. Just generosity in motion. Just people backing people.

Because Eddie didn't build his legacy on podiums alone.

He built it on people – people who went further because he saw them early, backed them fully, and brought them into the right room at the right time.

He understood that momentum isn't built in isolation. It's built in community. In chemistry. In trust. In talent that's seen, supported, and set free.

Because when you believe in people – and you bring them together – you don't just create talent. You create legacy.

The Principle as Philosophy

Eddie Jordan didn't wait for permission to believe in people. He didn't need a committee or a data pack – he trusted his gut.

Because talent isn't always obvious. It's not polished or ready-made. Sometimes it's raw, quiet, dressed in oil-stained overalls or playing guitar on a Dublin street. But when Eddie saw it – *really saw it* – he moved. Fast.

Spotting talent was only half the job. The rest was backing it – with trust, not conditions. With space, not ego.

That's what made him different. What made him great was what came next. Eddie built environments where talent could multiply. He didn't want to be the smartest in the room – he wanted to be surrounded by people who made him better and moved things faster.

"You are the sum of the people closest to you," he'd say. "So make sure they're go-getters. Brave. Progressive."

It wasn't just about skill – it was about energy. He was drawn to people who lit things up, who didn't wait to be asked, who were wired to care, build, move. And once he found them, he trusted them. He got out of the way.

Simple. Rare. Most want control, Eddie wanted momentum.

That extended to his network too. He didn't collect contacts – he built real relationships. He stayed in touch, remembered details, showed up when no one else did.

Because Eddie understood what many leaders miss: people aren't a cost.

They're the multiplier.

Spot them early. Back them fully. Build trust. And they won't just deliver.

They'll take you further than you could have gone alone.

Practical Translation

Eddie Jordan didn't overthink people. He felt them. He didn't build empires by himself – he built with people. And that's what made all the difference.

Here's how to bring that mindset into your own life and leadership:

1. Don't wait for perfect – spot potential early

Talent doesn't show up finished, it shows up curious. Rough. Ready to grow. Eddie looked for hunger, not headlines. Next time you're with someone new – watch for the spark. The posture. The honesty. The instinct. If you feel something, say something. That's how great partnerships start.

> **Ask yourself:** *Am I looking past polish to spot raw potential – and encouraging it when I do?*

2. Listen beyond the words

Eddie didn't just hear answers, he listened to how they were said. The pause before the sentence. The glance. The tone. The tension. Be fully present when you meet someone new. Ask a question that matters, and listen with everything you've got. People will tell you who they are – if you're paying attention.

> **Ask yourself:** *Am I really listening – not just to the words, but to what's underneath them?*

3. Build your inner circle like it's your engine

"You are the sum of the people closest to you." So check your circle. Are they go-getters? Builders? Doers? If not, change the mix. Invite in energy. Invite in action. Build around people who move forward – and take you with them.

> **Ask yourself:** *Are the people around me pulling me forward – or quietly holding me back?*

4. Hire smarter – then step back

Eddie didn't hire to feel powerful, he hired to create power. Find people smarter than you, braver than you, different from you – and get out of their way. No micromanagement. Just belief, clarity, and trust. Give them the keys. Give them the room. Watch what happens.

> **Ask yourself:** *Am I hiring people who stretch me – and trusting them enough to lead?*

5. Play the long game with people

Relationships don't pay off instantly. But over time? They're your greatest asset. Keep in touch. Remember details. Call when it matters. Be the one who shows up – even when there's nothing in it for you. You don't build trust on LinkedIn, you build it over time – with real action.

> **Ask yourself:** *Am I investing in real relationships – even when there's no quick win?*

6. Build your network like a living thing

Eddie didn't just collect contacts, he connected them. He didn't protect access – he shared it. He opened doors. So be generous. Introduce people. Recommend someone. Make that call. Be the reason someone else levels up – and your whole network levels up with them.

> **Ask yourself:** *Am I actively growing my network – adding value, making connections, creating movement?*

7. Don't chase stars. Cultivate them.

Everyone wants the finished article. Eddie invested early. He saw the mechanic, the junior, the busker – and said, "Let's go." Great teams aren't found. They're grown. Be the person who makes someone better – not just the one who notices them once they already are.

> **Ask yourself:** *Am I spotting early promise – or only recognizing greatness once it's obvious?*

8. Give first. Back first. Trust first.

Most people wait. Wait to see what you do. Wait to decide if they'll support you. Eddie didn't wait. He gave first. He trusted first. And it came back tenfold. When you find someone you believe in – go first. Make the offer. Be early. Be bold. Be clear. Because people never forget who backed them when no one else would.

Ask yourself: *Where could I move first – and be remembered for the belief I offered early?*

Bottom Line: People are the multiplier. Choose them well. Invest in them deeply. And if you do that, your legacy won't be built by what you did alone.

It'll be built by what they go on to do – because you believed.

Reflection

There's something quietly extraordinary about being seen before you're ready – before the results, the title, or the world gives you permission.

Most people don't know what that kind of belief feels like until someone offers it to them. Eddie Jordan did. Again and again.

He spotted people when they were still forming – still rough, still figuring it out. And instead of waiting for them to become someone worth backing, he backed them anyway.

He didn't need a polished pitch or perfect data. He needed a spark. A flicker of potential. And when he felt it, he moved before the world caught up.

Because for Eddie, spotting talent wasn't about luck: it was about looking differently.

It wasn't "What is this now?" but "What could this become?" – and making space for that answer to emerge.

That belief didn't stay private. He said something. He did something. He gave you the moment – and stood off to the side, proud.

And that changed things. Not just in careers – but in confidence, in courage, in how people carried themselves.

When someone like Eddie sees something in you, you start to see it too.

That's the real impact of this principle. It's not about recruitment or team building, it's about transformation.

Eddie didn't just spot talent. He backed it. He gave people time. Trust. Room to grow.

And in a world obsessed with finished products, that kind of belief is rare.

But when it's real? It's powerful. Because when you invest early – and stay – you don't just get performance. You build people.

So wherever you lead, ask yourself: What am I overlooking because it isn't polished yet? Who around me is carrying something special that hasn't been recognized?

Spotting potential isn't just perception. It's permission.

And when it's backed with trust, action, and presence – like Eddie backed it – it becomes one of the most generous and lasting things you can offer.

You don't need to wait for someone to prove they're ready.

Notice. Believe. Back them.

As Eddie put it: "I didn't need someone to be perfect. I just needed to believe they could go further than they thought possible – and then give them the space to prove it."

Section Four:
Authenticity, Energy, and Character

18. Show Up with a Smile

The Eddie Story

You could tell Eddie Jordan had arrived before you even saw him.

There was a lift in the room. A ripple of energy. A slight buzz in the air. He wasn't loud straight away – but his presence was. It was the feeling that someone had just shown up who wasn't pretending to be anyone but himself, and who, despite whatever was happening that day, had already decided he was going to enjoy it.

And at the centre of that feeling was the smile.

Eddie's smile wasn't a trick. It wasn't a sales move. It wasn't something he put on to seem approachable. It was who he was. It came from the inside – from presence, from choosing to be here fully, with his whole self. It was his signature – and his superpower.

He didn't smile because everything was perfect. He smiled because he knew how messy life could be – and chose to meet it with humour and humanity anyway.

And that disarming energy made all the difference.

Because Eddie understood something very few people really grasp: showing up with a smile is one of the most powerful techniques for dealing with people. It relaxes the room. It lowers defences. It puts people at ease. It opens the door to better relationships, better interactions, better deals.

When someone leads with genuine humour and warmth, they make it easier for others to be real. To think clearly. To trust faster. That was Eddie's edge – and he used it brilliantly.

People often thought Eddie smiled because he was successful. But in truth, he was successful because he smiled. Because he led with light, not with pressure. With truth, not with fear. And that made people want to work with him, laugh with him, fight for him.

His smile wasn't about "being nice", it was about being real.

It told people: *I'm here. I'm not hiding. I'm not performing. And I'm not afraid of you.*

He was genuinely interested in people. He tuned in. He empathized. He cared. He listened – properly. He remembered detail. He wasn't just waiting for his turn to talk – a habit so many people fall into without realizing.

We live in a world where many are tied up in their own self-consciousness, where insecurity makes conversation into performance. People love the sound of their own voice. They wait to speak rather than really listen. Eddie was different.

And while yes, Eddie loved the sound of his own voice – no question there – it was often to entertain, to mentor, or to spark an idea that might help you move forward.

He wasn't just talking, he was connecting.

A few years ago, a friend called Darren joined Eddie and me for a bike ride. Afterwards, over coffee, the two of them had a proper chat – about life, family, and everything in between.

Eddie, as always, sparked the laughter that made it easy to talk about anything.

Then, just before we left, Eddie placed a hand on Darren's belly – carrying a bit of extra weight at the time – looked him straight in the eye with that signature grin, and said:

"Lose that."

It was quick. Honest. Disarming. And it landed.

That day, Darren made a decision. He got serious about his health. Today, he's 32kg lighter – and he still credits that single moment, and Eddie's straight-shooting kindness, as the turning point.

That was Eddie. He had a gift for reading the room, tuning into the moment, and knowing the exact thing to say to unlock something important.

You can't fake being genuinely interested in people. It's a decision – and when you make it, it pays you back a hundredfold.

Eddie often said, "I'm the luckiest guy in the world." And he was – but it wasn't by accident.

He made his own luck. By showing up smiling. By trusting himself to find the path less travelled – and to make it more interesting every single time. By choosing presence over pretence. By choosing people over performance.

And that's what gave him power.

Whether he was walking into a tense sponsor meeting, surviving a chaotic travel day on three hours' sleep, or facing the fallout of a mechanical disaster on race weekend – Eddie arrived the same way: Smile first. Presence second. Fire third.

Not to mask the truth. To shift the truth – to a better rhythm.

He wasn't passive, he was alive.

And that smile? It was contagious.

One of his crew once said: "You'd be knee-deep in engine failure, the press circling like sharks, and Eddie would walk in with that grin and say, 'Lads, we're going to win this f**king race. COME ON!' And somehow – you'd believe him."

Because when Eddie smiled, it wasn't just a facial expression. It was a signal.

It was a choice to lead with light, not with panic. To create momentum, not fear.

And people mirrored it.

That was part of Eddie's leadership magic. He knew people are always scanning – looking for emotional cues. And if the leader walks in heavy, guarded, stressed – the team contracts. But if the leader walks in smiling?

Shoulders drop. Eyes lift. The room breathes again.

He wasn't pretending problems didn't exist. He was choosing not to let them define the energy.

One of Eddie's rare gifts was carrying pressure without passing it on. He could be juggling money issues, political dramas, driver problems, engineering failures – and still pause to check in on someone's family. Still crack a joke with a journalist. Still lift the room with a single smile.

He understood: a real smile changes you, too. It resets your system. Loosens the jaw. Opens the heart. Reminds you: you're still here. You're still moving. You're still choosing life over fear.

Even in his most intense moments – in the middle of big-money business deals, in the noise of Formula 1 negotiations, in the chaos of international travel – Eddie carried his rhythm: Smile. Connect. Move forward.

He let go faster than most. Let go of grudges. Let go of losses. Let go of fear.

Not by pretending. By choosing.

And that choice – to bring light, to bring rhythm, to bring energy – changed everything.

It changed how deals got done. It changed how teams survived the worst days. It changed how life felt for everyone lucky enough to be close to him.

He didn't have to say, "It's going to be ok." He smiled – and everyone knew. That was Eddie. That was the power of light. That was the power of a real smile.

The Principle as Philosophy

A real smile doesn't come from your mouth, it comes from your *soul*. It's more than an expression – it's a *decision*. A reset. A commitment to be here, fully. To bring your whole self, not just your smart self. To lead with presence, not pressure.

Eddie Jordan understood this instinctively. His smile wasn't painted on. It came from the deep confidence of someone who *wasn't pretending*. Someone who had nothing to prove – only something to offer.

And that's what made it land.

A real smile says: "I'm with you." It says: "We've got this." It makes the space safer, warmer, easier to breathe in. It lowers defences. It signals trust. And it lifts the whole room before a single task has started.

But it's not always easy. Especially when you're under pressure. Especially when you're tired, behind, or managing chaos.

That's where the real skill lives – not in grinning when everything's going well, but in *choosing* to bring light when things are heavy.

That's what Eddie did.

He didn't show up with a smile because things were easy. He smiled because he knew the room needed a rhythm – and he was willing to start it.

That's leadership. That's generosity. That's energy discipline.

And when done well, it's goes beyond being contagious – it's *transformational*.

Because a real smile isn't about being positive.

It's about being *present*.

Practical Translation

A real smile, like Eddie's, is a signal – to yourself and to others. It tells the world: I've arrived with my energy intact. And I'm not afraid to bring it.

Here's how to bring this into your day-to-day life, leadership, and presence:

1. Smile from the inside out

Don't force it. Feel it. A smile isn't about faking joy – it's about letting go of tension and being fully where your feet are.

Ask yourself: *What do I need to let go of to be here?*

2. Decide your energy before you enter

You can't control the room, but you can control what you walk in with.

> **Ask yourself:** *Am I bringing light or waiting for someone else to?*

3. Let it be the reset button

Under pressure? Frustrated? Burnt out? Pause. Breathe. Smile – not because you have to, but because you *can*.

> **Ask yourself:** *What would happen if I smiled right now?*

4. Notice the ripple effect

Real energy spreads. People feel it. And they give it back. Even a small smile can shift a whole team.

> **Ask yourself:** *Who could use my presence more than my plan today?*

5. Make it a habit of return

Smiling is not pretending everything's ok. It's *remembering* that you can face things with openness.

> **Ask yourself:** *What rhythm do I want people to remember me for?*

6. Smile when you're alone

Try it. On a walk. At your desk. In the mirror. Feel how it changes your posture, your breath, your state. Practise a natural smile – not the fake one for photos, but the kind that feels like a quiet yes. A smile is just a frown turned upside down. See how it makes you feel when you really smile.

> **Ask yourself:** *What if my own smile was the best company I could keep today?*

Reflection

Eddie's smile wasn't just a flash of charm, it was a signal. A spark. A starting gun. It told the room: something's about to happen. And it usually did. That grin carried more than mischief. It carried intent. Energy. A refusal to be small. A decision, every time, to lift the space rather than lean on it.

He didn't wait for someone else to set the tone. He was the tone. Whether in the pit lane, the boardroom, the bar, or backstage, Eddie showed up with rhythm, with heart, with a grin that said: "Let's get on with it." And people followed. Because when someone smiles like that – not to impress, but to ignite – it's hard not to believe again. In the moment. In each other. In yourself.

That was Eddie's power. Not just to perform, but to transform. With presence. With pulse. With that grin.

If you want to lead like Eddie, don't start with a script. Start with a spark. From the inside out.

As Eddie once said:

"You don't need permission to bring the energy. You just need the balls."

And he always had them.

19. No Dimmer Switch

The Eddie Story

If you ever had the joy – and I use that word deliberately – of spending time around Eddie Jordan, you'd know that he didn't just light up a room.

He lit *you* up too.

Eddie didn't slip quietly into the background. He didn't assess the temperature of a room before speaking. He didn't wait to be invited. He didn't play it cool.

He showed up.

With rhythm. With force. With a twinkle in his eye and a story just about to tumble out of his mouth. With his full self – every time.

He didn't have a dimmer switch. It was on or off. Awake or asleep. *Everything or nothing.* And he would never have lived any other way.

It didn't matter if you caught him at an Formula 1 event, in a business meeting, cycling in the Alps, or at a quiet dinner table – the same Eddie showed up every time. Not a toned-down version. Not a "weekend" version. Not a polished PR front. Just Eddie – vibrant, joyful, emotional, alive.

And often, musical.

Eddie had rhythm in his bones, and he couldn't help but let

it out. If there was a surface nearby, he'd find a way to drum on it – sometimes with his hands, sometimes with spoons, sometimes with whatever utensils were close enough to grab before the chorus hit.

One of the places where that joy came through most vividly was in Covent Garden, London – where, even in his seventies, you could sometimes find him on a street corner, busking with his dear friend Luca. Not for attention. Not for money. But just to *feel alive*.

Luca would set up the mic and the guitar, and Eddie would bring his Cajón – a hand percussion box that doubles as a seat – and often a pair of spoons. He'd tap out rhythms as people walked by, some smiling, some stopping, some filming without realizing who they were watching.

And if they asked? Luca would say, "That's John. Or maybe Eddie Irvine. Or Bernie Ecclestone's cousin. Depends on the day."

Eddie never corrected him. Never craved credit. He just grinned and kept the beat going.

Because he wasn't doing it to be recognized.

He was doing it to *live*.

In his last year, while already suffering through cancer, he went busking *multiple* times. Not for show. For soul. He cycled 110 kilometres in Cape Town and finished second in his age group. He sailed his boat. He travelled. He told stories. He created rhythm – because as long as there was a beat left, Eddie wasn't going to waste it.

And then there was the podcast.

In 2023, he and David Coulthard launched *Formula For Success*. Both of them agreed that F.F.S. didn't actually stand for "Formula for Success". He loved the name. The edginess of it. "We'll do ten episodes," he said. "I'll tell a few stories. We'll see what happens."

What happened was over 110 episodes. Global charts. Millions of listeners. And a legacy of storytelling that connected the world of motorsport to laughter, humility, and joy.

And Eddie committed to it.

He didn't miss a recording unless he was under anaesthetic. Literally.

He could be in a hotel in London, a boat in Monaco, a quiet flat in Dublin – it didn't matter. The mic came out. The headphones went on. The beat resumed.

I visited him once in Monaco when he was visibly unwell. In bed. In pain. Quiet. Slow. Sleepy.

I said, "Eddie, I'll leave you to rest."

He looked up at me with a flicker of the old spark and said: "Nope. I'm recording a podcast in an hour. You need to set it up for me."

Then, through a clenched jaw and a grin, added: "And stop being a dick."

I said, "Eddie . . . you're in no fit state to record anything. Let me cancel it."

His voice hardened. Teeth clenched, not with anger, but with grit. "I'm doing it."

And he did. He recorded the episode.

And when it aired, you wouldn't have known a thing. His voice was steady. His stories flowed. The mischief was intact. The rhythm was there.

That was Eddie. A *storyteller* to the very end – and, as he liked to say, "There's even some truth in nearly all of them."

But more than a performer, Eddie was *present*. He didn't just show up for the big things, he showed up for *everything*.

He went to bed early (when he wasn't out too late). He got up early. He planned his days. He checked in on people. He squeezed every drop of juice out of life.

And he never – not once – dimmed himself to make anyone else more comfortable.

He believed life gave you great opportunities. That you shouldn't stay stuck because of your past. Or your thinking. Or your habits.

"If you're alive," he'd say, "then live."

He didn't need the spotlight – but he *was* the light. And not because he demanded attention. Because he radiated *presence*. And presence like that changes a room. Changes a ride. Changes a dinner. Changes a friendship.

Eddie didn't have one personality for the public and another in private.

He had one setting: ON.

And when he was on – which was always – he didn't just walk into a moment. He brought the rhythm.

He brought the spoons. He brought the story. He brought the grin. He brought the craic. He brought the edge. He brought the madness.

And those of us lucky enough to stand beside him felt our own vibration lift, our own volume rise, our own story feel a little bit bolder.

Because when someone lives that brightly beside you – you stop hiding in the shadows.

You remember: This is what life can feel like.

And you turn up the dial.

The Principle as Philosophy

Most people learn to tone themselves down. To scan the room before they speak. To play small just enough to feel safe. It's like walking through life with one hand on a dimmer switch – constantly adjusting, rarely arriving as the full version of themselves.

Eddie Jordan never did that. He never wanted to.

He didn't self-edit. He didn't shrink to fit the space. He showed up – loud, warm, electric – because he understood something vital: presence is power. And rhythm is leadership. He lived in tune with himself and chose, moment after moment, to share that rhythm without apology.

Being fully expressed isn't about being the loudest. It's about being real. It's not recklessness – it's freedom. It's knowing who you are and being bold enough to bring that into every room, whether it's a race day, a dinner table, a stage, or a simple chat with a stranger.

Eddie didn't try to be unforgettable, he simply refused to be forgettable. And when he showed up like that – alive, unfiltered, present – it gave others permission to do the same. It made the space warmer. The energy higher. The moment matter more.

Because the world doesn't need your edited version. It needs your full frequency. It needs your colour, your humour, your honesty. Not to impress, but to connect.

So whatever room you walk into, whatever moment you face – don't dim. Don't hold back. Don't wait.

Let your rhythm lead.

As Eddie said: "If you've got a spark, don't sit on it. Light the bloody place up!"

Practical Translation

Living without a dimmer switch doesn't mean exhausting yourself. It means *aligning* yourself. It means living with integrity between your inner spark and your outer presence.

Here's how to turn this principle into action:

1. Check whether you're dimming — and why

Are you playing small to avoid attention? To make others comfortable? To avoid failure? Be honest.

> **Ask yourself:** *Am I editing myself to fit in — or expanding to be fully me?*

2. Find your rhythm — then trust it

Eddie didn't copy anyone's cadence. He moved to his own beat — and so can you. You don't need to be loud, you need to be *real*.

> **Ask yourself:** *What pace, tone, and energy feels most me — and am I living in that?*

3. Bring your energy to the room, not just your head

Don't be the person who waits to "feel the vibe". *Be the vibe*. Walk in awake. Lead with energy.

> **Ask yourself:** *What energy am I radiating today – and is it helping or holding back?*

4. Do the thing that lights you up, even if it makes no sense

Busk. Dance. Drum. Speak. Say yes. Start small – but start. It doesn't have to be productive, it just has to be *alive*.

> **Ask yourself:** *What would I do today if I stopped worrying what anyone else thought?*

5. Refuse to let illness, age, or fear silence you

If Eddie could busk in Covent Garden, record podcasts from bed, and cycle races in his seventies, what excuse are you still using?

> **Ask yourself:** *What story am I telling myself about why I can't – and is it true?*

6. Let your story be a signal, not a performance

When you share your truth, others recognize their own. You don't need to impress. Just show up with a grin and the courage to begin.

> **Ask yourself:** *If I lived today like it mattered, how would I walk into the room?*

Reflection

Eddie Jordan didn't just show people how to win, he showed them how to live.

With mischief. With rhythm. With truth. With timing. With brightness. With full, unapologetic presence.

He didn't tone it down to make others comfortable. He didn't wait for perfect moments. He *was* the moment – fully alive, fully there. Whether tapping spoons in Covent Garden, telling a story for the fiftieth time like it was the first, or lifting a room just by walking into it, Eddie made people feel more awake, more grounded, more themselves.

He didn't hold back his spark – he shared it. Freely. Joyfully. And in doing so, he gave everyone around him permission to show up fully too. That was his magic. Not performance: presence.

So, here's the invitation: Don't shrink. Don't edit. Don't wait.

Live now. Play your rhythm. Bring your energy. And when the moment calls – say yes, light it up, and go all in.

Just like Eddie did.

> *"It's not the podiums or the headlines you remember. It's the laughs, the risks, the music, the chaos. That's what makes a life."*
> – Eddie Jordan

20. Stay Humble

The Eddie Story

Eddie Jordan was many things – flamboyant, fearless, funny, sharp – but underneath it all, he was quietly and unshakeably humble.

It's easy to confuse confidence with ego. Eddie had plenty of the first, and none of the second. The public saw the colourful shirts, the big voice, the spotlight moments. But behind it all was a man deeply rooted in where he came from and crystal clear about what really mattered in life – and it was *never* the flash.

He may have once owned boats, travelled on private jets, and sat at the table with world champions and billionaires – but he was just as happy with a £1 coffee in a corner café with plastic chairs and a biscuit on the side. In fact, he preferred it. He loved finding the place off the beaten track, the kind of café that didn't have a loyalty app or uniform cups. That was where he felt most himself. He didn't need to be seen, he just wanted to connect.

When he was in London, you wouldn't find Eddie being chauffeured around in the back of a tinted car. *He took the bus.* Happily. Said he liked seeing what was going on. Said it beat sitting in traffic, trying to look important. While others were being driven, Eddie was chatting to people on the top deck, observing the city, still learning. He didn't want to get "soft" and lazy. He did enjoy it when people recognized him, as he said, "I can't believe that 20 years after I sold my Formula 1 team, I am still recognized so much." Except when someone came up and asked for a selfie and then said, "Thanks, Bernie [Ecclestone]" . . .

People throw around the phrase "a man of the people". But

Eddie was that – not in theory, but in practice. Every day. With everyone. From security guards to CEOs, from mechanics to presenters, from buskers to broadcasters. He treated them the same. He meant it when he asked how your day was. And he usually remembered what you told him.

I remember when my daughter Mia had just moved to London. She stayed with Eddie and Marie for a few weeks while she found her feet. One Sunday, around 12:30 p.m., my phone rang. It was Eddie. He said, "Mia's studying in her bedroom. I'm going to get lunch for her – she needs to eat something. Is there anything she likes or doesn't like?"

And I remember just stopping in that moment – thinking: This is a man who's lived one of the most extraordinary lives. He's scaled the heights of Formula 1, music, media, and business. And today he's walking to Tesco Express to pick up ingredients to make my daughter lunch.

That was Eddie.

He was the guy who remembered what mattered. The guy who didn't think he was too important to make someone a sandwich or carry his own bags, or ask for help. The guy who made the small things feel just as important as the big ones.

He always remembered his roots back in Ireland and did a lot to promote Ireland and Irish people. He would speak a few words in Irish. "*Conas ata tu?*" was often his greeting ("How are you?" in Irish). In his house in Spain, he had tiles on a huge open-plan floor downstairs, and right across the floor was a mosaic tile of the river Liffey in Dublin, to remind him of where home really was.

And despite the fact that he *had* accomplished so much – really, more than most could ever dream of – he never needed to show off about it. He owned his success, yes. He was proud of what he'd built. But he never acted like it made him better than anyone else.

He didn't let cockiness or ego get in the way of his growth. He always wanted to learn more. Do better. Live fuller. He stayed teachable. He stayed open. And most of all, he stayed *himself*. He would say, "Don't get high on your own supply."

When Eddie spoke to you, you always got the real thing. There was no mystery. No agenda. No politics. No double-talk. What he said was what he meant. If he liked you, you knew it. If he didn't – well, you probably knew that too.

People never walked away from Eddie wondering, *"What did he really think?"* Because he told you. With honesty. With humour. With heart. With no filter. If he thought someone was getting too cocky, he'd look them straight in the eye and say, "Do you think your sh*t doesn't stink?"

He didn't waste time being diplomatic if the truth would do. And he didn't play the room. He didn't say one thing and do another. He wasn't interested in managing impressions – he was interested in living with *integrity*.

He knew exactly who he was: a boy from Dublin who'd built a life on rhythm, risk, character, and community. A man who'd earned a seat at the biggest tables in the world – and never once forgot how he got there. Or who helped him. Or what it cost. Or what really mattered.

He never let the world convince him that success was about money or prestige or control. For Eddie, success was about *freedom*. The freedom to laugh. To tell stories. To create. To help someone out. To play a gig. To sit in a café and watch the world go by. To chat to a stranger who came up for a selfie.

That's what grounded him.

And that's why people trusted him – not just in business, or on stage, or on air, but in the quiet, human spaces where humility lives.

Eddie Jordan never needed to act like he was special.

He just knew that being *real* was enough. And that made him unforgettable.

> *"I always knew there were people smarter than me – that's why I listened, asked questions, and hired well. Humility isn't weakness. It's survival."*
> – Eddie Jordan

> *"You've got to stay humble, no matter how loud the world gets. In this sport, the moment you think you've cracked it, you're finished."*
> – Eddie Jordan

The Principle as Philosophy

Humility isn't about pretending you haven't achieved anything. It's about knowing that your achievements don't make you more valuable than anyone else.

Eddie Jordan understood that better than most. He was proud of what he'd done. He had every right to be. But his identity was never wrapped up in his resume. It was anchored in *who he was* – not what he had.

And that made all the difference.

He didn't have to perform modesty. He didn't have to play it down. He could tell you about the podium finishes, the TV shows, the multimillion-dollar deals – but you never got the sense he was trying to impress you.

Because he wasn't.

He was just sharing a story. Laughing at himself. Letting you in.

Eddie's version of humility wasn't about shrinking – it was about standing tall *and making room for others to stand tall too*. It was about keeping your feet on the ground even when the world keeps trying to put you on a pedestal.

Real humility is magnetic. And Eddie had it in spades.

Because people don't remember you for how loudly you talk about yourself. They remember how you made them feel.

And Eddie made people feel *seen*. Equal. Valued. From interns to icons, he showed up the same way.

That's what staying humble looks like: confidence without arrogance. Pride without pretension. Knowing who you are – without forgetting where you came from.

Practical Translation

Staying humble doesn't mean playing small. It means staying grounded – no matter how high you climb. Eddie used to say be nice to the people you meet on your way up the ladder as they are the people you will meet on the way down.

Here's how to practice it the Eddie way:

1. Talk to everyone like they matter — because they do

From the person bringing your coffee to the one signing the contract, treat people the same.

> **Ask yourself:** *Am I present with everyone, or only the people I think matter?*

2. Give credit. Take blame. Be fair.

When things go right, spread the credit. When they go wrong, take responsibility. That's leadership with humility.

> **Ask yourself:** *Do I own my mistakes as readily as I celebrate my wins?*

3. Be curious — even when you know a lot

Eddie never stopped learning. He never assumed he had all the answers. Stay curious, stay teachable.

> **Ask yourself:** *Who could I learn something from today — no matter their age or title?*

4. Let go of the image — be real

You don't need to be the polished version of yourself. Be the honest one. People will connect to that more than perfection.

> **Ask yourself:** *Am I being impressive — or being myself?*

5. Remember the journey

Wherever you are now, it wasn't always like this. Don't forget your roots – that's where your truth lives.

> **Ask yourself:** *Who helped me get here – and have I thanked them?*

6. Do the small things without needing credit

Walk to the shop. Make the lunch. Call your friend's kid. These things matter more than most people realize.

> **Ask yourself:** *What can I do today that shows someone I care – without needing to be noticed?*

Reflection

Eddie Jordan was a giant in so many worlds – motorsport, music, media, business – but his greatest strength wasn't his reach. It was his touch. The way he made people feel. The way he could talk to a billionaire and a bus driver the same way. The way he never stopped being the boy from Dublin, no matter how many countries he travelled or stages he stood on.

He lived big. He made noise. He brought rhythm. He stood out. But he never needed to be the centre of the story. He just wanted to be in the story – with you. Eddie didn't pretend to be less than he was, he just didn't believe he was better than anyone else.

He showed us that humility isn't weakness – it's strength with soul. It's presence without posture. It's being powerful and still choosing kindness. He didn't lead by status, he led by spirit. He didn't command loyalty, he inspired it. He didn't talk about humility, he lived it.

That's what made him admired but also loved.

So, if you've built something – a career, a name, a following – don't let it lift you above the people who helped you get there. Walk among them. Thank them. Listen to them. Learn from them. And every so often?

Take the bus.

Carry the bag.

Slip the waiter a tenner.

Because those are the moments that define you. Not the ones on the podium. But the ones when no one's watching.

That's where humility lives.

That's where Eddie lived.

And that's what made him unforgettable.

> *"You are the sum of the people closest to you, so make sure they're go-getters. Brave. Progressive."*
> – Eddie Jordan

21. Be Yourself and Inspire

The Eddie Story

From the moment Eddie Jordan stepped into a Formula 1 paddock, people knew he wasn't like the others.

Where the other team principals wore stiff suits and rehearsed corporate scripts, Eddie burst through the gates like a one-man carnival. Loud shirts, gold-rimmed glasses, wild hair, leather shoes with more character than some of the cars on the grid. He looked like he'd wandered in from backstage at a Rolling Stones gig – and often had. But he belonged. And more importantly, he made you believe he belonged.

Eddie didn't try to fit in.

He tried to be remembered.

And he was.

But here's the truth most people missed: it wasn't an act. It wasn't marketing. It wasn't contrived chaos to grab attention. It was just *him* – turned all the way up. Every colour, every laugh, every unexpected turn of phrase, every ridiculous shirt. Eddie Jordan, uncensored and unapologetic.

He was always authentic. Self-assured without arrogance. Direct without dominance. Funny without needing to be the centre of attention. He didn't act loud to cover insecurity – he just *was* loud, because that was his rhythm. He wasn't pretending to be confident. He just didn't spend any time wondering whether he should be.

He loved people – really loved them. Loved their quirks, their stories, their opinions. He didn't just tolerate personality, he encouraged it. Drew it out of people like a magician pulls scarves from a hat. One minute you were guarded, cautious, corporate – and by the end of the conversation, you were laughing, throwing ideas around, maybe even dancing. That's the effect Eddie had.

And he did it without a mask. Without shapeshifting. Without trying to fit anyone's mould. He didn't spend time worrying what others thought – not because he didn't care, but because he was already racing ahead. That kind of presence – that freedom – is contagious.

He didn't have to think about being "authentic". He just *was*. And in being so real, he made everyone else feel like they could breathe again.

He once said, "Why would you be shy?" Not as a dig. As an invitation. As a challenge. As a gift.

He wanted you to stop dimming your light. Stop tiptoeing. Be yourself – because when you are, you don't have to carry the burden of pretending. You free up your energy to *do*. To *move*. To *lead*.

That was Eddie's edge. He wasn't trying to impress you, he was trying to wake you up.

He knew that most people spent half their life trying to figure out who they are supposed to be. He didn't. He decided early – and lived it fully.

And he took that same principle into leadership.

He didn't want clones in his garage, he wanted misfits with magic. Characters with competence. People who swore, danced, argued, laughed, cried, cared. People who were human – and brought their full humanity into the mission.

That's why Jordan Grand Prix didn't just feel like a racing team. It felt like a tribe. A band. A place where you were expected to bring all of yourself – and no one asked you to leave the interesting parts at the door.

And that culture? It made them fast. Because when people are free, they commit harder. When they're trusted, they give more.

When they don't have to waste energy being someone else, they perform better as themselves.

Eddie was flawed, of course. He made mistakes. Said the wrong thing. Lost his temper. Got things spectacularly wrong. But here's the difference: he *owned it*. Learned from it. Laughed at himself. And then moved forward – sharper, humbler, more human.

He never let failure become shame. He never let mistakes become masks. He didn't believe in hiding the parts of yourself that were unfinished. He believed in movement.

Always forward.

He wanted to be the best version of himself – mentally, physically, spiritually. That's why he kept pushing into his seventies. Still riding bikes. Still playing gigs. Still doing business. Still mentoring. Still asking questions. Still full of music, motion, mischief.

Because being yourself doesn't mean staying still. It means staying true – even as you evolve.

And when you spent time with Eddie, you left braver. Not because he gave you advice. Because he showed you what it looked like to live *without apology.* And when someone does that in front of you – with joy, with power, with presence – it makes you want to do it too.

Eddie didn't just inspire others by being loud.

He inspired them by being *real.*

> *"Just be who you are – fully.*
> *People can feel when it's real."*
> – **Eddie Jordan**

The Principle as Philosophy

In a world where most people are scanning the room, trying to work out how they should behave, Eddie Jordan walked in already knowing. He was himself. Fully. Visibly. Loudly. And it changed the room every time.

That wasn't just charisma. It was leverage.

Eddie understood something most people miss: when you're yourself – truly, unapologetically – you become *undeniable*. You stop trying to manage your image. You stop second-guessing your words. You stop burning energy on pretence. And you start *leading*.

Authenticity isn't passivity. It's *power*. It's alignment. It's the fastest route to trust.

People didn't follow Eddie because he was perfect. They followed him because they knew what they were getting. He was consistent. You didn't need to decode him. You could relax – because the person across from you wasn't trying to manipulate or mould themselves. He was just *there* – honest, engaged, and real.

That realness gave others permission. It loosened collars. Unlocked voices. Invited courage. People stepped up around Eddie not only because he was a great leader – but because he made them feel safe enough to lead in their own way.

This wasn't about "personal branding". This was about *not leaving yourself behind*. Eddie didn't edit his essence to suit a sponsor or soften his tone for a boardroom. He brought energy and conviction wherever he went – because that's what gets remembered. That's what inspires people.

He wasn't perfect – but he was *present*. And in business, in leadership, and in life – that's the real leverage.

Practical Translation

Being yourself doesn't mean broadcasting every opinion or wearing loud shirts for the sake of it. It means *being aligned –* with your values, your style, your rhythm, your voice.

Here's how to put Eddie's authenticity into practice:

1. Drop the act — especially when it's tempting

When stakes are high, people tend to mask up. But that's exactly when you need to show up as yourself. That's when people are watching for truth.

> **Ask yourself:** *Am I trying to win this moment . . . or just to be liked?*

2. Let your personality come through the work

Eddie didn't separate who he was from what he did. His energy, humour, edge – it all flowed into the culture. Be real in how you lead. People will remember how you made them *feel.*

> **Ask yourself:** *Where am I flattening myself to appear "professional"?*

3. Don't spend energy managing what others think

Eddie wasn't careless – he just didn't carry unnecessary weight. You can't move fast if you're always trying to control perception.

> **Ask yourself:** *What could I build if I stopped worrying about my image?*

4. Create space for others to be real

When you're yourself, you create safety. People drop their guard. Ideas get sharper. Conversations go deeper. Culture becomes real.

> **Ask yourself:** *Am I creating environments where people feel free to be themselves?*

5. Be flawed — but be learning

Eddie never pretended to be flawless, but he *owned* his flaws and used them to grow. Don't chase perfection. Chase *presence*.

> **Ask yourself:** *Am I more focused on looking good or actually getting better?*

6. Celebrate what makes you different

Your quirks aren't liabilities, they're your edge. Your rhythm. Your code. Use them. Honour them. Let people connect to them.

> **Ask yourself:** *What part of me have I been hiding that could actually become a strength?*

Reflection

Eddie Jordan didn't lead with a title, he led with presence. He didn't enter a room to impress, but to connect. Fully himself. No mask. No softening of edges. And somehow, that gave everyone else permission to be themselves too.

That's the real impact of authenticity. It doesn't just ease the room, it energizes it. People lean in. They tell the truth. They take risks. They laugh again. That's not accidental, that's leadership of the rarest kind.

Eddie proved, again and again – team after team, gig after gig – that when you lead from who you truly are, the right people will find you, follow you, and build something that lasts. He didn't shrink to fit. He didn't bend to please. He didn't wear a version of himself that looked tidy on paper but rang hollow in real life.

He showed up as Eddie. Every time. And the world responded.

So, here's the invitation:

Be yourself.

Not the polished version. Not the strategic version. Not the version you think they want.

The real one.

Because that's the version people trust. That's the version people follow.

That's the version people remember.

22. Move Your Ass

The Eddie Story

Eddie Jordan never sat still for long. He wasn't restless – he was ready. Always. Because he knew something most people forget: your body is the ignition key for your mind. When you move, everything sharpens. Ideas come. Clarity returns. Energy finds its rhythm. And Eddie was all about rhythm.

He cycled. Swam. Walked hills. Lifted weights. Hit the gym early and often. Even when nobody was watching – especially then. Fitness for him wasn't about ego. It wasn't to impress. It was to *perform*. He kept his body tuned like an Formula 1 engine. Because when the body is fit, the mind fires faster. The confidence rises. The voice is clearer. The risks are cleaner. The decisions land.

And he never gave himself a free pass. He knew the buck stopped with him. Only *he* could let himself off the hook – and he never did. He kept himself accountable, always. He didn't duck out of training. He didn't coast through sessions. He didn't say, "I'll go tomorrow," because he knew what tomorrow becomes. Tomorrow turns into next week. And next week becomes never. And suddenly, you've lost it – your sharpness, your edge, your fitness. He never let that happen.

He swam in the sea whenever he could – cold or warm, didn't matter. The shock of the water reminded him he was alive. He rode bikes for hours, sometimes competitively, sometimes socially, but always with purpose. And he trained with discipline. Quietly. Consistently. Even in his seventies. Even when it hurt.

There's a story from Cape Town in 2024. Eddie signed up for

the 110km Cape Town Cycle Tour at 76 years old. He was in pain. He could have pulled out. Nobody would have questioned it. But that's not how Eddie moved. Helmet on. Jersey zipped. Ready to go. He didn't just ride, he *raced*. Finished second in his age category. And when one of his friends was ahead of him, all you could hear was Eddie's voice: "Faster, Peter! Faster!"

He trained like that because he lived like that. High tempo. Fully in. He knew the days you *don't* feel like moving are the ones you *have* to. He didn't wait for motivation – he created it by taking action. A quick gym session before a broadcast. A walk to shift the jet lag. A stretch in a hotel room before a meeting. Nothing complicated. Just consistent. Just focused. Just enough to keep the system lit.

Even at the Monaco Grand Prix, where others sat still and soaked it up, Eddie was moving. Sometimes 20 gigs in four days. Walking boat to boat. Playing drums. Climbing ladders. Laughing. Riding the beat. Tipping staff between sets. Sweating. Performing. Moving. Always moving.

Because here's the thing – Eddie understood that movement keeps you young. Not because it adds years to your life, but because it fills the years with momentum. And momentum is everything. It lifts you out of doubt. It clears the fog. It reminds you what you're made of.

He didn't need science to tell him that. He lived it. He felt it. And he built his life around it.

So when people asked Eddie, "How do you stay sharp?", he didn't give them a lecture. He gave them a shrug and said, "I'm always moving." And that was the secret.

As he got older, he used to say, "Don't let the old man in." It was a mantra. He lived it. It was about conditioning yourself to keep your thinking youthful and your body in shape. Once you start to think "I'm too old" or "I can't do that", it becomes a self-fulfilling prophecy.

During his illness, he became a strong advocate for regular check-ups and early testing. He firmly believed that health is the most valuable thing you have – without it, everything else becomes a struggle.

Stay young. Stay active. Don't let the old man in. FTB.

The Principle as Philosophy

Eddie Jordan believed movement was more than fitness.

It was a mindset.

He understood what most people forget: your body isn't just transportation – it's *ignition*. It's how you prime the system. How you unlock energy, sharpen thinking, restore confidence, shift your state. When the body moves, the fog clears. The noise fades. The mind *fires*.

He didn't move for vanity, he moved for *velocity*. For clarity. For presence. For edge.

Because the truth is, when you stop moving, you start dulling.

Not only your body – your decisions. Your sharpness. Your instincts. Your emotional capacity. Your voice.

That's why Eddie stayed fit – not for appearance, but for *performance*. So he could lead better, speak clearer, work smarter, live louder. So he could say yes to one more gig, one more trip, one more risk, one more story.

Movement wasn't about being ripped, it was about being *ready*.

And Eddie didn't wait to feel like moving. He moved *first*. And the feeling followed.

He built his discipline like a Formula 1 car – not to show off, but to go further, faster, smoother, sharper. That's the philosophy.

If you want a better mind, *start with the body*. If you want more energy, *move*. If you want to live sharper, *train like it matters*.

Because it *does*.

Practical Translation

You don't need a spinning class or a personal trainer. You just need to *move like your mind depends on it* – because it does.

Here's how to bring this principle to life:

1. Move every day – no matter what

It doesn't have to be long. And it doesn't have to be hard. Just get your body in motion – even if it's just a stretch, a walk, or a set of squats. Make it part of your day. No debate.

> **Ask yourself:** *What's my minimum movement today – and have I done it yet?*

2. Train for clarity, not just calories

Eddie didn't work out to burn, he worked out to *think*. Use movement to reset your brain, not punish your body.

> **Ask yourself:** *When I feel stuck, do I move or scroll?*

3. Move before motivation shows up

Don't wait to feel ready. Move *first*, and the rest will follow. Eddie didn't wait – he acted.

> **Ask yourself:** *Am I delaying because I'm tired – or because I've forgotten what movement gives me?*

4. Use movement to shift mood

Bad day? Go for a walk. Foggy mind? Go for a ride. Sluggish before a meeting? Stretch. Train to *feel* better – not just to look better.

> **Ask yourself:** *What movement will give me momentum right now?*

5. Build movement into the life you already live

Don't overthink it. Climb stairs. Dance. Carry the bags. Walk to the shop. Cycle to the coffee. Keep the engine running.

> **Ask yourself:** *Where's the next chance to move – and will I take it?*

Reflection

Eddie Jordan never gave health advice. He didn't talk about reps or routines. He didn't preach. He just moved.

He swam in cold seas. Rode hills. Did push-ups in tuxedos. Walked at dawn. Lifted weights in hotel gyms. Carried his own bags. Jumped on stage, pounded the drums, sweated through the beat. Motion was built into him – not for show, but because it made him feel alive.

That was the magic. Eddie didn't move to perform. He moved to connect – to himself, to the moment, to the world. And people noticed. They mirrored him. Because when you move with purpose, people feel it. They remember it. And more importantly, you remember who you are: sharp, strong, alive, capable.

Movement was how Eddie tuned his mind. It was how he cleared the fog, stayed in rhythm, stayed in the race. Not for applause. Not for aesthetics. But to stay ready. To live sharper. To show up with energy when it mattered.

And that's the lesson.

Move your body, especially when you don't feel like it.

Not to impress anyone. Not to prove anything.

But because you want to live fully.

Because you want to be ready.

Because you want to be here – really here – for everything that counts.

Eddie never sat still for long.

Not because he was restless.

Because he was ready.

And that's why the sharpness never left.

"Never let the old man in."
– Eddie Jordan

23. Don't Carry Baggage

The Eddie Story

If there's one principle that defined how Eddie Jordan navigated the world – in sport, in business, in friendship, and on the open road – it's this: don't carry what doesn't help you move faster.

That's not a slogan, that's how he lived.

For Eddie, the past was useful only as a reference point – never as a weight. He didn't believe in dragging regrets, grudges, or guilt behind him. Life was already fast and unpredictable. The last thing you needed was to race while hauling yesterday's baggage over your shoulder.

He was emotional, yes. Fierce, passionate, vocal – no one would ever accuse Eddie Jordan of being a calm sea. But his magic wasn't in avoiding conflict or discomfort. His gift was in *clearing the air and moving forward*. Quickly. Fully. Without residue.

People who worked with him learned this fast. If you made a mistake – on the car, in strategy, with a sponsor – he would *tell you*. Loudly. Colourfully. In stereo. His anger, when it came, wasn't subtle. It was immediate, physical, sometimes theatrical.

But once he got it out of his system, it was *over*. Truly over.

He didn't hold it against you. He didn't build a quiet case behind your back. He didn't sulk or stew, or send someone else to do his talking for him. He'd blast you, and then he'd be back five minutes later with a pint, a story, and a grin.

That was Eddie's rhythm. That was his emotional hygiene.

And it made him not just a better leader – it made him *light to be around*. Even when things were high-stakes. Even when the pressure was building. You could always feel that Eddie was present. Not holding onto things. Not secretly angry. Not quietly unravelling. He was *clean*. Current. All in.

You saw this in racing. You saw it in meetings. You saw it most vividly on a bike.

Out on the road, cycling with friends or pushing himself solo, Eddie rode like he lived – all in. But if a car cut too close, or a driver opened a door without looking, the reaction was immediate. A blast of fury, a wave of arms, a tirade of outrage echoing off the tarmac. He'd sometimes take both hands off the handlebars just to properly gesticulate.

You'd think he was about to follow the car home and knock on the driver's door. But seconds later, he'd pedal past you, laughing, cheeks flushed with adrenaline, and say:

"I love aggro."

He meant it. He wasn't pretending to enjoy conflict – he was celebrating the *aliveness of it*. The spark. The emotional honesty of it. And then, like a good storm, it was gone. Cleared. Forgotten.

What made it all so memorable was the *speed of the reset*. Most people hold onto their anger. It lingers, leaks, poisons the mood. Not Eddie. He let it pass *through* him, not *into* him. His outbursts were intense, but never personal. Once it was out, it didn't linger. It didn't rot.

In fact, the people who caught the sharpest end of his anger were often the same ones he called later that day to check in on – or the ones he brought along on his next big adventure.

His team understood this. That's why people stayed at Jordan Grand Prix longer than they had to. Why so many of them stayed loyal to him even after the team changed hands. Because they knew: Eddie didn't carry baggage. He didn't play power games. If he had a problem with you, he'd let you know. If he didn't, he wouldn't pretend he did.

That authenticity was a rare kind of leadership.

It also gave people around him permission to fail. To try again. To recover quickly. He wasn't a man who judged you on your last mistake. He was watching your next move. You could screw up, fix it, and move on without shame. That's rare in high-pressure environments. It's almost unheard of in Formula 1.

But Eddie cultivated it, because it's how *he* operated.

There were bigger tests of this principle too – defining moments when Eddie had every right to hold a grudge, to play the victim, to make enemies for life.

The most famous was, of course, the Michael Schumacher story at Spa in 1991. Eddie took a gamble on a young German driver who had never raced in Formula 1 before. Michael turned up, put in a dazzling qualifying lap, and stunned the sport. Everyone saw it: this kid was special. It was Eddie's talent-scouting at its finest.

And then, just as quickly, it was over. Schumacher's management team – backed by Benetton and some clever legal footwork – snatched him away before he could race again for Jordan. It was brutal. Eddie had discovered him, given him the shot, and was rewarded with a door slammed in his face.

And yes, he fought it. But he didn't let it define him. He didn't moan for years in the press or take subtle jabs in interviews. He *moved on*. Found other talent. Kept building.

In the long run, it *enhanced* his legacy – because it showed that Eddie didn't just have an eye for talent. He had a *backbone for recovery*.

You saw the same thing when the Jordan Formula 1 team – his life's work – was sold. When it was rebranded, reshaped, absorbed into the machinery of modern Formula 1. That would have broken many people. And maybe, for a few quiet weeks, it did. But then he re-emerged. With music. With business. With his trademark Irish twinkle.

Eddie didn't carry the sadness of losing his team into the next chapter. He used the freedom. He opened himself up to new roads, new stories, new people. He became a broadcaster, a drummer, a mentor. He kept showing up – curious, laughing, unpredictable, *alive.*

The same story played out in business. Eddie wasn't immune to betrayal, to being let down. But he never let the bruises become beliefs. He didn't start saying, "You can't trust anyone." He didn't shut down. He stayed open. Still bet on people. Still moved forward.

Even in his friendships, he forgave quickly. It was never about being right, it was about keeping life *moving.*

Because Eddie understood something at a deep, instinctive level – something that people in high-stakes environments often forget: you cannot perform if you're holding on. You cannot lead if you're dragging old hurt into the room. You cannot enjoy the present if you're weighed down by the past.

Eddie's life was full of friction – but empty of baggage. Full of storms – but never stuck in them.

That's why, if you spent time with him, you *felt better.* Not because he fixed everything, but because he didn't bring his old wounds to the table. He was *with you* – fully. Loud, yes. Demanding, yes. But *free.*

And that's rare. That's special. That's a legacy in itself.

Because it's one thing to win races.

It's another to be the kind of person who makes everyone around them lighter – just by choosing not to carry what they don't need.

The Principle as Philosophy

There's a reason Eddie Jordan could move so fast – not only on the track, but through life: he wasn't weighed down.

You make bad decisions when you are emotional. You lose objectivity and the consequences can be dire.

He didn't carry grudges like trophies. He didn't drag regret from one chapter to the next. And he never let a moment of conflict turn into a lifelong feud. His fire was fierce, but his forgiveness was *faster.*

For Eddie, letting go wasn't about forgetting. It was about *not being defined by what no longer served him.* The loss, the failure, the argument – they had their moment. He learned what he could. Then he let them go. He didn't repress emotion, and he didn't pretend not to care. He just understood when the moment had passed, and when it was time to move on.

That emotional agility is easy to admire but hard to practice. Most people carry too much. A remark that cut too deep. A betrayal that still burns. A version of themselves they can't seem to outgrow. Over time, it becomes instinct to carry it all – like protection. Like proof.

But in reality, it's just *drag.* You can't accelerate with the handbrake on. You can't grow if you're gripping what hurt you.

Eddie understood this. He felt things fully – often louder, faster, and more colourfully than most. But he let those emotions *move through* him, not *stay with* him. It's why he could rage at a driver in the morning and toast them at dinner. Why he could lose the biggest deal of his life and still laugh with you an hour later.

It wasn't that the moment didn't matter, it was that it didn't own the next one.

Letting go wasn't a tactic. It was *trust.* Trust that life would bring something new. That the future still had space for magic. That if you stayed light, you could move quicker – towards better.

This wasn't about being unbothered. Eddie wasn't cold. He cared deeply. That's why he needed to move – so the caring didn't curdle into bitterness.

And that's the core of the principle: Feel what you need to feel. Then release it. Cleanly. Deliberately. Without apology.

Because the cost of carrying baggage isn't just heaviness. It's missing what's happening right in front of you.

If you're holding onto the last corner, you miss the next one.

If you're focused on the last punch, you drop your guard for the one that's coming.

If you're stuck in a story about who wronged you, you stop writing new ones.

Eddie's life – wild, unfiltered, alive – was powered by momentum. And momentum only survives when you're brave enough to travel light.

Practical Translation

After the fire, Eddie always found his freedom. That wasn't just temperament, it was intentional. He knew how to return to joy after the storm, how to clear the emotional air so the next moment could breathe. His resets weren't by accident – they were *habit*. And if you want to lead, build, live, or love the way Eddie did, that habit can be yours too.

You don't need to become someone who never gets angry. You don't need to avoid conflict or pretend you're fine when you're not. That's not the point.

The point is to feel what you feel – and then not let it fester.

It's the festering that gets heavy. That turns friction into fracture. That turns one bad moment into a pattern you start calling your personality.

So, here's how to live lighter, the Eddie way:

1. Let the emotion move through, not in

When something stings – say it. Own it. Acknowledge it. Don't push it down, and don't wrap it in fake politeness. But once it's expressed, give yourself permission to *let it pass.*

Eddie could rage in full stereo and be smiling minutes later – not because he didn't mean it, but because he didn't *need* to hold it.

> **Ask yourself:** Am I letting this pass through me – or letting it build inside me?

2. Close the loop before you move on

Don't pretend everything's fine if it's not. Eddie was brilliant at clearing the air. Fast. Direct. No guessing games. That's why people trusted him – they knew where they stood.

If you've got an unresolved conversation, have it. If you owe someone an apology, give it. If you need to call something out, do so with courage. And then – move on.

> **Ask yourself:** *What's hanging open that I can finally close, cleanly?*

3. Don't turn a moment into an identity

A mistake is something that happened, it's not who you are.

Eddie lost deals, got stitched up, backed the wrong people. But he didn't turn that into bitterness. He didn't retreat into caution or resentment. He learned, recalibrated, and kept showing up.

> **Ask yourself:** *Is there something I'm still carrying because I've mistaken it for part of me?*

4. Name it, then dump it

Write it down. Speak it out loud. Let it go.

Sometimes the only thing keeping you stuck is that you haven't acknowledged what's still weighing you down. Eddie's freedom came from being *honest*. Not polite. Not guarded. Honest.

> **Ask yourself:** *What am I still mad about, embarrassed by, or afraid to name – and what would happen if I just said it?*

5. Learn the rhythm of reset

You don't need a dramatic ritual to reset. Eddie used movement. Music. Laughter. A change of scene. A story. A song. A burst of speed. The moment the emotion passed, he shifted his energy too.

You can do the same. Find your rhythm. When you feel the weight creeping back in – *change state*. Don't sit in the fog.

> **Ask yourself:** *What's one small thing I can do to shift this energy right now?*

6. Build the muscle of lightness

Letting go is not passive – it's a practice. It's noticing when you're rehashing the argument. Replaying the slight. Re-opening a wound. And gently, firmly, telling yourself: *We don't need this today.*

> **Ask yourself:** *What would it feel like if I carried 20 per cent less emotional weight this week?*

7. Hold people loosely, love them fully

Eddie didn't cling. He didn't try to control what people did with his loyalty. He gave it freely – and when people let him down, he moved on. Not with coldness, but with clarity.

Some people won't handle your trust well. Some will disappoint you. Some will surprise you again. But none of them are worth carrying around forever in your head.

> **Ask yourself:** *Am I letting someone else's mistake take up more space in my life than it deserves?*

8. Forgive fast – even if they don't deserve it

Forgiveness doesn't mean agreement, it means *liberation*. It means you get your energy back. Eddie didn't wait for perfect apologies. He let people go with grace – because he didn't want to carry the drama. He wanted to *ride free*.

> **Ask yourself:** *What am I still holding because I'm waiting to be proven right?*

Letting go isn't weakness. It's what allows you to be fully present.

And Eddie Jordan didn't just want to win. He wanted to be *alive*. Right here. In this moment. Clean. Sharp. Smiling.

You can too.

Reflection

Some people walk into a room and bring the last five arguments with them. The tension sits in their shoulders. The silence drags. The energy is heavy with what wasn't said – or what was said too many times.

Eddie Jordan wasn't one of those people.

He didn't carry it. Not the grudge, not the drama, not the echo of yesterday's conflict. He dealt with the moment in the moment – and once it was done, it was done. That gave him an edge, but not the sharp kind that cuts. The clear kind that moves.

That emotional clarity made him fast. Light. Free. His energy wasn't caught in old conversations, it was available. For the next deal. The next idea. The next laugh. And the people around him felt it too. His team didn't have to tiptoe. They knew the heat would pass. The relationship would hold.

That's more than a personality trait. It's a discipline. A rhythm. A principle.

Eddie didn't drag the past behind him. He let it rise like a wave – said what needed saying, sometimes in language only a Dublin lad could get away with – and then let it fall. Whole. Finished.

He didn't weaponize silence. He didn't keep people guessing. He didn't let resentment linger and call it toughness. He cleared the air. Breathed again. Smiled again. Moved.

And that, more than anything, was his secret. Not simply the fire, but the way he cleared the smoke.

He knew that anger has its place – but not a permanent one. That mistakes are lessons, not identities. That forgiveness is not weakness, but wisdom. He let go – not because he didn't care, but because he cared about what came next even more.

The next race.

The next riff.

The next glass of wine in the sun.

The next smile that hadn't happened yet.

He didn't waste time looking back.

He had too much road ahead.

So, if something's slowing you down, something you can't stop thinking about, ask the question Eddie always answered without words:

Do I need this for where I'm going?

If the answer is no, drop it.
Say what needs to be said.
Then smile.
Then move on.
There's life up ahead.
Ride light.

> *"I confronted the moment head-on.*
> *Then I let it go. What matters is what you do next."*
> — **Eddie Jordan**

Final Lap –
The Eddie Code Wrapped Up

24. Keep Attacking

The Eddie Story

Eddie Jordan believed that commitment wasn't just about starting well – it was about finishing. And finishing strong. You could have the best start in the world, but if you faded in the final lap, it was wasted energy.

He said it often and clearly: "Races are won on the last lap. You've got to be in contention when it counts."

That wasn't just about Formula 1. That was life. It was business. It was leadership. A good start means nothing if you're not there when it matters most. Eddie knew that endurance mattered more than excitement – because the race isn't won on the grid, it's won in the grit.

In business, he was just as relentless: "If the money's not in the bank, the deal's not done."

It didn't matter how good the meeting felt or how confident the other party seemed. Until the contract was signed and the money cleared, nothing counted. Eddie had seen too many people declare victory too early. And that was a mistake he refused to make.

"Don't tell me we've won any deal until it's real."

"You can't bank promises."

That mindset saved Jordan Grand Prix more than once.

One of the most dramatic moments came when the UK Commercial Court issued a winding-up order. The team had just 24 hours to come up with £1 million to meet its creditors. Eddie had no money. No resources. No backers left to call. It looked like the end.

And then – out of nowhere – his childhood friend Mick Tunney arrived at the factory with a cheque for the full amount. "I had no idea where he got it," Eddie said. "I didn't sign anything. We stayed alive. And I repaid him a few weeks later."

That wasn't just financial survival, that was belief. That was friendship at full throttle. That was never giving up.

It wasn't the only time the walls closed in. During other tough moments, Eddie learned the court officers often delivered legal notices late on Friday afternoons. So, he made himself unavailable. Disappeared. Everyone at the factory knew: *Don't. Open. The. Door. TO ANYONE.*

There was hustle. There was mischief. But there was also deep responsibility. Eddie carried pressure so others didn't have to. He showed up with fire and confidence, but underneath it all, he felt the weight. He worried. He scrambled. He carried more than most people ever saw.

And it's important to say this, too: Eddie wasn't perfect. He made mistakes. He got it wrong. He trusted the wrong people. Overcommitted. Overpromised. He could be a pain in the ass – stubborn, unpredictable, impossible to pin down.

But he got away with nearly all of it – because deep down,

people knew he had a big heart. He didn't just fight for himself, he fought for you. In researching this book, so many people said the same thing: *If I was in a real crisis, Eddie would be one of the first five people I'd call.* He might kick your ass afterwards, but first, he'd show up. Fully. No questions asked. And his friends knew it.

He was told he'd never make it to the Formula 1 grid. He did. He lost Michael Schumacher after one race. He bounced back. He faced legal action, financial ruin, press heat, walkouts, and exits. And he kept going.

Because Eddie didn't flinch. He adapted. He attacked. He stayed in the ring – when others faded, when the road turned ugly, when the odds said stop.

That's the power of this principle. "Never give up" wasn't a slogan for Eddie. It was a strategy. It was how underdogs win. How things get finished. How people go from nearly to actually.

He didn't wait for perfect plans, he moved with what he had – courage, energy, grit, mischief. That mindset made people believe. It made teams go further. It made fans fall in love with Jordan Grand Prix – not because they always won, but because they never stopped trying.

That relentlessness didn't just change results. It changed people.

Because when you watch someone keep showing up, no matter the punches – they don't just inspire you, they challenge you. To dig deeper. To rise again. To keep going.

Eddie didn't coast. He didn't promise smooth roads. He promised it would be worth it. He promised presence. He stayed in – fully, fiercely, unflinchingly. And when everything looked lost, he was still there. Sleeves rolled up. Heart in it. Asking the only question that mattered:

"What's the move?"

That's what *Keep Attacking* means. Not blind hope. Not false drama. But belief, in motion.

So whatever you're facing, don't procrastinate at the start, don't stall when things get tricky, and don't wait for the perfect moment that never comes. Do it. Now.

> *"Attack. Stay. Finish. Believe. Keep attacking.*
> *FTB. Never give up. Keep attacking."*
> **– Eddie Jordan**

The Principle as Philosophy

Every other principle in this book rests on this one.

Thinking big, committing fully, trusting people, staying humble – none of it matters if you give up when it gets hard. None of it works if you stop showing up. None of it delivers if you check out before the job is done.

That's why Eddie Jordan never coasted. Never cruised. Never assumed anything was finished until it truly was.

He believed that the winners weren't just the fastest – they were the most relentless. The ones who stayed in the fight when others folded. The ones who took the hits and kept their head in the game.

"You don't need to win every lap," he said. "You just need to be in it when it counts."

It was a mindset built on grit, timing, and instinct. But more than that, it was built on *presence*. The kind of full-throttle awareness that says: *I'm still here. I'm still coming. I'm not done yet.*

This wasn't about blind optimism. It wasn't about naivety.

Eddie knew the numbers. He knew the risks. He knew how bad things could get. He just chose to stay in the game anyway.

He believed in movement. In staying active. In staying alert. In keeping your hands on the wheel, even when the engine was stalling.

Because when you quit, you're out. But when you stay in, even barely – you still have a shot.

This principle was Eddie's compass. The thing he came back to when everything else was falling apart. The through-line in every crazy comeback, every late-night negotiation, every last-lap overtake.

Stay in the game. Don't give up. Keep attacking.

Practical Translation

This principle isn't just about survival – it's about strategy. It's about how you keep your energy up, your head clear, and your grip tight when most people would already have let go.

Here's how to embed Eddie Jordan's never-give-up mindset into your world – whether you're running a team, leading a business, chasing a goal, or climbing a personal hill.

1. Don't ease up just because things look good

Too many people back off when the signs turn positive. Eddie didn't. He kept the pressure on until the contract was signed, the cheque cleared, the tyres were rolling.

"Looks good" is not the same as done. Stay sharp until it's real.

Ask yourself: *Am I coasting before the finish line?*

2. Finish what you start – like the result depends on it

Because it does. Anyone can start something. Eddie believed what mattered was how you *finish*. That's where trust is earned. That's where results happen. That's where your edge lives.

> **Ask yourself:** *Where have I let something drift that I need to complete?*

3. When you're out of options, find another angle

Ask. Call. Show up. Look ridiculous if you have to. Eddie once saved his team because an old friend believed in him. The door is never as closed as it looks.
FIND. A. WAY.

> **Ask yourself:** *What haven't I tried yet?*

4. Never confuse silence with surrender

Just because Eddie didn't shout about his problems didn't mean he wasn't fighting. He carried burdens quietly and sought counsel from the right people. You don't have to suffer out loud to stay in the game – you just have to keep moving.

> **Ask yourself:** *Am I mistaking quiet for weakness – in myself or others?*

5. Treat pressure as proof that you're close

If it's heavy, it's probably important. Eddie didn't run from pressure – he ran into it. He carried responsibility for his people and his purpose.

> **Ask yourself:** *What am I avoiding that I should be embracing?*

6. Stay in the room when others leave

In deals, in debates, in dreams. Most people check out when it gets awkward or uncertain. Eddie stayed. Even when the odds were ridiculous. Especially then.

> **Ask yourself:** *Where do I tend to exit early – and why?*

7. Seek counsel, not comfort

Eddie wasn't afraid to admit what he didn't know. He asked questions. He sought clarity – not sympathy. He didn't want to be rescued. He wanted direction.

> **Ask yourself:** *Am I looking for advice, or just reassurance?*

8. Remember the rule: B-E-L-I-E-V-E

Say it. Spell it. Mean it. If you don't believe you can pull it off, no one else will. Eddie lived and breathed that word. Even when it was hard. Especially then.

> **Ask yourself:** *Do I really believe I can do this – and if not, why not?*

9. Keep attacking, even if it's messy

Don't wait to feel 100 per cent. Don't wait for a perfect moment. Don't back off just because you've hit resistance. Push. Nudge. Pivot. Hustle.

If you're still breathing, you're still in it.

> **Ask yourself:** *What small move can I make right now to keep going?*

10. Show others what staying looks like

When you don't quit, you give the people around you permission to stay strong too. And that might change everything – for them, and for you.

> **Ask yourself:** *Who's watching me right now – and what example am I setting?*

Reflection

Eddie Jordan's life wasn't smooth. It was jagged, fast, unpredictable. His career – across racing, business, media, and music – was marked by soaring highs and crushing setbacks. But the one thing that never changed? He refused to quit.

He was told he'd never make it to the Formula 1 grid. But he did.

He lost Michael Schumacher after one race. He bounced back.

He faced financial ruin, legal battles, sponsorship exits. He kept going.

Because Eddie didn't flinch. He adapted. He attacked. He stayed in the ring – when others faded, when the road turned ugly, when the odds said stop.

That's the power of this principle. "Never give up" wasn't a slogan for Eddie. It was a strategy. It was resilience in action. It's how underdogs win. It's how things get finished. It's how you earn the right to say, "I gave everything."

Eddie didn't wait for perfect plans. He moved with what he had – courage, energy, grit, mischief. That mindset made people believe. It made teams go further. It made fans fall in love with Jordan Grand Prix – not because they always won, but because they never stopped trying.

That relentlessness didn't just change results, it changed people.

Because when you watch someone keep showing up, no matter the punches, they don't just inspire you.

They challenge you.

To dig deeper.

To rise again.

To keep going.

Eddie didn't coast. He didn't promise smooth roads. He promised presence. He stayed in – fully, fiercely, unflinchingly. And if the wheels came off? He was still there. Sleeves rolled. Eyes locked. Asking the only question that mattered:

"What's the move?"

Because that's what this principle really means: Not drama. Not defiance. Not blind hope.

But belief in motion. Belief that rises again.

Belief that carries the pressure, the doubt, and the dream – all at once.

So whatever you're facing, don't fantasize the start. Don't coast on early progress. Don't wait for the perfect moment.

Attack. Stay. Finish. Believe.

Because the win may not come when you want it. But it will come – if you keep chasing it like Eddie did. Winners don't quit . . . and quitters don't win.

25. Think Outside the Box

The Eddie Story

Eddie Jordan built his whole life by refusing to follow the standard path. For him, "thinking outside the box" wasn't a nice-to-have – it was how he operated. Not occasionally. Not when stuck. But all the time.

He didn't wait for permission. He didn't ask what was normal. He just looked at the challenge, tilted his head slightly, and found a new way through.

Like the day he strolled into the clubhouse at Wentworth Golf Club wearing his golf shoes. "Sir, you can't come in here wearing golf shoes," came the voice at the door. It wasn't aggressive, just a rule. But rules didn't rattle Eddie. He smiled, bent down, and calmly took off his shoes – then walked through the clubhouse in his socks, nodding at people as though nothing was out of place. The woman who stopped him was Amanda Newey, wife of legendary Formula 1 designer Adrian Newey. And instead of it becoming a stand-off, it sparked a friendship. Amanda and Eddie stayed close for years after. That was the thing with Eddie – even when the rules said no, he made people smile, and he moved forward anyway.

This was his pattern. If someone said, "That's not allowed," Eddie's brain lit up. If someone said, "That's impossible," he became more interested, not less.

In 1994, a major oil company came calling with sponsorship money. The problem? Eddie already had a title sponsor on the side of the car. Most teams would have walked away from one of them, but not Eddie. He stuck one sponsor on the left side of the car, the other on the right. Then he went further – placing each sponsor's hospitality suite on opposite sides of the track, so whichever direction the car passed, each brand saw their own logo in full view. It was cheeky. It was smart. It was totally Eddie.

Same with DHL. They wanted the car to be white. Eddie said no: "If you want in, the car stays yellow." But he didn't stop there. He pitched something even bolder: "Don't change the car – change your brand." And DHL did. They changed their global branding to yellow. Not only did Eddie keep the sponsorship, he licensed the colour "Jordan Yellow" and got paid for years after.

It was the same playbook with Puma. They weren't even in Formula 1 at the time, but Eddie convinced them to sponsor Jordan and co-brand the race kit – even though Puma didn't make FIA-compliant gear. His workaround? Partner quietly with Sparco behind the scenes to meet safety standards, while Puma took the spotlight. Puma broke into Formula 1. Sparco delivered the performance. Eddie got both. That wasn't luck, that was a new route no one else had spotted.

And then there was the Jordan 191 – the debut car. Eddie wanted it green. Not just because it looked good, but because he was already thinking three steps ahead. He went after sponsors who used green in their branding – like 7UP and Fujifilm – *before* they were ever signed. He didn't just build a car and then pitch it, he built the car *for the pitch*. He designed the livery to match the cheque. Most people chase sponsorship, Eddie created a magnet for it.

This wasn't rebellion for its own sake. It was belief. A deep, unshakeable confidence that with the right attitude and enough imagination, there's always a way through.

He didn't just hear "no" and stop. He heard "no" and started looking. If someone said something was impossible, it only made him more determined. That energy – that hunger to solve things differently – came from a lifetime of backing himself. Not with ego, but with creativity.

And no, not every idea worked. But Eddie understood the maths of momentum. If you think differently, challenge the obvious, and keep going past the first hurdle, you'll find a solution five times out of ten. But if you stop at the first "no", you'll find a solution *zero* times out of ten.

That's why this principle lives last in The Jordan Code – because in many ways, it lives inside all the others. The code doesn't work without it. At first, it takes practice. But for Eddie, it became a way of life. A way of leading. A way of being.

Because the best way to break the rules . . . is to make better ones.

The Principle as Philosophy

Thinking outside the box wasn't one of Eddie's tools – it was the fuel that powered them all. It's the reason this is the final principle: not because it came last in his approach, but because it *ran through everything*. It was the thread that held the whole Jordan Code together.

Every single principle – from Think Big to Pull the Same Way, from Back Yourself to Steal the Deal, Keep Your Honour – is shaped by this deeper mindset: *don't accept the obvious, don't accept the rules, don't accept "no" at face value.* If something wasn't working, Eddie didn't wait for someone to fix it. He flipped the angle and found another way in.

He didn't believe in the status quo. He didn't respect "how it's always been done". He challenged it. Every time.

Eddie trained himself to look at things sideways – not with cynicism, but with curiosity. What if we tried it backwards? What if we brought in a partner nobody expects? What if we did the opposite of what we're told? That's not rebellion – that's *problem-solving with rhythm*.

It wasn't about showing off, it was about outcomes. For Eddie, the goal was always clear – and if the normal route didn't get you there, you tried another one. You tried five. You tried ten. Because here's the truth: you won't find a solution every time. But if you try, you'll find a new answer five times out of ten. And that's enough to change everything. But if you stop at the first hurdle, if you accept "no" or "not allowed" or "too hard", then you find a solution zero times out of ten. Guaranteed.

This mindset came from belief – belief that if you stayed with a challenge long enough, your brain *would* come up with something. It wasn't talent, it was repetition. A habit. A refusal to walk away when the door was shut. Eddie just looked for a window. Or a side gate. Or a wall he could climb.

That's what made him different. Not just how he moved – but how he thought. Constantly asking:

– What's the outcome we need?

– What's standing in the way?

– What if we rewired the whole thing?

"Think Outside the Box" isn't a principle for emergencies, it's a principle for every day. It's how Eddie approached meetings, setbacks, deals, designs, gigs, and friendships. It's how he lived – full of angles, options, and cheeky shortcuts that somehow worked.

So if you remember nothing else, remember this: *Most people stop at the obvious. Eddie never did. He kept going. And that's why he got further.*

Practical Translation

Thinking outside the box isn't about being quirky or creative for the sake of it. It's about refusing to stop when the standard answers fall short. It's about training your brain to look again – not just once, but every time.

You don't have to be in Formula 1 to think like Eddie. You don't need sponsors or pit lanes or live TV. You just need a mindset that says: *there's always another angle.*

Here's how to build that muscle – and use it every day:

25 Principles to Live and Lead

1. Focus on the outcome, not the method

Don't get stuck on how things are *usually* done. Start with what needs to be achieved – then ask, "What's every possible way to get there?" You'll be surprised what appears once you stop limiting yourself to what's familiar.

> **Ask yourself:** *Am I fixated on how it's done, or on what I'm trying to achieve?*

2. When you hear "no", treat it as a signal to look harder

Eddie heard "no" as "not yet" or "try another route". Every "no" became energy. If someone shuts a door, knock again. Or try the window. Or build your own door.

> **Ask yourself:** *What other way could I try if this door is closed?*

3. List at least five ways to solve the problem – including the mad ones

Train yourself to go beyond the first idea. Even if the fourth or fifth sounds absurd, it might unlock something the safe option never will.

> **Ask yourself:** *Have I explored beyond the obvious ideas?*

4. Challenge every assumption — especially your own

Ask: "Why are we doing it this way?" "Who says that's not allowed?" "Is that a rule, or just a habit?" Most systems run on auto-pilot. Eddie didn't.

> **Ask yourself:** *What belief or assumption here needs challenging?*

5. Reframe the problem entirely

Instead of "How do I solve this?" ask, "What if the problem itself is the wrong one?" Eddie didn't tweak. He flipped the question.

> **Ask yourself:** *Am I solving the right problem — or just the one in front of me?*

6. Use friction as fuel

If you're getting resistance, that's a sign you're close to something worth doing. Most breakthroughs come just past the point others gave up.

> **Ask yourself:** *What's the resistance telling me — and how can I use it?*

7. Make it a daily habit, not a last resort

Don't wait until you're stuck. Ask different questions in every meeting. Flip the process every week. Try weird ideas every morning. Eddie didn't think sideways only when he had to – he did it because he *could*.

> **Ask yourself:** *When did I last try something different – just to see what might happen?*

8. Take full responsibility for finding a way

This is the part most people skip. They wait for someone else to fix it, or blame the process, or give up too soon. Eddie didn't. He owned the challenge. If something wasn't working, he didn't moan – he moved. *If you want a better answer, take responsibility for finding one.*

> **Ask yourself:** *Am I waiting for someone else – or am I owning the outcome?*

9. Ask yourself this – what would Eddie do here?

And answer it honestly. Then smile, trust your gut . . . and do that.

> **Ask yourself:** *Am I being bold enough – or is there a wilder, wiser move I'm avoiding?*

Reflection

Eddie Jordan never waited for the perfect answer – he moved towards a better one. That mindset made him dangerous. Not because he broke the rules recklessly, but because he never believed the rules were the whole story.

He didn't sit in meetings saying, "That's not how it's done." He walked in and said, "What if we tried it another way?" He didn't coast through life waiting for someone to solve it. He took responsibility, turned the problem over in his hands, and kept going until a new path showed itself.

He trained his brain to look again. To push one step further than most people dared. And that's why he built what others couldn't.

Thinking outside the box isn't about being clever, it's about being *committed*. Committed to finding a way. Committed to not giving up at the first sign of resistance. Committed to believing that something better is possible – even if you're the only one who sees it yet.

Most people give up too early. Eddie didn't. He kept looking. He kept pushing. And five times out of ten, he found a better way. That was enough to change the game. Over and over again.

That's why this principle comes last – because in many ways, it lives *inside* every other one.

Eddie thought differently. That's what made him *move* differently.

So don't wait.

Don't shrink.

Don't ask what's allowed.

Don't be put off by resistance or barriers.

Ask: *What's possible?*

And when you feel stuck or the world says no – smile.

Then take your shoes off, walk in anyway . . .

. . . and think like Eddie.

The Full Throttle Code –
25 Principles to Live and Lead with

Eddie Jordan didn't follow rules, he made his own. These 25 principles aren't theories. They're lived truths – tested in garages, gigs, boardrooms, boats, on bikes, and in bars.

They're how he led teams, made deals, backed people, built loyalty, and kept his edge.

They're practical. They're personal. And they still hold.

Every one of them was earned the hard way – through wins, wild turns, and more than a few mistakes. They cost time, energy, and plenty of money to figure out. This book exists so you don't have to pay the same price. Use them in your career. In your business. In your life.

Read them. Live them. Pass them on. Make them louder. And whatever you do – bring your full self to the grid.

Don't try and be Eddie. Just try to be the best version of you. That's where all the magic happens.

FTB.

What Eddie Learned
from Bernie Ecclestone

If Eddie Jordan was the soul of Formula 1 – vibrant, loud, impulsive, full of heart – then Bernie Ecclestone was the mind: calculating, quiet, always two or three moves ahead.

Eddie didn't just respect Bernie, he studied him – not in classrooms or mentorship programmes, but in hotel bars, pit lanes, boardrooms, and off-the-record dinners where real deals happened. Bernie never taught. But if you watched closely, you walked away with a black belt in power, timing, and control.

> *"Watching Bernie was the best MBA*
> *I never paid for."*
> – Eddie Jordan

For those who didn't grow up in the paddock, here's the short version: Bernie Ecclestone turned Formula 1 from a travelling circus into a global commercial empire.

He started as a driver, became a team owner, and then rewired the sport. He controlled TV rights, set the calendar, brokered the sponsorships – and made it all pay. Quietly. Precisely. With total control.

He negotiated with governments, billionaires, broadcasters, and race promoters – and almost always walked away with the better deal. Five foot nothing, and yet he owned every room. While others made noise, Bernie made moves.

If Formula 1 was chess, Bernie was the only one who knew where all the pieces really were.

When he sold Formula 1 to Liberty Media in 2016 for $8 billion, it ended a four-decade reign. He walked away with an estimated $1 billion – and didn't flinch once.

But this chapter – and this book – isn't only about what Eddie did. It's about how he learned. From pain, from mistakes, and from people. Especially people like Bernie.

Eddie watched. He listened. He learned from Bernie, Niki Lauda, Damon Hill, Jean Alesi, and his mother Eileen and others.

Then he passed those lessons on – usually in the most chaotic and unforgettable way possible.

This book reflects those principles – some learned the hard way, some borrowed, all lived. You don't need to follow them all. Some will stick. Some will challenge you. A few might not be for you.

That's the point.

We learn to make fewer mistakes. To fail forward, not fall flat.

So take what works. Pass it on. And remember: the best teachers don't give answers. They live them – just like Bernie did.

1. Control the Game

Bernie didn't play the game – he built the board and handed out the dice. From media rights to team deals, he structured the system around himself.

Eddie learned: If you want lasting power, don't just play. Control the pitch.

"Bernie showed me that being a player isn't enough. You've got to own the pitch, the ball, and the bloody referee. That's how you survive."

2. Know More Than You Say

Bernie spoke quietly and rarely – which made people listen more. He never rushed to fill the silence, he let it work for him.

Eddie learned: Mystery is power. Let others guess what you're thinking.

"Bernie never filled the silence. He used it. That's when you knew he was thinking five steps ahead."

3. Stay in the Room

Bernie was always there – not loud, not centre stage, but present. He made sure no major decision happened without him in the room.

Eddie learned: Proximity is power. Be where it happens.

"Bernie didn't chase influence. He positioned himself so nothing happened without him. I learned: presence is power."

4. Loyalty Over Ladders

Bernie kept the same people around for years – they earned his trust. He didn't care about titles, he cared about character.

Eddie learned: Build your team on loyalty, not CVs.

"If Bernie trusted you, that was worth more than any promotion. I built my team the same way – loyalty first, ego second."

5. Simplicity Wins

While others wrapped things in data and jargon, Bernie stripped them down. He made huge deals feel like pub conversations.

Eddie learned: Clarity cuts through. Say less, mean more.

"I once saw Bernie reduce a four-hour meeting into one sentence. It wasn't magic – it was clarity."

6. Be Indispensable

Bernie made himself so central that no one could imagine Formula 1 without him. He didn't just hold power, he became necessary.

Eddie learned: Make yourself the one thing they can't replace.

"Bernie didn't chase relevance – he built it. If you make yourself indispensable, they can't sideline you."

7. Negotiate from Strength

Bernie didn't blink first. He set the tempo and controlled the terms. He never needed a deal more than the other side.

Eddie learned: Know your value. Be willing to walk.

"Bernie made you sweat – because he never looked like he needed the deal. That's how you hold your ground."

8. Respect, Then Ruthlessness

Bernie could be warm – but he was never soft. If someone couldn't deliver, he moved on.

Eddie learned: Be fair, but don't flinch.

"Bernie had a soft side, but he wouldn't let it cost the business. I learned to separate kindness from compromise."

9. Know the Whole Business

Bernie understood everything   from tax structures to tyre pressures. You couldn't bluff him.

Eddie learned: Don't just lead – understand.

"Bernie didn't just know the business – he *was* the business. That's why no one could bluff him."

10. Master the Media

Bernie made Formula 1 global because he understood drama, characters, story. He didn't hide from the cameras, he directed the show.

Eddie learned: Make your brand bigger than your title.

"Bernie turned drivers into stars and deals into drama. He made Formula 1 sexy – and I loved that."

11. Pick Up the Phone

Bernie didn't hide behind email. He called. He understood that tone, trust, and timing lived in voice – not text.

Eddie learned: If it matters, speak it.

"Bernie didn't do long emails. If it mattered, he rang you. He knew tone mattered more than clever typing."

12. Business is Human

Behind the strategy, Bernie understood people – their pride, fear, and patterns. That's why he always won.

Eddie learned: You're not managing systems, you're managing people.

"Bernie knew everyone's weakness – and their birthday. That's power: knowing the numbers and the people."

Final Reflection: The Greatest Teacher Never Tried to Teach

Eddie never got a formal lesson from Bernie. He didn't need one. Bernie taught by doing – and if you were paying attention, you learned everything.

"Bernie never sat me down and said 'here's how to do it.' He just lived it. And if you had your eyes open, you'd walk away smarter."

PART III

Side Roads and Legacy

7

Business, Boats, and Bids

The Oyster Story – Open Waters, Open Heart

Eddie Jordan didn't come to sailing late, he came to it fully. For all the speed and pressure of racing, sailing gave him something different – freedom. Stillness. Time to think, move, laugh, and live at the rhythm of the wind. It wasn't about slowing down, it was about shifting gears.

He'd always loved the sea – the openness, the vastness, the sense that anything was possible. But in 2013, that love became something more. That's when he joined the inaugural Oyster World Rally, a 27-month, 33,000-nautical-mile circumnavigation of the globe. His yacht? *Lush*, a bespoke Oyster 885, built for distance, comfort, and performance.

Lush wasn't just a boat. It was a stage, a sanctuary, a story. Eddie brought the full EJ experience with him: spoons, drums, mayhem, and soul. He didn't just sail her, he animated her. *Lush* became Jordan Grand Prix on water – a travelling theatre of mischief and momentum, powered by instinct, humour, and a very real sense of purpose.

The trip forged bonds. Tested character. Created memories and chaos in equal measure. But more than that, it revealed how Eddie led – whether in boardrooms or pit lanes – or across oceans. He pushed people to be better. Expected them to step up. And celebrated the moments when they did.

That belief in people was exactly why, years later, when Oyster Yachts fell into administration, Eddie didn't walk away. Instead, he stepped in. He got the call from Richard Hadida, a self-made British tech entrepreneur and fellow Oyster owner – someone Eddie had known, trusted, and respected for years.

Richard wanted to buy the business. Revive the legacy. Save the workforce. Eddie didn't hesitate. He joined the mission. Became a director and brand ambassador. A force in the rebuild.

Because Eddie didn't invest in balance sheets. He invested in belief – in teams, in momentum, in bold bets backed by real vision. Together, he and Richard rebuilt Oyster from the keel up – modernizing the factory, redesigning the fleet, and reigniting the culture.

Eddie didn't just lend his name, he lent his energy. He toured the yards, met apprentices, listened to engineers, sat in design meetings. He wasn't a figurehead. He was a teammate – someone who knew what it meant to build something great, and fight like hell to keep it alive.

He became Oyster's most visible ambassador. He hosted guests on *Lush*, played drums at events, shared stories of the World Rally, and proudly backed the brand with action, not ego. Behind the charm was insight. Behind the rhythm was substance. He knew this world. He understood what high-end buyers wanted – and how to lead a team through storms, literal and otherwise.

In 2023, Eddie stepped down as a director. The brand was back. The team was strong. His work was done. But his legacy remains written into the wood, the culture, the spirit of the place.

Because *Lush* wasn't just a yacht. It was a floating expression of Eddie's philosophy: go all in, back brilliant people, and never let the wind decide where you stop.

The Playtech Bid – Betting on the Impossible

Eddie Jordan always believed that "impossible" just means nobody's tried hard enough. So when the chance came to buy Playtech – one of the world's most influential gambling tech firms – he didn't flinch. He leaned in.

It started, like most bold ventures do, with a conversation.

I'd spent years inside the gambling industry. Built platforms. Led teams. I knew Playtech was a sleeping giant: rock-solid infrastructure, but it was stuck – and had incredible potential. It didn't just need money – it needed belief. Energy. Urgency.

I brought the idea to Eddie. We were aligned immediately – two people built on instinct, speed, and the ability to rattle a boardroom. I was ready. Eddie was interested: "I've been an investor in gambling businesses for years. Let's go."

We phoned his financial team.

Their response: "Lads, ye are bonkers if you think you can raise the support and £3 billion needed to buy the company."

Eddie's face changed. His jaw tightened. Through gritted teeth he said, "Nobody tells me I can't do something. We're doing it. I'll find a way. Come on."

That was it. We were off.

"Eddie, we need a name."

"Let's use JKO – J for Jordan and KO for you. Next question."

So we set up JKO Play Ltd. as the bidding vehicle and built a heavyweight team. It became a full-blown operation. At one stage, 40 of us were flat-out, working across time zones. We called it *Project Cape*. It was chaos – in the best sense.

One night I was pacing around Eddie's apartment, hammering out a deal to pre-sell a division of Playtech. The numbers were flying: £1.3 billion, then £1.4 billion. Eddie listened. Calm. Focused. Afterwards, we sat back and I said, "We just argued about £100 million like it was £1,000." It felt surreal. Paper money. That's how big this was.

We weren't alone. Aristocrat Leisure had already tabled a £2.7 billion bid. Gopher Investments was circling too. But we had something different: momentum. Eddie's grit and charm opened doors money couldn't. He knew the players. He could read a room. And he ran on belief when others played it safe.

At our first meeting with Playtech's board, Brian Mattingley – the chairman – paused and looked at Eddie: "You may not remember me, but when you moved to Oxford, you used to drink with us at The White Horse on Friday nights. You had us in stitches. Our wives even played basketball together."

Eddie grinned. "I remember. I didn't have a pot to piss in back then – probably made you pay for the drinks too."

Fifty years later: one man chairing a £3 billion company, the other trying to buy it. A full-circle moment. Pure Eddie.

By early 2022, we were five days from the formal bid. The team was ready. Financing, legal, vision – all lined up. It was David versus Goliath. But then came the twist.

A shareholder group holding 30 per cent announced they'd block any deal. They didn't care about the upside, they wanted things to stay exactly as they were.

Momentum stalled. The structure stopped working. We couldn't go public. We had to step back. Not because we didn't believe – but because the politics just wouldn't shift.

It stung. We'd come so close. Five days from the shot that could have rewritten the gaming industry's playbook.

But Eddie didn't sulk. He just looked at me and said, "Move on. Things happen for the best. We'll get the next one. We've learned a lot, had some real fun – and we'll 100 per cent get our investment back in other ways."

Because for Eddie – and for me – the win isn't always the outcome. It's the swing. It's having the guts to go all in when everyone else is hedging. That's what made him who he was.

The Playtech bid didn't land, but it proved, yet again, what Eddie Jordan always knew:

When someone says, "You can't," that's the time to back yourself and go all in. And when you go all in, you don't lose. You just reload for the next one.

The London Irish Story – We Had to Try

Drink may have been consumed when EJ, Nigel Northridge, Mike Farnan, and I met in a Paris bar during the 2023 Rugby World Cup. By the end of the night, we'd made a pact – to try and bring London Irish back. At the very least, to give this hallowed name a shot at returning to the pitch.

It was a Jordan Grand Prix reunion of sorts. EJ. Nigel – once the boss of Benson & Hedges and one of Eddie's earliest backers. Mike – who ran global marketing for Jordan before reshaping Manchester United's international fan base. And me – someone who had stood beside Eddie across multiple ventures, wins, and wild swings.

Nigel and Mike had been close to London Irish for years. The club had gone into administration just months earlier. Suspended from the Premiership. Staff and players dismissed overnight. Like Wasps and Worcester, it had become another victim of professional rugby's broken business model – a slow collapse accelerated by Covid.

There are moves you make because they're strategic – and moves you make because they matter. For Eddie, this was mostly the latter. But he also knew how to play the angles. He'd had past wins pulling brands out of the fire.

London Irish wasn't just a rugby club, it was a flag. Founded in 1898 by Irish grads in London, with a £10 grant from the IRFU, it stood for identity, belonging, and defiant pride. For Irish families in Britain, it was a parish without walls. A club that nurtured talent, welcomed all comers, and earned the nickname "The Exiles". It was everyone's second team. And it mattered.

Yes, it was messy. The administrators wanted £20 million for the assets. There was no guarantee what league the team would play in. Most investors would walk.

But not Eddie.

He didn't see a dead end, he saw a blank canvas. A brand

with no baggage. A story worth saving. And maybe, a little bit of himself in it too – the Irishman who moved to London, made something out of nothing, and never stopped believing in where he came from.

He picked up the phone. First to his son, Kyle. Then to Daniel McKeown – a long-time friend and co-investor from the Playtech deal. Someone he trusted. Someone who got things done. "Even when you lose a deal," Eddie had always said, "you get it back in the next one." London Irish was the next one.

They started building. What would it take to bring this club back – to play – yes – but to matter again?

This wasn't nostalgia. It was a reset. A chance to rebuild professional rugby in a smarter way. Eddie knew the old model was broken. But with the right people, structure, and belief, it could work. And London Irish could lead the way.

He also saw the potential most missed. The Exiles had a dormant global fanbase of 200,000. Over a million Londoners claim Irish descent. More than 80 million people worldwide do. London Irish had always been a symbol, now it could be a movement.

Eddie spoke to former players, supporters, and staff. What he found wasn't bitterness – it was loyalty. People were waiting. Waiting for someone to care. To fight. To believe. The response was the same across his rugby network: "If you're in, we're in."

So he was.

Because to Eddie, sport wasn't about trophies. It was about rhythm. Community. Identity. A reason to show up. And when a club like London Irish falls, it's not just the players who lose – it's every kid who wore the shirt, every family that stood in the stands, every grandparent who passed the stories on.

And when something like that is at risk, you don't wait. You act.

That's what Eddie did. With Jordan Grand Prix. With Oyster Yachts. And now, with London Irish. Not for the headlines. Not for the money. But because some things are worth trying for – especially when the world says it's too late.

Fifteen months of back-and-forth led to a breakthrough in February 2025 – on a call between Eddie, mid-chemo, and Mick Crossan, the club's former owner and largest creditor. Eddie was in pain. He lost his train of thought more than once. But he stayed on the call. Spoke from the heart. And persuaded Mick to give his team a shot.

It took five more weeks just to get the website and social logins, but Eddie wasn't letting go. He wanted the relaunch to happen on St Patrick's Day weekend – the emotional high point of the club's calendar. On 15 March, he was still finalizing the press release. The announcement went live: Eddie named patron. Daniel as chairman. Kyle stepping up as CEO.

The impact was massive. Over £25 million in earned media value. The social media accounts – silent for two years – surged past a million views. London Irish was alive again. Because Eddie made it matter.

Three days later, on 18 March, his health took a turn. He passed away less than 48 hours later.

As we write, the future of London Irish is still uncertain. The team is working to secure a league, union approval, a venue, and a training base. But they keep going – fuelled by Eddie's fire. And by one word he gave them, every day:

"B E L I E V E. Believe. F***ing believe."

Mentoring Across Industries – Spark, Then Step Back

Eddie's advice didn't come wrapped in jargon or self-help slogans. That wasn't his style. No PowerPoints. No leadership frameworks. But if you spent five minutes with him – in a pub, backstage, on a walk, or at lunch in Monaco – you left changed.

Not because he fixed your problems.

But because he believed in you before you did.

That was the Eddie effect. He didn't mentor through manuals. He mentored through momentum. He listened – properly – and landed the insight that cut straight through the noise. No fluff. No filter. Just truth, direct to the gut.

In motorsport, the names are famous now – Schumacher, Hill, Alesi, Irvine, Fisichella. But back then? They were raw. Unpolished. Unfinished. Eddie spotted something – a stillness, a spark, a flicker of potential. He gave them a shot. A test. A seat. A stage. Then stepped back and let them rise. He didn't need the credit, he just wanted to watch.

And it wasn't just in racing.

He saw it in business founders, journalists, buskers, broadcasters, chefs. If they had fire, he felt it. He didn't care what industry they came from. He cared about hunger. Energy. Rhythm.

In media, Formula 1 presenters and commentators still credit Eddie for helping them find their voice. He didn't care if you nailed the line, he cared if you meant it. His advice? "Don't just report the sport – feel it. Then make the audience feel you."

He played gigs around the world with a street musician named Luca, whom he'd spotted busking on Grafton Street in Dublin.

Not because he needed a guitarist. Because he believed in what happens when someone feels seen.

In business? Same thing. Entrepreneurs would pitch ideas, expecting pushback. Instead, Eddie leaned in: "If you believe it, I'll back you. Just don't waste my time." His belief wasn't soft. It came with pressure. Accountability. Expectation. He didn't let people coast. He pushed them – then let go.

Mentorship, for Eddie, was never about control. It was about ignition. He saw potential like a drummer feels tempo – instinctively. And when he felt it, he acted. Fast. Decisively. He gave people something they didn't even realize they needed: permission.

Permission to try. Permission to fail.

Permission to go bigger than anyone else thought reasonable.

He didn't hover. He didn't micromanage. He gave you the tools, the challenge, and the belief – and then he got out of the way. And when you pulled it off? He'd smile, say "Told you", and pour another glass.

He didn't need a formal title. He didn't wait to be asked. If he saw something in you, that was it.

And if he didn't?

Well . . . you'd know.

What made Eddie's mentorship rare wasn't just his eye for talent. It was his heart. He cared. Not performatively. Properly. He turned up at 2 a.m. He called when others didn't. He gave people back to themselves – not with lectures, but with belief.

And maybe that's the biggest lesson he left across every industry, every jam session, every boardroom, and garage:

Mentorship isn't about telling someone where to go. It's about helping them find their own direction – and the confidence to take it.

It's standing beside them at the start line and saying: "Go on, then. I'm watching."

Summary – The Edge of Belief

Whether it was crossing oceans, chasing billion-pound deals, reviving a fallen club, or backing someone with nothing but instinct and fire – Eddie Jordan didn't do things by the book, he did them by belief.

He didn't wait for permission, he moved on feel. He didn't ask for consensus, he backed his gut – and he brought people with him.

This chapter isn't about safe bets. It's about full swings. With boats. With bids. With people. With purpose.

And if it didn't work out? He kept going.

That was the edge. Not status. Not polish. Not a perfect plan. It was belief – in the person, in the moment, in what could be built out of chaos. That's what gave him his rhythm.

Because Eddie knew the real advantage is this: move before you're certain. Believe before the outcome. Start when others are still stalling.

That's where the edge lives.

So if you're sitting on an idea, a deal, a hunch   stop waiting for the green light.

Back it.

Build it.

Go.

JFDI (Just F***ing Do It!).

FTB.

8

Music, Rhythm, and Relationships

Eddie's Bands – From V10 to The Robbers

Eddie Jordan didn't just love music – he needed it. And when the rhythm inside him got too loud to ignore, he did what any music-obsessed, madness-prone ex-Formula 1 team boss might do: he started a band. Then another.

The first was called V10, a nod to the thundering ten-cylinder engines of Eddie's favourite Formula 1 era. Like the engines, the band was loud, unpredictable, and occasionally on the verge of explosion. They played Irish rock, classic anthems, whatever felt good – fuelled by energy, not polish.

Eddie was always behind the kit. Arms flailing. Grin wide. Shirt untucked. He wasn't trying to be the best drummer in the world, he was trying to light the place up. And it worked. V10 played charity gigs, sponsor parties, backroom jams, and hotel ballrooms where people came for the cars and stayed for the chaos.

Eventually, V10 evolved into Eddie and The Robbers – less a

band, more a travelling circus. A loose, joyful collective of musicians, mates, and misfits who played not for deals or labels, but to get the room moving. And move it did.

They played Monaco. Cape Town. London. Rome. Singapore. Japan. Boats. Vineyards. Weddings. Hospitality suites. They played in places no one expected music – and suddenly, it was a party.

What made it work wasn't precision. It was permission. Permission to mess up. To miss a beat. To play with heart. If the bass player was off or Eddie lost time mid-fill, no one cared. The energy never dropped. Everyone got involved.

It wasn't just music. It was release. It was community. It was joy.

Because Eddie wasn't in it for the applause.

He was in it for the rhythm. And the reminder that no matter how serious life gets, you can always make a bit of noise and have a bit of fun.

Busking and Mayhem with Spoons

Eddie didn't perform at you, he pulled you in.

Sometimes he busked properly – on the street. Other times, he'd jump in mid-set with a band or bang spoons at a train station. Once, outside a venue in Lisbon, he sat on the kerb, spooning along to music blaring from inside. A semi-circle of confused tourists gathered. He didn't care. He was alive. That was the point: he was in the Zone.

The spoons weren't a gimmick, they were his release. His reset. When pressure built – when the cameras stopped and the deals were done – he found rhythm. Not in silence. In noise.

It was his way back to himself. Like some people run. Or meditate. Eddie spooned. It brought him back to the tempo that mattered.

Rock 'n' Roll – Drumming with the Stars

Only Eddie Jordan could go from a Dublin bank clerk to jamming with Bryan Adams, Mike Rutherford, Chris Rea, and Bob Geldof – not by begging his way in, but by showing up with presence and not caring if he missed a beat.

He started small. Borrowed kits. Local gigs. But the confidence was always there – the same kind he brought to the Formula 1 grid. He wasn't the best, but he had feel. He had joy. And he had groove.

That combination? Irresistible.

He played private gigs, charity concerts, yacht parties, jam sessions that ran into the early hours. And it didn't matter who was in the crowd – GRAMMY winners, billionaires, drivers, legends – they all caught the vibe.

He wasn't "that Formula 1 guy trying to be a rock star", he was a man in love with rhythm, unfiltered and unapologetic.

The stars loved him for it. Because in a world full of polish, Eddie brought soul. He wasn't trying to lead, he was just trying to stay in the pocket – and make everyone else sound better.

There was one night he never forgot. A small club in Cape Town, drumming alongside a local jazz trio. No cameras. No VIPs. Just rhythm. After the set, the bandleader leaned in and said, "You've got feel, man. You listen."

Eddie never forgot that. Because it wasn't flattery, it was truth.

339

Why Music Matters – The Beat Beneath It All

For Eddie Jordan, music wasn't a hobby. It wasn't a side project. It wasn't even about performance.

It was air.

It was honesty. No masks. No spin. No titles. Just rhythm. You're either in time or you're not. You're either present or you're not. That rawness always called to him.

Even after decades of racing, investing, mentoring, and negotiating, he felt most himself behind a kit. Not chasing applause – just chasing the beat.

Music gave him flow. It gave him lightness. And it gave him joy.

Because racing is pressure. Business is politics. But music? Music is fun. It's soul-first. It's human.

From banging spoons in Bray to jamming with rock legends in Monaco, from busking in Lisbon to playing late-night sets with The Robbers, the beat never left him. It was the throughline. The safe place. The party and the prayer.

And maybe most importantly – music was how Eddie connected. It was how he mentored. How he celebrated. How he let people in. A harmony out of nowhere. A chorus shared by strangers. That's where walls dropped and friendships formed.

So why does music matter?

Because it brings people together. Because it kept Eddie grounded. Because even when the world got heavy, music reminded him not to take it all too seriously.

And because somewhere in the crash of cymbals, the rattle of a spoon, the hum of a bassline – is the rhythm of a life lived fast, lived loud, and lived fully.

Summary – A Life in Rhythm

Eddie Jordan's life didn't follow a traditional score, but through all the deals, races, dinners, and stories there was always one constant: rhythm.

Music wasn't a side gig. It was a second heartbeat.

From the chaos of The Robbers to the quiet jams in Cape Town, from spoon-shaking mayhem to sober, soulful sessions with real musicians – Eddie didn't just play music, he lived in it.

It was how he stayed human when the world turned clinical. How he built trust. How he mentored outsiders and made them feel part of the band.

And it taught him something that business never could:

When you stop trying to lead every moment . . . the magic finds you.

That's why music mattered.

Because in the rhythm, Eddie didn't just find the beat.

He found himself.

9

Monaco, Friendship, and the Long Game

Monaco and Unretiring

Eddie Jordan didn't retire to Monaco. He lived it. Fully. Loudly. Daily. It was his stage.

To most people, Monaco looks like a postcard – yachts in the harbour, slow Rolls-Royces crawling along the boulevard, champagne catching the afternoon sun. But for Eddie, it wasn't a retreat. It was another kind of circuit – alive, unpredictable, always moving. And he was its ringmaster. No fancy car for him. He cycled or walked everywhere.

He loved the randomness. The energy. The ability to walk or cycle everywhere – to jump from coffee to chaos, from boat to boardroom, from breakfast to a late-night jam without missing a beat.

His Monaco didn't run on schedules, it ran on rhythm.

You'd spot him cycling through the backstreets, shirt flapping, legs pumping, wind in his hair. Then he'd stop, mid-ride, to shout a joke to a concierge or wave to a maître d' like they were team-mates from the paddock. Because they were. Every few minutes someone would call out: "Eddieeeee!" A driver. A doorman. A billionaire. A busker. He knew them all – and if he didn't, he made it feel like he did.

He packed Monaco into his bones. Grand Prix weekends were his favourite – not just for the racing, but for the electricity. The boats. The noise. The people. It was a living version of what he'd built with Jordan GP: chaos with purpose, speed with soul, fun with an edge.

For Eddie, Monaco wasn't about wealth. It was about motion. It wasn't about status. It was about connection. The best moments weren't in the boardroom – they happened during a quick espresso with a sailor or a drink at sunset with a Saudi investor. He treated the city like a stage. And he played it like no one else could.

Monaco may be full of characters. But Eddie? He became part of the architecture.

Lessons on Friendship –
The Long Game of Showing Up

Eddie Jordan didn't build a network. He built friendships. Real ones. Loud ones. Lifelong, messy, hilarious, loyal ones. The kind that showed up in crisis – and somehow turned it into a party.

Friendship, for Eddie, wasn't small talk or check-ins. It was presence. It was *showing up*. For a pint, a phone call, a moment – or a full-on disaster. His circle cut across generations, industries, and continents: drivers, engineers, musicians, chefs, sailors, waiters, billionaires. If you were in his world, you mattered.

And here's the thing – it wasn't just the inner circle. Eddie had that rare gift: he made everyone feel like they were in the circle. Whether you were a champion or a stranger, a bellhop or a busker, if you crossed his path, he gave you time. A joke. A look that said, *I see you*. And you remembered it.

That's why when he passed away, the response came from every corner. Yes, from rock stars and racing legends. But also from fans who met him once. Waiters who remembered a smile and a tip. Someone who took a selfie with him in Monaco and walked away feeling like they'd just spoken to a lifelong friend.

Because that's what Eddie made people feel. You didn't need history. Just a moment. And he'd make it matter.

He wasn't trying to impress. He was being human – properly, unapologetically, joyfully human.

And that's what his mates – the old ones, the wildcard ones, and the once-in-a-lifetime ones – will never forget.

You don't remember what people say, you remember how they made you feel. And Eddie Jordan was a master at that – without ever trying to be.

Sailing –
Freedom, Rhythm, and the Wild Open Blue

Eddie Jordan didn't just own boats. He lived them. Sailing wasn't a hobby or a retirement fantasy. It was his space to breathe, move, think, laugh, and live without noise. When the world got too loud or too fast, the sea gave him stillness. And presence.

But more than anything, it gave him time with the people who mattered.

Eddie didn't sail to isolate. He sailed to connect. His boats were floating kitchens, jam venues, storytelling stages, and laughter factories. He cooked on board. Played spoons after dinner. Sat up late with a glass of red, asking how you really were. The next morning? You were up and cycling at 08:00 sharp – no excuses, even if he'd gone to bed at ten and you hadn't.

He always said boats were the best way to get real time with people. More than just time – quality time. No rush, no roles, no interruptions. Just rhythm, wind, food, and music.

And then there was *Lush* – his beloved Oyster 885. In 2013, Eddie joined the inaugural Oyster World Rally, a 33,000-nautical-mile journey around the globe. Unlike others who flew in for the PR photo, Eddie did every leg. Fully. Passionately. He wasn't there to tick a box – he was there to live it. *Lush* became his memory machine.

He loved that sailing was free. No fuel bills. No engines guzzling diesel. Just wind and motion. "Why pay when the wind will take you?" he'd say, half-grinning, half-serious. That thrifty Irish streak ran deep – the same part of him that turned off lights at home and negotiated everything down to the last cent.

Later came *Blush* – a 45m Perini Navi, fast and elegant, designed by Ed Dubois. Then his mighty Sunseeker 155 – a stage for Grand Prix weekends, band sessions, and quiet coffees at sunrise. Every boat had a story. Every journey had a soundtrack. And Eddie was always at the helm – of the boat and the moment.

His love for sailing didn't end at the deck. He wrote a regular column for *Boat International* under the title "Lippy from the Liffey". The writing was pure Eddie: sharp, funny, heartfelt, and unfiltered. He didn't write to show off, he wrote to show up – to remind people that the joy of boats wasn't in the speed or the size. It was in the people you brought along.

Because to Eddie, boats weren't toys or trophies: they were vessels. For presence. For connection. For joy.

"Racing was how I lived fast," he once said. "But sailing is how I live free."

Anyone who shared a deck, a dinner, or a dawn with him at sea would tell you: he meant every word.

Cycling – Speed, Sanity, and the Joy of the Ride

When Eddie Jordan had to give up running because of his knees, he didn't slow down. He just found another gear. Enter cycling – the perfect blend of speed, scenery, and sanity.

It started as a way to stay fit. But like most things with Eddie, it became so much more. Cycling wasn't just physical, it was mental. It was his mobile meditation – a way to move through the world while making sense of it.

And of course, it became social. Deeply, hilariously, beautifully social.

He loved riding with friends. Loved the rhythm of it. The easy banter on the bike. The "quick coffee" that turned into four hours of storytelling, arguments, dreaming, laughter, and big, messy, honest life chat.

For Eddie, the road was just the warm-up. The real ride started at the café table.

Beachside cafés in France. Hillside haunts near Bray. Old favourites in Cape Town. They weren't just pit stops – they were his office, his think tank, his roundtable. Espresso in hand, sunglasses on his head, Lycra on show, and mischief in his grin.

If you rode with Eddie, you knew what was coming: a few updates on the bike ... then a free-range download of ideas, opinions, provocations, and perspective.

Business. Music. Family. Ambition. Fear. Philosophy. Politics. Football. Formula 1.

No topic was off-limits. No opinion too strong. No laugh too loud.

It wasn't just a conversation. It was a reset. A rhythm. A ride for the soul.

And it always felt important – because Eddie made you feel like it was. Whether you were a CEO or someone who'd never clipped into a bike in your life, if you were at that table, you were in the circle.

He didn't lecture. He listened. He challenged. And when he did, it came with humour and heart. A push and a wink.

Cycling gave him momentum – for his body, but as much for his ideas. It kept him sharp. Kept him honest. Kept him moving forward in a world that often pushes people to sit still.

Because for Eddie Jordan, a great day wasn't just a good ride. It was a good ride with better company – and a coffee that turned into a conversation you'd never forget. He especially loved the ride from Monaco to Dolceacqua in Italy: "I just cycled across three countries and had coffee for one euro in the centre of the village."

Family – The Sanctuary Behind the Speed

For a man who lived most of his life at 100 miles an hour, Eddie Jordan had surprisingly strong boundaries when it came to one thing: family.

He didn't bring the Formula 1 circus home with him. He didn't need to. Because home – real home – wasn't a shrine to his success. It was a sanctuary. A place where the world didn't need to watch, and he didn't need to perform.

There were no trophies in the house. No helmets. No framed photos of podiums or trackside glory. No memorabilia, not a single memento. In fact, unless you really knew what to look for, you'd never guess you were standing in the home of one of the most colourful, successful team owners in Formula 1 history.

That was by design.

The house was about life. Their life. Marie, the kids, the grandkids, and the constant rhythm of real family moments – noisy, honest, beautifully unfiltered.

And at the centre of every house – whether it was in Cape Town, Monaco, or Sotogrande – was the table.

Not simply any table. A huge one. The kind that could seat 12 without blinking, and 16 if people didn't mind getting a little closer. And they always did. Because that table wasn't just furniture – it was the heartbeat of the house.

Meals, stories, debates, laughter, birthdays, ideas, music, confessions, toasts, tears, deals – it all happened there.

Eddie loved having his people around that table. The loud ones. The cheeky ones. The unexpected drop-ins. It didn't matter who you were – if you were in, you were welcome. And it wasn't unusual to sit down for lunch and realize you were breaking bread with a musician, a neighbour, a racing legend, and someone who just popped in to say hi.

The front door was almost always unlocked. That was Eddie's style. Everyone was welcome. Everyone had a place.

There's a now-classic story that sums it up perfectly. One day, when Kyle was a young boy, he came into the kitchen and said to Marie, a little unsure,

"Mum . . . I let a homeless man in to use the toilet. He said he knew you and Dad, so I thought it was ok."

A few minutes later, George Harrison walked out of the bathroom.

Yes – that George Harrison. The Beatles' George. A close family friend. With his rock star dishevelled look – the designer homeless look you might call it.

That was the Jordan house. Unexpected. Open. Generous. Unpredictable. And unforgettable.

Eddie kept that same energy with his own traditions. Every summer, he brought the whole family together in Sotogrande, Spain – kids, grandkids, partners, friends. Bikes and beach walks, wine and music, storytelling and late-night laughter. And every Christmas, they'd do it all again somewhere else. Different setting. Same heartbeat.

He kept that rhythm going year after year. Because no matter how big his life got – no matter the stages, the stakes, the speed – this was what grounded him.

Family wasn't a performance. It was the one place he didn't have to be "Eddie Jordan". He could just be Dad. Grandad. Husband. Host. Friend. The guy at the head of the table making sure your glass was full and that you were having fun.

He didn't talk about family values. He lived them. Was he perfect? No, but he did his best. And in a world full of noise, ego, and acceleration, the most remarkable thing was how still and real it all felt around that table.

No trophies. No titles. No closed doors. Everyone welcome.

Just the people he loved – gathered, fed, laughing, together.

And in the end, that was the legacy that mattered most.

10

Life at 100 Beats Per Minute

This was never going to be the full story.

To truly capture Eddie Jordan – in all his rhythm, wildness, heart, and heat – you'd need ten volumes, and even then, you'd still be missing something. He was too fast, too layered, too alive to ever be pinned down on paper.

And that's just the part you could publish. The rest? Let's just say there are stories – legendary ones – still echoing around paddocks, boats, bars, and backrooms that no editor would ever dare approve. Half the best ones never made it past the cutting room floor. The other half can only be told over a drink, in low lighting, with no microphones anywhere nearby.

Because with Eddie, the real magic wasn't always in the head-lines. It was in the in-between. The moments you had to be there for. The ones that left you laughing, speechless, or a little bit changed.

That's why this book was never meant to be definitive. It was meant to be useful.

An invitation.

A guide.

A pause in the middle of a high-speed life – where you pull off the track, sit down, and hear the stories that shaped a man who shaped so many others.

Because Eddie Jordan was one of a kind. He wasn't just a team boss. He wasn't just a drummer. Or a dealmaker. Or a sailor. Or a mentor. He was all of it – and somehow more. A walking contradiction, a magnetic force, a high-octane mix of instinct, humour, loyalty, and vision. He could go from joking with a concierge to bidding on a billion-pound company within the same hour – and make both people feel seen and important.

This book exists to show you how.

How he thought. What he cared about. What drove him. What he believed made people great. What he learned the hard way. What he passed on the easy way – over a pint, a coffee, or a late-night jam session.

You've read about the roots of rebellion, how a boy from Bray swapped a bank desk for a kart track and never looked back. You've followed the path of Jordan Grand Prix – how Eddie built a Formula 1 team on energy, guts, and gumption, and made it a family, not just a garage. You've seen how he spotted talent, before the world caught up. Senna. Schumacher. Hill. Irvine. Alesi. Brundle. Fisichella. Ralf. You've felt his fire in business, boats, and bids – from world rallies on *Lush*, to the audacious £3 billion Playtech takeover attempt, to trying to rescue London Irish out of pure belief. You've seen what mattered – music, friendship, rhythm, and realness. And above all, you've seen family – the one thing that grounded him, defined him, and kept his heart bigger than any deal he ever closed.

This book is more than a biography. It's a study guide. A reference. A little black box you can dip into when you're stuck. When you're looking for a push, a laugh, a principle to hang your day on.

Whether you're building a team, leading a company, picking yourself up from failure, or chasing your next adventure – The Jordan Code applies.

It's not about being Eddie.

It's about being you, fully.

This book is here to remind you that greatness doesn't come from playing safe. It comes from backing yourself, committing fully, trusting your gut, and treating people properly. It comes from being present, showing up, and refusing to let yourself off the hook.

Eddie believed that if you gave something your full self – your rhythm, your energy, your madness, your attention – you *couldn't fail*. Because success wasn't always a trophy. Sometimes it was a story, a connection, a lesson, a laugh.

In his later years, he quoted Warren Buffett when he said, "Basically, when you get to my age, you'll really measure your success in life by how many of the people you want to have love you actually do love you." Success in life is about happiness, contentment, people, and having fun.

And it had to be fun. Always fun.

Because if you're not enjoying it, what's the point?

So, what now?

Now it's your turn.

Whatever you're chasing, building, dreaming about – keep your eye on the prize and go and do it.

Don't hesitate. Don't ask for permission.

So JFDI!

Go.

Because life isn't meant to be observed. It's meant to be a challenge. It's meant to have momentum. It's meant to push boundaries. It's meant to be *lived*.

At full throttle.

At 100 beats per minute.

Every. Single. Day.

FTB!

Tributes and Reflections

List of Contributors

Bernie Ecclestone

Bono

Flavio Briatore

Roger Taylor

Richard Branson

Mark Webber

Alain Prost

Nico Roche

Adrian Newey

Jeremy Clarkson

Natalie Pinkham

Shane Lowry

Nigel Northridge

Zoe Jordan

Jaime Bergel

Stephen Roche

Ian Phillips

Kevin Moran

Dr Michael Smurfit

Denis O'Brien

Liam Tomlin

Giselle Pettyfer (née Davies)

Eddie Irvine

Gary Anderson

Martin McCarthy

Ard Matthews

Nick Mason

Michael Flatley

Gavin Kelly

Mike Rutherford

Daniel McKeown

Leonard and Reneé Feinstein

Derek Daly

Tony Kilduff

Keith Wood

Paul van der Horst Bruyn

Paul Adamson

Karun Chandhok

Dermot Desmond

Martin Donnelly

Pat Brazel

Patrick Guilbaud

Liam Cunningham

J.P. Fitzgerald

Mike Brady

Ian Poulter

Lee Mutch

Jake Humphrey

Adrian Lazarus

Wade Ormsby

Darren Petersen

Mark Gallagher

Paul McGinley

Michael Chester

Richard Hadida

PJ Fallon

Barry Grinham

Stuart Makin

Peter Young

Dr Costa Kapnias

Luca Pachetti

Henri Leconte

Stefan Johansson

Mick Tunney

Michael D. Higgins

Enda Kenny

Micheál Martin

Bernie Ecclestone

The driving force behind Formula 1's rise to global prominence, shaping its commercial empire with unmatched deal-making and control.

Eddie was a super guy. I loved him – and, truthfully, everybody did. No one ever stayed upset with Eddie for long. And if they were, somehow, he always found a way to charm his way out of it.

We worked together on all sorts of things over the years. One episode – very naughty on my part – was the Michael Schumacher situation. I stole Michael from Eddie. It all happened in one night. I had to persuade Flavio to take him – he wasn't keen at first. He had to stand down one of his drivers to make space. Tom Walkinshaw, who was engineering director at Benetton, played a key role in getting it done.

Eddie didn't want to let Michael go. He was helpful, but he knew what he had. I honestly don't know what would've happened if that deal hadn't happened. Would Michael have stayed with Eddie? Would he have gone on to be as successful? We'll never know. But what we do know is that it all started thanks to Eddie.

He did a lot of jobs for me over the years – and he was really good at them. When we were considering taking Formula 1 to China, I sent Eddie over to see if it would work . . . and to make sure we wouldn't have to live on fried rice! He went – and in 2004, we had our first Grand Prix in China. It's strangely fitting that the minute's silence for Eddie was held at the Chinese Grand Prix, just days after he passed.

Eddie helped people. He did a lot behind the scenes, without fuss and without reward.

He was wonderful.

I miss him dearly.

Bono

U2 frontman and long-time friend of Eddie.

Eddie Jordan. EJ. Faster than life. Will never die around anyone who loves racing.

The gift from the gods with the gift of the gab. A heart as big as his mouth and that mouth was large.

The governor. The gaffer. Living it large. In charge.

Oh boy. A Dublin boy with a lot to say. So bubbling in Dublin. He moved to Bray.

Who could control or contain and restrain him? A boy racer. Dream chaser.

Formula fun to Formula 1.

A friend to all. And an enemy to none.

They say the pinnacle for Eddie was in '98. Jordan one and two. Who knew? EJ knew. He discovered Michael Schumacher. Or maybe Michael Schumacher discovered EJ!

Bringing the best out of everyone is everyone's job. Eddie was just better at it than most of us.

Eddie was the epitome of the epigram that "worried money never wins".

His joy infectious. Outrageous. Contagious.

Yeah, a little dangerous. Never reckless. Never couldn't care less. Never feckless. And never unkind.

Eddie Jordan cared deeply for everyone around him which is why he is loved by people who never got near him. Fearless, funny and generous.

But God *is* fair. So Eddie wasn't allowed to be the greatest drummer in the world. But no drummer in the world has ever had more fun. EJ, serious fun.

Living for love, laughter, noise, speed, loyalty. The man was Irish royalty.

Eddie was a joy. Eddie brought joy.

I will. We will. Miss you.

No one could keep up with you. This life or the next.

May you rest in peace but more likely "at pace".

Flavio Briatore

Italian businessman best known for leading Benetton and Renault to Formula 1 world titles.

Eddie was one of a kind. In a paddock that sometimes took itself far too seriously, Eddie brought colour, mischief, and real soul. He didn't follow the script – he rewrote it. We were competitors, friends, rivals, co-conspirators – and always entertained by each other.

He had the heart of a rockstar and the brain of a streetwise dealmaker. When Eddie walked into a room, things got louder, funnier, and more unpredictable – in the best possible way. He could charm a crowd, negotiate a deal, mentor a driver, and still find time to play the spoons after dinner.

We argued, we laughed, we tried to steal each other's sponsors – and drivers! And then we had dinner. I shared holidays and trips with Eddie and Marie too – always great company. That was the magic of Eddie. He had an incredible instinct for people – and if he believed in you, you felt ten feet tall.

He gave the sport its heartbeat. He gave it flair. And in his own Irish way, he reminded all of us not to take life – or ourselves – too seriously.

The grid feels quieter without him. But his rhythm, his spirit, and his chaos will echo for a long time.

Grazie, Eddie.

Roger Taylor

Queen's drummer.

I think of Eddie as an electric fizzing firework of a man!

His heroic achievements in the cutthroat world of motor racing at the highest level bear witness to his extraordinary creativity and tireless tenacity when pitched against the moneyed, powerful giants of Formula 1. Truly great achievements!

And obviously a man of impeccable taste, given his love of rock 'n' roll music – in particular the drums, and his passion for boats and sailing the world. Definitely a man after my own heart!

I last saw him at Stamford Bridge at a Chelsea game, shortly before he left us – still cheerful, with a wonderful zest for life in all its twists and turns.

He will be sorely missed – we are diminished!

Richard Branson

Founder of the Virgin Group.

As a fellow entrepreneur, it was always delightful to cross paths with Eddie Jordan – as we always said, us bearded businessmen have to stick together! As well as being a smart, talented leader, it was the way Eddie did things differently that stood out. He always had a smile and a story, and you could tell the people around him loved working together.

Once I gifted him some clapped-out old vans, which one of his new mechanics, Andy, fixed up. I just learned that 37 years later, he's still with the team, now its longest-serving member. That sounds like Eddie Jordan.

Mark Webber

Nine-time Formula 1 Grand Prix winner.

Eddie showed me light at the end of the tunnel at a critical point in 1999 when I was on the bones of my ass.

He gave me critical advice and sent me on my way when I really needed it. He was always in my corner and brilliant with my wife Ann and my family. He was an absolute dynamo and always a pleasure to be around.

I loved his great sayings:

- Never let the old guy in.
- F**k the begrudgers.

I'll never forget him – great man, great friend.

Alain Prost

Four-time Formula 1 world champion and one of the most successful and respected drivers in the history of the sport.

I was honoured to have Eddie as a friend.

I knew him a long time, all the way back to when we were racing in Formula 3. We had our own teams and competed against each other. For maybe five years, it was just small teams – Eddie's and mine. It was a tough time for both of us, but also a special one.

We had many meetings with the other teams, but Eddie and I always sat together. I trusted him. He was clever, and he was a very good businessman.

Many people saw the showman – the controversial figure, the man with the band – but behind all of that was a truly incredible man. He had great depth, a strong understanding of people and situations. When I needed advice, I turned to him – and I really listened.

We'd often be in serious meetings, discussing serious matters, sitting side by side – and then Eddie would suddenly lean over and whisper a joke or a funny comment, right in the middle of a tense moment. It was so hard not to laugh. He had that effect – he could change the mood in an instant.

There are not many people in life who leave an impact like Eddie did. He always said kind things about me as a driver, and I appreciated that very much – because he really knew what he was talking about. Praise from Eddie meant something.

We always had fun. Being around him was a pleasure.

And we never had an argument. Not once. Even though we were competitors, sometimes chasing the same sponsors, we never clashed. I think it was the deep mutual respect and the friendship underneath that meant more than any rivalry.

When I was under pressure or stressed, I would talk to Eddie. We might start with serious business, but soon he'd tell a story and we'd be laughing together. I always felt better after seeing him.

He was a true gentleman – a lovely man.

The last time I saw him was on a bike in Monaco. We had dinner later, just the two of us. When you spent one-on-one time with Eddie, he was different – more quiet, engaged, thoughtful. He really listened, and he gave advice you could trust. I can't even remember what we talked about that night – and that was the magic of Eddie. You remembered the feeling, the warmth, not the details.

Others might give you advice to suit themselves. Eddie gave you the advice you needed – even if it wasn't what you wanted to hear. He was honest. He was someone you could trust. And I always did.

I was always amazed how he could be a showman, then switch to deep business talk, then pick up a guitar – all in the same restaurant, in one evening.

I sent him a message just two or three weeks before his passing. He replied to say he was fighting his battle with courage – the only way he knew.

He was unique. A great friend. And I miss him.

Nico Roche

Former Irish pro cyclist, national champion, and veteran of 24 Grand Tours.

I had the privilege to meet Eddie for the first time when I moved to Monaco. I grew up watching and following Eddie all my childhood as an Formula 1 fan and a proud young compatriot.

I remember that particular day. He was playing the spoons with his band in a local pub. I couldn't believe the energy and the vibes he brought to the room – it was highly contagious.

They often say, don't meet your idols. I can say this is wrong!

I admired Eddie for his success story, and I got to meet an incredible genuine sports enthusiast that I got lucky enough to call a friend.

Adrian Newey

Formula 1 car designer and engineer, winner of championships with Williams, McLaren, and Red Bull. Currently technical director and co-owner of Aston Martin Formula 1.

I first met Eddie in the summer of 1993 while I was at Williams.

At that time, I lived in Fyfield, which had a small pub. One Saturday, it hosted a hog roast, which the family and I all went to. While queuing for said roast, pint in hand, EJ appeared, brandishing an envelope! How he had tracked down where I was, I have no idea, but he made a big theatre of ripping open the envelope and handing me a cheque for £500,000: "Yours if you join Jordan."

Of course, we chatted for a while – also with Ian Phillips, my old colleague from my Leyton House days, who was now working as EJ's sporting director. Unsurprisingly, the cheque was not signed, and I chose to stay at Williams. But for years afterwards, at every chance encounter in an Formula 1 paddock, I would hear, "I fuckin' own ya," accompanied by the cheeky smile.

And so it was until my wife, Amanda, and I bought a house in Cape Town – which happened to be about a mile from Eddie and Marie's. Turned out that Eddie was effectively the mayor of Cape Town and appeared to know everyone there. He introduced us to his closest friends down there, giving us a great social circle. Two to three times a week, Eddie and I – often just the two of us, other times with other cycling buddies – used to go cycling the 16-mile trip to Noordhoek along a stunning hilly seaside route for coffee and scrambled eggs on toast. The ride back was always slower!

We chatted about everything on those rides and became very good friends. One day, the wind had been too strong in the morning for our usual breakfast run, so we elected instead to leave at 4 o'clock. As we reached the top of the first long climb, the heavens opened and the wind strengthened again as a huge front came in. We turned back to Camps Bay and stopped at a bar named Cause & Effect – a very apt name, as it turned out.

Two of Eddie's *FFS* podcast team turned up, and Amanda came down to join us. As we got stuck into the margaritas with the lightning storm raging outside, talk turned to my concerns at Red Bull Racing and why, for a number of reasons, I felt I needed to resign. "Don't worry, I'll be your fucking manager."

What happened from there is quite well publicized, but the immediate footnote was that Eddie decided he would cycle the one mile back to his house. Let's just say his balance had become somewhat compromised, and despite imploring him to walk, it appears he got on his bike as soon as he was out of sight.

Meeting two days later for our normal breakfast ride, Eddie was a little sheepish – his arm and leg scraped up. That was Eddie: instinctive, immaculate in his timing for spotting a business opportunity, incorrigible, and always his own man.

Jeremy Clarkson

British TV presenter and motoring journalist known for Top Gear *and* The Grand Tour.

The most terrifying day of my life – genuinely. I was on holiday in the south of France when Eddie rings me up.

"Do you want to borrow a boat?"

I said, "No thanks, I've already got one."

"You'll want this one," he says. "It's a really lovely sailing boat."

So I took it. Just for a day or two. All the kids on board. No mention of money. No terms. Nothing. And the whole time I was thinking – I am absolutely screwed. Because I knew what was coming. Might be a week, might be a year, but one day I'd get the call. And I'd be expected to do something I absolutely didn't want to do – and I'd have to say yes, because of the bloody boat.

But the call never came. It never came.

That was Eddie. Staggering generosity, hidden behind all the chaos and volume.

Natalie Pinkham

British television presenter and journalist, best known for her work in Formula 1 broadcasting.

Eddie always championed others. He actually helped me get my job at Sky Sports – he grabbed my arm in the paddock back in Abu Dhabi 2011 and said we are going to talk to the Sky bosses about your career. He marched me over to the head of Sky Sports and said, now you wouldn't dare take me, but you have to take

Pinky for your coverage from next year ... or words to that effect. I'll be forever grateful.

He had one of those faces which made you smile before he had even spoken ... you just knew he was about to say something funny and mischievous; and it was always underpinned by incredible kindness. EJ was a rare treasure.

Shane Lowry

Irish professional golfer, 2019 Open Champion and member of multiple Ryder Cup teams.

Eddie Jordan was an absolute legend of Irish sport. What he achieved in Formula 1 and beyond really put Ireland on the global map – he showed the world what Irish ambition and talent looked like. I was lucky enough to get to know Eddie over the years and he even hosted me at a Grand Prix in Abu Dhabi, which was an unbelievable experience. He truly was one of a kind.

Nigel Northridge

Former CEO of Gallaher Group PLC.

No matter the differences in views on value, return, or execution, Eddie always believed that any successful deal had to deliver a win/win for both parties. He was the arch dealmaker, but his negotiation technique was rooted in mutual respect – and often led to genuine, enduring friendships. Ours was one of those.

In a lifetime, you meet precious few people with true charisma.

Eddie was one of those rare creatures. Over ten years as Primary Sponsor of Jordan Grand Prix, we fought and laughed – and then fought and laughed all over again. That emotional cocktail was often infuriating but always thrilling and completely addictive.

Eddie had a unique ability to align his heart and head. Determined, single-minded and incorrigible in adversity – but, most importantly, loyal to eternity.

Every deal we made together came with a story I've wanted to tell ever since. Often, Eddie's version would differ from mine – and that was part of the charm. He had an unrivalled ability to create his own version of history.

But what mattered most was that we always made our deals work – by appreciating each other's point of view and finding compromise in common ground.

In his own words, "he was an absolute mega," and I will deeply miss his remarkable and unique sense of humour, combined with that relentless drive to succeed – and that infectious twinkle in his eye.

Zoe Jordan

Eddie's eldest daughter. Award-winning fashion designer, creative entrepreneur, and performance coach. Zoe also serves as a trustee of the Eddie Jordan Foundation.

To the world, he was Eddie Jordan – the rule-breaker, the risk-taker, the renegade in racing leathers or loud shirts. But to me, he was Dad. The main man in my life. The one who taught me how to live freely, laugh loudly, and trust my gut. Who never turned down an adventure, never slowed down, and never let a storm pass without chasing it head-on.

Our life was never ordinary. It was more caravan than cul-de-sac – nomadic and chaotic, trailing racetracks across Europe, living out of bags, befriending the ants in muddy paddocks. But he balanced it all. He gave everything to his work, but when he switched off, he was truly present. Time with him was golden.

He was always a hustler. As a teenager, he stood outside Lansdowne Road selling questionably dated smoked salmon to rugby fans, charming punters and striking deals long before the Formula 1 paddock knew his name. Classic Dad – spotting an angle, taking the risk, and making it all look effortless.

Some of my earliest memories are of tailing him around Silverstone, watching him weave through drivers, mechanics, and businessmen with that unstoppable energy. He had magnetism – a kind of "anything is possible" attitude that pulled people in, including me. I'd sit quietly in the corner of his office, listening to wild ideas or the next big deal. Sometimes he'd catch my eye and give me a cheeky wink – letting me know I was in on it too. That spirit, that belief in making your own luck, was his gift to us all.

Dad used to say, "F*** the begrudgers." It wasn't just a motto, it was a philosophy. That mindset became my wings.

Our house was always open – full of friends, family, chaos, and characters. Johnny Herbert used to do my hair before school, complete with bows. Life was electric. That was Dad's doing. He lit everything up. Made the dullest day sunny.

He was colourblind, so from the age of ten I picked out his shirts and ties. Sometimes I wonder if that's where my love of fabric and colour began – laying out his outfits each night, styling my dad before he went out to do deals that would reshape motorsport. Looking back, maybe that was my first fashion internship.

There's an old Irish saying: "Briseann an dúchas trí shúile an chait" – what's in the cat is in the kitten. We were often called twins, not just because of the matching big shnozzes, as he liked to say, but because we mirrored each other – in energy, in defiance, in spirit. We clashed often, especially when I left my safe banking job to launch my fashion brand. He gave me the silent treatment. Couldn't understand why I'd walk away from security. Until I reminded him: he did exactly the same when he left the Bank of Ireland to chase cars. He grinned, twinkle in his eye, and conceded the point.

We were fire on fire sometimes. We'd argue, blow up, and always find our way back – usually over lunch or a football match. That was Dad. Fierce heat, but fiercer loyalty underneath.

He adored my girls – Eden (named for him), Dylan, and Inez. They were enchanted by him. He was a big kid: mischief, madness, and F-bombs. He'd show up unannounced – once on my doorstep in Hong Kong, just after the Australian Grand Prix, wanting to steal a few days with me and my newborn. We'd walk, talk, brunch. He'd cradle little Edie in his arms, soft and quiet in those rare private moments. He could be tough – but for his girls, he cracked like an eggshell.

He sat front row at my shows, beaming in his FTB bomber. He saw the parallels between our worlds – the pit lane and the catwalk. Both fast, brutal, brilliant. Both needing vision, teams, sponsors, and steel. I think he respected that I carved my own path into one of the toughest games – just as he had.

He taught me to be brave. To follow the energy. To take chances. To laugh at the odds and keep going when others would quit. And to never, ever listen to the begrudgers.

He was the spark. The noise. The pulse. Young and free – too wild a spirit to tame.

If you knew him, you know there's no way he's missing out.

He'll be riding shotgun as we chase our dreams – hollering from the sidelines, forever and always.

Jaime Bergel

Jaime Bergel is a Spanish private equity investor.

My dear Eddie,

We met over 25 years ago in Southern Spain. After approximately two minutes of talking, you called me a "f-ing petrolhead!" Over two decades later – a friendship I've treasured every step of the way – and you were still calling me a "f-ing" everything. And how I would love to hear those words again today.

We became close friends. We talked about everything – our families, sometimes business, Formula 1 gossip, the world's problems, friendship. You called often to ask for a favour – never for yourself, always for someone you wanted to help.

There were so many unforgettable nights. Parties at home in Sotogrande, those magic white nights with family and friends – nights my daughters loved, and that your energy and enthusiasm made truly special. They adored you. Everyone did. But my girls had a special bond with you – you made them laugh so much from the time they were little.

I'll never forget Barcelona, during the Grand Prix in May, when you shut down the whole team and everyone around to sing happy 14th birthday to my daughter Teresa. She turned 34 recently and still talks about that birthday.

When you left us, my daughters called to comfort me. They knew I had lost a dear friend – someone who had become part of the family. There was never a dinner planned in our home where they didn't ask, "Are Eddie and Marie coming?"

The last time we saw each other was in Monaco, when I raced in the Historic Grand Prix. You made a superhuman effort to participate in a talk with Adrian Newey, just days after surgery. You kept your spirit and humour as always – teasing everyone, and as ever, making fun of yourself. Those of us who really knew you could see how much effort it took, and I saw it in Marie's eyes when I went to check on you both.

After that, when you were in your beloved South Africa, we spoke often. You didn't want to talk much about your illness – you just kept urging me to get tested and take care of myself. Always thinking of others. Always generous. Our last conversation, just days before you went to play the drums at a gig, had the taste of goodbye. And for me, an enormous sadness.

We all miss you, Eddie. I still hear your voice, see you show up at the house unannounced on your bicycle, asking for a drink. I keep so many memories of you close in my heart.

You were the f***ing greatest, my friend.

Stephen Roche

Former professional cyclist. Winner of the Tour de France, Giro d'Italia, and World Championship in 1987.

I first met Eddie when he was running a Formula Ford team and racing at Mondello Park. I loved going down there – the buzz of the track, the energy of the place. And I loved jumping into the car whenever I got the chance. I was hooked.

Eddie and I crossed paths at various events over the years, and we'd always have a chat. I remember talking to him as I was starting to get big results in cycling. I told him I was dreaming of even bigger things ahead. I'll never forget what he said to me – it stuck with me, and I've passed it on to others so many times since.

He said, "If you tell someone your dreams and they don't laugh, you're not dreaming big enough."

It was so Eddie – bold, unapologetic, and full of belief. That idea meant a lot to me. I was a dreamer, but I didn't always voice it. Eddie reminded me that dreaming isn't just allowed – it's essential. If you don't dream it, you've no chance of doing it.

Later, during and after my career, I'd see him down in Antibes. He'd be on his boat, and I'd turn up on a bike. We'd sit for a coffee in a simple café and talk about everything and nothing. That was the thing about Eddie – he had all the success, the lifestyle, the showmanship, but he never lost his humility or his openness. He made you feel like an equal, no matter who you were.

His energy was infectious. His will to succeed, his vision, and his generosity of spirit – it all made him such an admired figure.

Back in the '80s and early '90s, Ireland was going through tough times. But we had Eddie. We had great footballers, golfers, Sean Kelly and myself in cycling – people who gave Ireland something to believe in. Proof that you could come from this little country and make it on the world stage.

I think we inspired a generation – and I hope we gave business leaders and young dreamers the confidence to think big, to go global, to take their shot. At the end of the day, we were all just down-to-earth people. The lads next door. And Eddie – even with the flash and the fame – never stopped being that.

Rest in peace, Eddie. Thanks for the belief, the wisdom, and the dreams.

Ian Phillips

Former editor of Autosport *magazine and commercial and marketing director at Jordan Grand Prix.*

I first met Eddie in 1975, when I was editor of *Autosport* magazine. We hosted weekly socials in London, and if you wanted a mention, you came along and bought a round. One night, a group of Irish lads turned up – and by the end of it, Eddie Jordan was on my sofa, telling me he was going to be Ireland's first Formula 1 world champion.

We crossed paths often after that, especially around Donnington Park, where I lived. Whenever there was a race, the Irish descended in full force – led by Eddie, of course. They'd drink the bars dry and pay in punts, worth half a pound. Eddie was at the heart of it all: mischievous, full of charm, impossible not to like.

Years later, I was running the Leyton House team when Eddie tried to poach some of my staff. I gave him a telling-off – three weeks later I was sacked, and within days, Eddie hired me. I later learned he was told he wouldn't get the 7UP sponsorship unless he brought me on. He always denied it with a grin, but I'm convinced it's true. I started in January 1991, only to find the team wasn't remotely ready. But that was Eddie – spinning dreams into action with nothing but belief and energy.

He could convince you of anything. His enthusiasm was out-rageous and somehow irresistible. We followed him not because we had to, but because we wanted to. He didn't say no to good ideas – even if it took a while to get a yes, especially if money was involved.

I was employee number 39 at Jordan. By the first race, we were just 50 people. Yet by 1999, we were fighting Ferrari, McLaren, and Williams for the championship. We didn't win it, but we proved that courage, belief, and togetherness could take you far.

Eddie had big dreams and pulled people into them. We worked like mad – and every night, he'd ring me at 11 p.m., asking, "You coming in tomorrow?" I'd say, "Yes, and I'll be there before you." That was the spirit – relentless but joyful.

He had a natural bond with fans. For years, Jordan Grand Prix was second only to Ferrari in popularity. Eddie loved reminding Ron Dennis of that. McLaren had the trophies, but we had the hearts.

We brought colour, humour, and music to Formula 1. Eddie's band played at races. The yellow cars stood out. We weren't just racing – we were connecting. Bernie loved it. We gave the sport a human side.

Eddie was brilliant, bold, and completely unique. He made things happen that shouldn't have been possible. We didn't just build a team. We built something unforgettable – because of Eddie.

Kevin Moran

Former Irish football and GAA star, who won two FA Cups with Manchester United.

Eddie was a true Dub. He was immensely proud of Dublin, often talking fondly about his teenage years and "Dublin in the rare aul' times". He went to school in Synge Street, while I was just down the road at Drimnagh – very close indeed.

What Eddie did for Ireland on the world stage was extraordinary, but it was never just about the fame or the achievements. At his core, he was proud to be a Dub. That sense of identity, loyalty, and pride never left him.

He dabbled in Gaelic football when he was young, but it was karting that stole his heart. Those school days were different times – tougher times, with the odd clatter from the Christian Brothers that would not be tolerated today. Looking back, Eddie would often smile and wince at the same time and say, "Those were tough times, but we had great fun." We both left Dublin in our early twenties and when we met up, it was typically in some far-flung country. But he would always say, "Look at us, two Dubs" when we were doing anything.

I first met Eddie properly in Spain, playing golf, and from there a great friendship grew. We had some brilliant ski trips with a bunch of lads. Of course, the skiing became competitive – Eddie would throw himself down the mountain at full tilt, barely a turn in sight, determined to be the fastest down, even though gravity was against his lighter frame!

I spent many great days sailing with him too. His hospitality was second to none. His attention to detail made you feel so welcome, so valued. When he spoke to you, it was as if you were the only person in the room. And he was always direct – you never left a conversation wondering what Eddie really thought!

I last had a proper catch-up with him at the Ryder Cup in Rome in 2023. I had just sold a business with my brother. Eddie's first question was, "How much did you make?" I gave him a round figure. He laughed, shook his head, and said, "I didn't ask you for a round number, ffs – how much did you really make?" – all with that big, mischievous grin. Moments later, he just got up and left, saying, "I'm off to play with the band at the Hospitality area." Sure enough, within ten minutes, Eddie and The Robbers were blasting across the venue!

Even when he was shouting and barking orders on his boat, his crew adored him. They knew it was all banter. They knew he cared. Eddie had that rare ability to bring people with him – through humour, through spirit, through heart.

Life aboard with him was always full of stories and craic. He was clever too – he would leave his wine glass full so no one would top it up, allowing him to pace himself without ever making a fuss.

One trip I will never forget was when we stopped at Komodo Island. I went for a swim, unaware of Eddie's next move. He quickly spread the "word" that the water had crocodiles – a story he told to anyone who would listen to him for years! He loved a good story, and an audience to share it with.

But what I will remember most about Eddie is his grit. His determination to win. It was part of his DNA. Formula 1 gave him the perfect stage for that, and he grabbed the opportunity with both hands. And he did win – in business, in sport, and in life.

Rest easy, Eddie. Thank you for the laughs, the lessons, the loyalty, and the lifetime of memories.

Dr Michael Smurfit

Irish businessman, known for his philanthropy and for building Smurfit Kappa into a global leader.

Eddie came to see me one afternoon in my office in Clonskeagh, Dublin. He wanted to talk about something important – sponsorship for his Formula 1 team. I still remember his energy that day, the spark in his eyes, the urgency in his voice.

"Have you thought about it?" he asked, hopeful.

I had. For several months, in fact. Despite my deep and long-standing interest in car racing – a passion I'd pursued myself in my twenties – I ultimately declined. Still, Eddie's enthusiasm was contagious.

A while later, he called me again, this time with more urgency in his voice.

"Michael, I need to see you," he said. "It's important."

We met. He sat across from me and got straight to the point.

"You have experience buying and selling companies," he said. "I've received an offer for my team. What do you think?"

He told me the number. I listened carefully.

Then I told him – clearly and firmly – that, in my strong opinion, he was selling far too cheap.

"You should ask at least double," I said.

He hesitated. "I'm afraid they'll walk away."

"I don't think so," I said. "But even if they do, you'll know you stood your ground."

To his credit, Eddie took my advice. He went back, asked for more, and ended up receiving nearly what he requested.

From that moment on, every time I ran into Eddie – whether in Ireland or here in Monaco – he'd insist on buying me a bottle of wine. He never stopped thanking me. Over the years, he told me more than once that the deal helped set his family on the road to real financial success.

Eddie was a lovely man in every way. Kind, driven, generous. I miss him already.

Monaco won't be quite the same without him.

Rest in peace, Eddie.

Denis O'Brien

Irish entrepreneur, best known for founding Digicel and his invest-ments in media, telecoms, and infrastructure.

Eddie and I used to go to all the Irish football matches together. Once, we didn't go – and Cyprus were beating us 3–0. I got a message from Eddie:

"Are you watching this shite?"

I said yes.

He replied, "You need to hire a manager for this team. This is bullshit."

I said, "Ok, I will – if you put some money towards it."

He shot back: "Fuck off, you've enough money."

I rang John Delaney and left a message. He thought it was a hoax. Four days later, I got a call when he realized it was serious. I ended up paying for the Irish manager, assistant, and the full backroom team for several years. Eddie's brilliant idea cost me €13 million. Thanks, Eddie.

He was a genius. He was like Peter Pan – he never grew old. Even in his seventies, he dressed like someone in their twenties. His heart had a youthful spirit.

I spent so much time with him, and I loved every minute. I was on his boat many, many times. Eventually, I realized our dietary styles weren't exactly aligned – Eddie didn't eat much and was incredibly disciplined, whereas we were a bit more loose on that front. So I found my own accommodation and just visited his boat instead! I told him his boat was now called *The Famine Ship*.

For my fiftieth, I happened to mention I liked Bryan Adams. Eddie rang Bryan and told him he had to come to Dublin. We sent a plane – my plane – to pick him up in Mexico and bring him over. Eddie arranged the whole thing. That was just him.

The first time I met him was in 1995. Dermot Desmond rang and said, "Come down to my office, I have someone I want you to meet." When I arrived at Dermot's IIU Offices in the IFSC, Dublin, Eddie Jordan was already there, and was in full flight. He was trying to convince us we couldn't possibly miss the opportunity of sponsoring his team. We, as Esat Digifone, ended up sponsoring him to the tune of something like £100,000. I asked what I'd get for that. He said, "I'll put you on my headphones." I don't know if he ever listened to me, but at least my logo was on his ears.

He was proudly Irish, but he lived by the FTB energy. He didn't let anyone tell him what to do – he just did what he wanted, full throttle, no brakes. He lived life to the full, and he loved people. He was incredibly generous with his time.

And here's the truth: he didn't have an ounce of the "FTB" spirit. He championed others. He loved to see people succeed. He thrived on it. It gave him energy. That made him unique.

I loved him. And I miss him.

Liam Tomlin

Award-winning chef and restaurateur, based in South Africa.

In life, if you're fortunate, you'll meet a few people who leave a lasting impression. Eddie was one of those guys – a man I held in great admiration. He approached everything with unwavering dedication and passion.

I first met Eddie at the original Chefs Warehouse in Cape Town. He arrived late one evening, looking for a table in a packed room. The front of house politely informed him that we were fully booked and couldn't accommodate him. Undeterred, Eddie made his way to the kitchen pass and introduced himself in his signature Eddie Jordan style. "How ya!" he interrupted my concentration as I was plating food and running a busy kitchen. He asked for a table and proceeded to tell me that he was in Cape Town, having taken over from Jeremy Clarkson and was filming for *Top Gear*. I wished him luck, acknowledging the big boots he had to fill, and apologized for the lack of a table. After some good-humoured banter, Eddie left.

The next day, Eddie and Marie arrived for lunch and we laughed about the previous evening. That moment marked the beginning of a wonderful friendship. Eddie became a staunch supporter of our restaurants and actively promoted them. He was an enthusiastic advocate for any product or service he believed in, sharing his passion with the world.

Formula 1 and high-end restaurants share many similarities. Both rely heavily on teamwork and timing. The entire team must be aligned and focused on achieving the same goal. Success in either field hinges on individual commitment and consistent performance. Each team member contributes uniquely; you have one chance at winning a race or winning a customer, and a team or business is not dependent on a single individual. This understanding was something Eddie truly grasped. Like Eddie, I have always surrounded myself with positive and talented people, which results in great teams. I've always had a knack for identifying talent, providing opportunities for growth, and nurturing it. He was a master of this.

Despite his international success and his life of globe-trotting, he never forgot his roots; he remained grounded and connected to his origins. Eddie treated everyone equally, regardless of their status or the occasion. He actively listened and showed genuine interest in what others had to say. He always involved you. I was once invited to be part of Eddie and The Robbers at a function they were performing at . . . I played the tambourine.

Confidence was a defining characteristic of Eddie. He wasn't afraid to share his successes without coming across as arrogant. He also wasn't afraid to acknowledge the challenges and hardships he had overcome.

Although our time together was limited, it was truly memorable and valuable. After time spent with Eddie, I always felt a little wiser and richer.

Giselle Pettyfer (née Davies)

Former head of press at Jordan Grand Prix and communications director at the IOC.

I was warned about Eddie before I met him. "Make sure you get business travel in your contract," advised my Benetton boss, John Postlethwaite. I was interviewing with Jordan Grand Prix – they were on the up and had a vacancy because Louise Goodman was moving to ITV. Benetton, meanwhile, were slipping down the grid and cutting back. So, I was trying to move teams. "Louise Goodman has business travel," said John. "But it's paid by Peugeot. Eddie will try to cut it for the new press officer."

John was right. And that was my first taste of EJ the hustler.

Six seasons later, Eddie tried another hustle when I left Jordan to join the International Olympic Committee. The new job offer would mean my leaving mid-season, so Eddie expected payback in the form of tickets for the Olympics. His tenacity nearly scuppered the move! You've got to love him. And the thing is, we all did. He would say, "I made you." And though I'd protest and say I had a fair part to play in making him (since my job was to get him in the media), there's no question that had I not worked for the most charismatic boss in the paddock, the head-hunter recruiting the IOC's director of communications would never have come knocking on my door.

I lived so many crazy experiences, thanks to Eddie and six years at Jordan Grand Prix. What comes to mind most, though, isn't the glamour or the glory. It's the little things. Like the time we were going down to the lobby of our hotel in Monza and a gorgeous girl walked into the lift – and Eddie actually said aloud what came into his mind. I'm gasping, laughing, and cringing just typing this – and that's without quoting what he said. Luckily, she didn't speak English. And anyway, even if she did, she would have laughed. Because that's how it was with Eddie. He could be so outrageous, but we all loved him.

The Eddie that stays with me most is the one who was really thoughtful. The one who cared, and mentored, and gave advice. The one who loved his family and talked about them all the time – who we'd hear calling his mum (my desk was outside his office). Jordan Grand Prix was a big family. I was there for six seasons, but Eddie remained part of my life over the nearly 30 years that followed. He still does, and always will.

Eddie Irvine

Former Formula 1 driver with Jordan and Ferrari.

EJ gave me and many others the keys to a magic world, one he loved to live in. Eternally grateful.

Gary Anderson

Race engineer and technical director. A core figure at Jordan Grand Prix.

I'm honoured to share a few memories of my time working with Eddie Jordan, a man who remains, even in his passing, a force of nature in my mind.

I first met Eddie during the days of Formula 3 in Europe, and one thing was clear from the outset – Eddie simply did not know how to give up. That relentlessness defined everything he touched, from our earliest conversations about starting a Formula 1 team to the incredible season we had in 1991.

At first, I was hesitant to join him on the Formula 1 project. I doubted myself more than anything, but Eddie's unique gift was his ability to see something in people that they couldn't yet see in themselves. He believed in me when I struggled to believe in myself, and that made all the difference. Even in the toughest moments, when it looked like we might not even make it to the starting grid, Eddie's unshakeable optimism and refusal to let go of the dream kept us all moving forward.

He never once burdened me with the reality that we were constantly close to the edge financially. His attitude was always, "It'll be ok." He had an uncanny ability to find a solution when others would give up. And somehow, he did – again and again. Eddie's success wasn't built on luck. It came from a deep-rooted set of principles. He was never late – not once. He respected time and expected the same from others. Even when he had money, he treated it with respect, turning off every light before bed and remembering his humble beginnings. That grounding never left him, and I think it's one of the things that made him such a genuine leader.

We had our ups and downs – how could we not, given the pressures of Formula 1? – but through it all, we stood by each other. When people gossiped or criticized Eddie, I often found myself defending him, because I knew the man behind the public persona: a man of integrity, of vision, and of heart.

There are countless stories that bring a smile even now. I remember one particular weekend when Eddie concocted a plan to sneak Heinz-Harald Frentzen into the car after our driver crashed and couldn't race. Honda were adamantly against it, and tensions were running high. When I went to confront Eddie about it, he'd escaped – quite literally – climbing out of the top of the motorhome and down the back ladder to avoid me! It was classic Eddie – always wriggling out of a tight spot, always one step ahead.

And who could forget our final victory in Brazil in 2003? We had plotted a strategy around the possibility of a red flag, refu-elling at exactly the right moment. Even after hours of planning and agreement, as the rain poured and the safety car led the field, Eddie turned to me on the pit wall and asked, "Are you sure?" It was pure Eddie – questioning, challenging, pushing to get the absolute best.

Eddie was a dreamer, yes, but not a fantasist. His dreams always had a backbone of reality; he could see a path where others saw only fog. And more importantly, he could inspire others to walk that path with him.

I owe a huge part of my career to Eddie Jordan. He gave me the chance to achieve more than I ever thought possible. I still fly economy, I still search for the best deal on a car – because like Eddie, I remember where I came from.

I miss him greatly. The world feels a little duller without him – that unpredictable, mischievous, unstoppable spirit.

Rest easy, Eddie. You made us all believe.

Martin McCarthy

Former racing driver and Formula 1 correspondent for the Irish Times.

The whole Formula 1 Grand Prix world stood still for three minutes at the 2025 Chinese Grand Prix to watch and listen to a powerful tribute by Bono to Eddie Jordan, who had died in Cape Town just three days earlier. Hundreds of millions watched it on television.

Eddie wasn't born in Bray, but he spent much of his childhood there. His father, Paddy, was a Bray native, and Paddy's sister Lilian – Eddie's favourite aunt – spoilt him rotten. Eddie, his parents, and his sister Helen lived in Dartry, South Dublin, which was directly connected to Bray by train via the Harcourt Street line. Almost every weekend, Eddie would travel down to stay with his beloved Aunt Lilian.

He loved Bray and its surroundings. He learned to drive the family's Ford Anglia while his parents played golf at the old Bray Golf Club by the river Dargle. He spent winters and summers in Bray and developed his love of motorsport through his Bray-born cousin Noel Smith, a rally champion and solicitor.

Although the Rathdrum and Wicklow road races were gone

by the time Eddie came of age, he competed in hill climbs at Callery (near the Sugar Loaf), Enniskerry, and other spots across the county. His mother, Eileen, was a dedicated member of Bray Golf Club and continued to play into her 80s.

Eddie's achievements were remarkable. He became a champion driver, winning the premier-class Formula Atlantic Irish Championship in 1978. In 1979, he left a ten-year career at the Bank of Ireland and moved to England to become a professional driver. But at 29, he was considered too old for the top ranks, so he started his own race team, running it successfully through the 1980s.

In 1990, he risked everything – every penny he had, and more – to start his own Formula 1 Grand Prix team. It became a glittering success, winning multiple Grands Prix and coming close to winning the 1999 World Championship. The team was powered in part by Benson & Hedges sponsorship, led by Greystones man Nigel Northridge.

Eddie also had a deep love for the sea and sailing. He spent his final three months at his villa in Clifton, Cape Town, overlooking the ocean – a love that stretched back to his early days on Bray's beachfront.

His autobiography, *An Independent Man*, recalls how his passion for music also emerged from the vibrant band scene in Bray during the 1970s.

Though he lived abroad for many years, Eddie remained Irish to the core. He cherished every return to Ireland – especially time spent in the seaside town he adored: Bray.

Ard Matthews

South African musician, best known as the lead singer of Just Jinjer.

Fate alone put Eddie and me into a round of golf in South Africa, and by the time the round ended we were thick as thieves, instant fellow robbers one might say.

Any time he came to his beloved Cape Town, we always made time for lunch, which with Eddie was never just a meal. It was a story, a spark, a memory in the making. He had a way of making you feel like the centre of the universe while, of course, keeping the whole room orbiting around him.

We shared so many fun moments on stage, and his belief in me and my music meant more to me than he may have ever known. He stood with me at the start line of my Cape to Rio voyage in 2023 and, as only Eddie would, turned to his mate and said with a grin, "This guy is an absolute nutter." What a compliment, coming from a man such as he. That was his humour, sharp but always loving.

Eddie was a highly respected sailor himself, having done many crossings long before I ever dreamed of mine. He was passionate about life, fearless in the face of it, and full of warmth in a way that left a lasting mark on everyone lucky enough to cross his path.

Though our time together was short, the impact was profound. His spirit, his laughter, and his friendship remain with me and always will.

Rest well, legend. Have spoons from The Big Dining Hall at the ready for when next we meet.

Nick Mason

Drummer and founding member of Pink Floyd.

I have so many happy memories of Eddie – with both music and cars never far from the frame.

He was the only man I knew who could outwit Ron Dennis and Steve O'Rourke – probably at the same time. That tells you everything about his charm, speed, and mischief.

And the spoons! Eddie was a perfectly good drummer, but he was a maestro on the spoons. Plus, no need for a drum tech – just cutlery and chaos, delivered with rhythm and a grin.

He made every room louder, funnier and more human. We'll miss that rhythm.

Michael Flatley

International dance icon and creator of Riverdance *and* Lord of the Dance.

Eddie Jordan was my best friend – and I don't say that lightly. Throughout all the ups and downs of my life, EJ was one of the few who was always there. Kings, politicians, lawyers, doctors – they all sought him out for advice, and I was no different.

He was a true, green-blooded Irishman in every sense – every inch a warrior. If you found yourself anywhere near him in a bar or a restaurant, there was no escaping without sharing a drink. He had the heart of a poet and the spirit of one of the toughest men I have ever known. He went into a room full of lawyers and he'd go through them for a shortcut. Eddie had that rare gift of telling you to go to hell – and making you look forward to the journey.

When I first met Eddie, it was 1996, and he asked me for tickets to my *Lord of the Dance* show in Hammersmith, London. I gave him a few – and in true Eddie style, he asked for a few more. He turned up with an entourage of Formula 1 greats, James Bond, billionaires, and a string of supermodels including Helena Christensen. That's who the man was. Afterwards, he told me that Helena had been so enamoured with the show that she rang her answering machine in Paris and recorded the show onto it so she could listen back whenever she wanted. Fun times. From that day on, a great friendship was born.

He was deeply romantic with Marie, and a truly brilliant musician. He stood head and shoulders above the rest. We shared so many memories together. I would play the flute, and he would play the spoons – our own little duo. Last year, we even played together with Rod Stewart in London – just the three of us. It was magic.

Eddie loved sport – especially rugby – and we spent many a day shouting for Ireland at matches, with Eddie's voice always the loudest in the stadium.

We sailed together, travelled together, and every step of the way he showed nothing but generosity and kindness.

Since the day he left, I have missed him terribly.

You may have gone on to the next world, Eddie, but you'll not be forgotten in this one. I'll see you on the other side, mate.

Love you.

Gavin Kelly

Founder of Kinmont, a corporate advisory firm. One of Eddie's most trusted confidants.

Eddie was a dear friend to my family and I, and a big part of our lives – from fantastic sailing trips to shared moments through our connection with Celtic Football Club and many business dealings. He left a mark wherever he went. Among many other things, I learned these from Eddie:

- Be a good listener, especially when people think you are not paying attention. It's like spying in plain sight.
- Take everyone as you find them – and once you've found them, help them take journeys to better places. Have soul.

He was one of a kind. I miss him deeply.

Mike Rutherford

English musician and founding member of Genesis and Mike + The Mechanics, known for his songwriting, guitar, and bass work.

Eddie was a unique friend. Our families have known each other for nearly three decades, and when you were with him, you had 100 per cent of his attention – for about five minutes – while he was already thinking about the next music gig or charity event we could pull together!

We cycled, skied, played music, and shared family time – everything was at full throttle, just the way he liked to live his life.

A few weeks before he passed away, when he was already very

ill, he played his last gig with us as part of Mike + The Mechanics. He played the drums for "Over My Shoulder" and received a standing ovation. It was a special evening. His courage to be on stage and hold his own in that moment was remarkable.

We spent a lot of time in Cape Town with Eddie and Marie, and all I know is that life isn't going to be the same without him. It might be a quieter place now – but certainly not as exciting.

We're going to miss him very much.

Daniel McKeown

Financier and strategic advisor. Partner in Jordan Associates with Kyle Jordan.

My relationship with EJ started in business but quickly turned personal. In his final five years, we spoke almost daily – usually with my kids in the car, so he became part of the family soundtrack, colourful language and all. They still quote his mantra: "Believe. F-ing believe." We first worked together on the bold Playtech bid with Keith O'Loughlin. EJ brought drive and connections; Keith knew the sector; I handled the UK takeover side of things. I told them they were deluded – but might just do it. Over two years, we nearly did, taking on Goldman Sachs and Morgan Stanley with sheer force of belief. EJ was relentless. Not the smartest in the room, he'd say – but always the fastest and toughest. He once told me to "be more of a bollocks"; I told him to try being less of one. We laughed, but the point stuck. Confidence means holding your ground, believing in your gut. Backing yourself.

Outside business, we cycled (his only advice: "Don't blow up on the first hill"), watched rugby, and sailed. He lent us *Tuga* – his smallest, scruffiest yacht – but perfect. In Palma, when a gin palace rocked every boat, he demanded a ruck. None came, but the drinks flowed. Even in his last days, he never stopped – closing Adrian Newey's deal with Aston Martin, and plotting the return of London Irish RFC. With his son Kyle, we had set up Jordan Associates to carry on his sports work, and that now survives him.

What EJ left behind wasn't just memories – but momentum. Always believing. Always moving. Always all-in. I miss him greatly.

Leonard and Reneé Feinstein

Entrepreneurs, philanthropists, and part of the family legacy behind Cap Estel.

EJ . . . the one and only. The world's beloved EJ. Our lives changed for the better after meeting him. We'd never encountered – and haven't since – anyone quite like him. His heart overflowed with love. First and always for his Marie, his cherished children and grandchildren, then for the friends and businesses who became family. He walked through life with his heart wide open, treating everyone as if they were the most important person he'd ever met. He was the light – no shadows.

He was the mightiest of souls. His life elevated ours – and every life he touched. That will be his legacy across the world. No one is saying a rich man passed away. Everyone is saying a good man, a great human, has gone. That's rare – especially for someone with wealth. If you learn one thing from EJ, let it be how to be a good person. A truly inspiring man. A life fully lived.

Surviving grief goes something like this – and we've seen just how many lives he touched through the overwhelming tributes that followed his passing:

Instead of assuming to know another's pain, let's honour the depth of it with empathy.

Instead of offering false reassurances, let's stand by them – steady and present.

Instead of imposing a timeline on healing, let's give it space to unfold.

Instead of searching for meaning in platitudes, let's acknowledge the rawness and the fact that sometimes there is no sense.

In the silence of grief, let love fill the space with quiet comfort.

Rest in the fast lane, EJ – drumming those spoons and lighting up the heavens. Thank you for the memories we've stacked in our hearts, till we meet again. We "fokin" loved you too – and always will. #FTB. May your memory be a blessing.

Derek Daly

Former Irish Formula 1 driver, later a US-based commentator and motivational speaker.

I bought my first race car from Eddie Jordan. He was a charming, sleight-of-hand wheeler-dealer. He promised more than he could deliver but was likable nonetheless.

Eddie's real day job was that of a banker, but he also sold

carpets from "around the corner". My deal was to pay him £400 (approx. $800) plus my pristine purple Ford Anglia in exchange for his Lotus 61 Formula Ford, albeit, without an engine. Part of the deal was the promise of the use of a specially tuned racing engine from Aldon Engineering, a British racing engine builder that he had a relationship with. To me this was an attractive deal, but truth be told, Eddie had no intention of honouring the Aldon part of the deal.

We became good friends nonetheless and cut our teeth together as scruffy wannabes in Mondello Park, racing against each other. He did pay me back for the bogus engine deal however, some 30 years later when I tested a Jordan Formula 1 car at Silverstone. The moral of the story was that trust is a must, and honourable people find a way.

Tony Kilduff

Entrepreneur, philanthropist, and longtime friend of Eddie and the Jordan family.

The Jordans and the Kilduffs met in 1992 during our first summer holiday in Sotogrande. By then, the Jordans were old hands there.

Jordan Formula 1 was still a toddler, and we marvelled as EJ – as we call him – nurtured it, charmed the sponsors, grew it, sold it, bought it back, won Grand Prix races, and sold it again. The stories, the robberies, the times spent in the pit lane at races all over the world, the intrigues and the ups and downs – they were absorbing and hilarious. Always fun! And a few of us were there that day in Spa!

EJ kept the fun going, ably assisted by the lovely, calm, relaxed Marie. So many CLIC (Cancer and Leukaemia in Childhood) events over the years – golf at Sunningdale, walking the Great Wall, cycling all over the world. The word of the event would go out, and so many said yes immediately, just to be near that spark. Word was it would be gruelling and hard – but also fun, amazing, and unforgettable.

And then the AMBER events. Who in rock 'n' roll managed to avoid performing on that stage?

And the family holidays! Skiing, safari, boating – all those Sunseekers, all those Oysters.

Then we thought he might take it easy – but no! TV, punditry, breaking new stories and analysis based on his unique understanding of Formula 1, music with The Robbers, constantly turning up with Luca, filming car programmes, podcasts, and deal-making right to the end. What energy, what an indefatigable spirit!

We have wonderful memories. When I think of EJ, I think of striving, success, happiness, graciousness, wit, experience, loyalty, steadfastness – and above all, good humour. A man of many talents.

Ar dheis Dé go raibh a anam.

Keith Wood

Former Irish rugby captain.

I've never seen a man join the dots like Eddie. It was his superpower – made all the more impressive considering that, most of the time, he resembled a bottle of fizzy Coke shaken aggressively.

To borrow from Ray Davies, he flitted from person to person like a butterfly. Exhausting to watch, essential for Eddie. His flitting was never random – it was instinctive, purposeful, and became the art of connection. And when he settled, even for a moment, you felt like the centre of the world.

We first met – as all good friendships should – in No. 10 Downing Street. It was an auspicious occasion: Britain's sports stars invited by Tony Blair after his sweeping election victory. Eddie's team was based in England, I had just returned from the Lions tour in South Africa, and we were both swept up in the celebratory mood. For a callow 25-year-old, the room was intimidating. But Eddie made a beeline for me, grabbed Ken Doherty (the reigning World Snooker Champion), and we snuck behind a paravent to chat among ourselves. By the end of the night, we strolled out through a silent and empty No. 10 – no security in sight – and let ourselves out through the famous black door.

Eddie's "dot-joining" kicked in not long after. I was invited to the Jordan team car launch with Cirque du Soleil at the Royal Albert Hall that January. Damon Hill and Ralf Schumacher were unveiled. I arrived straight from Harlequins training in shorts and a hoodie, feeling entirely out of place. As I made my way out, Dave Marren from M&C Saatchi pulled me back down to Eddie on stage. They tried (unsuccessfully) to wedge me into the car. Then Eddie insisted on lunch. I refused – my hairy white legs and silver service don't mix – but, as ever, Eddie got his way.

We lunched around the corner with his commercial director, Ian Phillips. I was seated between Eddie and Ian as three sharply dressed Japanese men arrived. All the questions were directed at me. Embarrassed and unsure, I bluffed a few answers and deflected the rest. Forty minutes later, after polite bows and handshakes, they left. Eddie and Ian erupted in celebration and ordered champagne. Turns out it was Mr Honda himself. They'd just signed a three-year engine deal. Mr Honda was a huge rugby fan – and directing questions to me was a mark of respect. Eddie had orchestrated the entire thing.

He always found the edge. Whatever was needed, he'd find it. It was the start of a special friendship. Marie and Eddie took Nicola and me under their wings. We played golf in Sunningdale, sailed the Med, skied in Switzerland, supported each other's causes, and made each other's friends our own.

Our last time together was a long, laughter-filled lunch in Paris – with Nicola, Eddie, Mick Tunney, and Ralph Parkes. His last text to me was about my sons. Typical Eddie. His dot-joining always came back to family.

Paul van der Horst Bruyn

Professional yacht captain, former skipper of Eddie Jordan's Blush *yacht.*

Working for Eddie wasn't your typical setup – but if you thrived under pressure and could handle a strong personality, it was unforgettable.

Eddie had a rare gift for spotting potential where others saw none. He took chances on people others overlooked and pushed them hard – but only if they were up for the challenge.

That was true not just in Formula 1, but also aboard *Blush*, where I had the privilege of serving as captain. It was my first time leading a large yacht, and the experience was intense. Eddie ran a high-pressure operation on a tighter budget than most, but expected more than double the return. And somehow, he got it. *Blush* became one of the most successful charter yachts of its kind.

Eddie was a mentor who led by example – whether running a race team, a business, or a boat. He pushed you to give 150 per cent, while he gave 200 per cent in everything: business, music, cycling, life.

From him, I gained knowledge, opportunity, and unforgettable memories. But the lesson that sticks with me most? If you want to succeed, you need to give everything – and truly believe you can make it happen.

Paul Adamson

Business advisor, executive coach and former superyacht captain.

"Paul, this is your lucky day . . . call me back now."

That was the first message I ever got from Eddie Jordan. I was go-karting on a stag in North Wales and thought it was a prank. But no – it was EJ. And yes – it was my lucky day.

Weeks later, my wife Audrey and I joined Eddie and Marie aboard their brand-new Oyster 885, *Lush*, for the inaugural Oyster World Rally. I was skipper, Audrey first mate – and Eddie? Part rockstar, part rogue, pure energy. Over 33,000 nautical miles, we sailed through remote islands and unforgettable moments. Working with Eddie was like sailing in 40 knots with every sail up – thrilling, intense, never dull.

What defined him was belief. He didn't care where you came from, only who you were. He gave me the helm of *Lush*, and later backed me again to become chief commercial officer at Oyster Yachts. That was the Eddie effect: give someone a shot, back them, expect them to rise.

One story says it all.

We were anchored off Moorea. He was due at the ferry terminal at 11 a.m., but landed at 4:30 a.m. Waiting wasn't an option. He hitched a ride with a fisherman, ended up on the wrong side of the island, stole a bike, cycled across Moorea, found a kayak and paddled out to *Lush*.

He burst into my cabin at 6:30 a.m., yelling:

"PAUL! WHERE THE F*&^! WERE YOU? WHY DIDN'T YOU ANSWER YOUR F*!KING PHONE?"

I was half-asleep, stunned by the Polynesian Ironman he'd just completed.

That was Eddie. He didn't wait for life – he made it happen. He believed, he pushed, he created momentum.

He changed my life. So, sail on, EJ. Full tilt. Always.

Karun Chandhok

Former racing driver and Formula 1 analyst.

It's 6:30 a.m. and the phone rings. "You know I'm only calling you because I want something. I'm recording a podcast today – what's that French f***ker's name in charge of Ferrari?" Only a loveable rogue like Eddie would get you out of bed, having woken up the newborn with his phone call and still make you smile.

401

There are several people who were closer to Eddie and knew him for longer than me, but I count myself very fortunate to have gotten to know Eddie well during our time doing TV together for Channel 4 and remained friends since then.

Eddie was a force of nature who loved the bustle of the paddock with all the gossip and wheeling and dealings that went on inside. He would wander around the Channel 4 office in his pink underpants trying to explain a left field theory about McLaren while of course pretending he couldn't hear all the rational bits he didn't want to hear! Of course, he was sharp as a knife and knew exactly the game he was playing by winding people up all the time.

His big heart and that warm hug that came with it will be what I miss the most. There's no doubt that he's up there doing all sorts of deals with God and creating a wave of amusing chaos that only he can get away with, but the world down here is a much poorer place without him.

Dermot Desmond

Irish businessman and financier with a wide-reaching impact across the worlds of finance, sport, and media.

I always said that any stories I have are for the rocking chair and until that time they are sealed in a vault and buried! I'm sure Eddie would agree that the best stories are sometimes best left untold!

As all his friends know, Eddie was a force of nature, unapologetically bold, endlessly energetic, and infectiously charismatic.

From his maverick days as a Formula 1 team boss to his vibrant presence in broadcasting and business, he always played by his own rules. A natural showman with a sharp mind, Eddie didn't just walk into a room – he took it over, leaving stories, laughter, and a bit of chaos in his wake. You didn't just meet Eddie Jordan – you experienced him.

Martin Donnelly

Former Formula 1 driver from Belfast.

For me, Eddie Jordan was a mentor, manager, and friend. I've shared many unforgettable moments with Eddie over the years, and when I look back, they're often equal parts hilarious, touching, and totally unique to the world of EJ. Here are just a few that always make me smile.

Jerez, 1989: We were out in Spain for a general Formula 3000 test in the Camel EJR Reynard. One evening, EJ was sharing my twin room – probably because I was footing the bill! I had what you'd call a classic "curtains" hairstyle at the time, and after stepping out of the shower, I was drying my hair when I noticed EJ lying on the bed in his boxers, Cuprinol tan on show, chest hair out, chatting to Marie back in Ireland.

As I unplugged the hairdryer, he covered the phone and asked if I'd leave it out for him. Now, we all knew Eddie wore a wig, so I cheekily told him I'd left it basking in the Spanish sun on the window ledge. His response? Classic EJ: "Feck off, Donnelly, I feckin' own you."

Dodgy Mags: Back in 1987/88, the EJR workshop inside

Silverstone Circuit was a modest unit next to Alan Docking's. It had a mezzanine level with offices, including EJ's. One of the mechanics, Little Ed, thought it'd be a laugh to secretly subscribe Eddie to *Transvestite Monthly*. Each month, it landed squarely on his desk. You can imagine the meltdown. EJ would storm out onto the balcony, red-faced and furious, barking about drivers, their dads, business meetings – even his own kids walking into the office.

He swore heads would roll. But the magazines kept coming . . . for six months. He never found out who was behind it.

Elton John in Rome: At the opening weekend of the 1989 FIA Formula 3000 Championship in Vallelunga, EJ took me aside. "If you do well in qualifying," he said, "I've got a treat lined up." I stuck the car on pole and, true to his word, he grabbed me after Park Fermé and told me to get changed – quick.

We drove into Rome, stopped at a suburban café, and met two friends and two stunning women. Then a black limo pulled up. Still clueless, I jumped in. Eventually, we pulled up at a backstage entrance. A man handed me a lanyard, and a security guard ushered us through corridors and lifts to a door marked with a star and one name: ELTON JOHN.

Inside, Elton was sipping red wine. He poured us each a glass and we chatted for 20 magical minutes before he went on stage. EJ invited him to the race – he couldn't make it, but sent me the biggest bouquet I received after my accident in Jerez the following year.

Pat Brazel

Fintech entrepreneur and longstanding friend.

Everyone knew Eddie was a force – a rare mix of guile, resilience, vision, and relentless energy.

He could be vulgar, dangerously funny, and had an ego the size of a planet. One of his favourite lines was "It's not about you" – though that never quite applied to him. He loved the spotlight, but no one minded, because he always made things better – whether leading a team, a charity, or a party.

We first met skiing, guests of a mutual friend. We volunteered to share a room – Eddie had no airs or graces. He could slum it or lord it, and did both. That started an annual ski trip that lasted over 20 years. Even when we didn't have to, we roomed together. His stories were wild, often unrepeatable, and always hilarious. I hope they were true – but with Eddie, a good story always beat a true one.

We also shared a love of music. Eddie could play – and with that ego, he had to play. Anywhere. Stadiums, restaurants, dive bars – it didn't matter. I knew the words, so when no real singer was available, I became his wingman. He banged the drums or rattled spoons while the house band scrambled to find a song and key we could half-manage. "Honky Tonk Women" met "Galway Girl" via "Rockin' in the Free World".

It was chaos – but people loved it. He brought joy, energy, and momentum.

That was Eddie. Always planning, giving, making things happen. One in a million? No – one in a hundred million.

Patrick Guilbaud

Award-winning chef and founder of Ireland's only two-Michelin-star restaurant.

Dear Eddie. It's hard to put into words how I feel, knowing that you are no longer with us.

From the day we met in the restaurant in the '80s – when you complained that the food was cold, despite the fact that you ordered a cold dish!

I didn't realize that we would meet again in the '90s in Sotogrande, where our friendship really began. This is when I discovered the real Eddie. Full of life, wit, and warmth. Mind you, you could be a real pain in the neck but you were our pain in the neck! So we didn't mind. I learned to cope with your special ways on the golf course – the lunches in Gigi's – the cycling and the skiing.

Always full of energy and great fun, you were unpredictable but my God, I miss you. Au revoir, Eddie.

Liam Cunningham

Irish actor known for The Wind That Shakes the Barley, Hunger, *and* Game of Thrones *(Ser Davos Seaworth).*

Silverstone Grand Prix 1995. Bernie Ecclestone introduces me to EJ. When he finds out I'm from Dublin, I'm taken under his wing for the next 30 years. You didn't have to be Irish to be taken care of by Eddie, but it helped.

His recollection of our first meeting needed correction regularly. Eddie never let the truth get in the way of a good story.

I travelled with Eddie to many Grand Prix and once you joined him, life started moving at 200mph. You needed to be, as we say in Ireland, "in the full of your health" just to keep up with him. He adored life and wrung the neck out of his time on this planet. His band regularly played "Lust for Life" by Iggy Pop for good reason.

His love for his family, the achievements of his kids, his charitable work, and his loyalty and generosity are unmatched.

The last time we were together was at my gym in Dublin last year. "Watch this," he says, and proceeds to bang out and count 30 pushups at top speed without stopping.

"Not bad for an old bastard in his 70s, huh?"

Four-letter words and abuse are liberally used if you're a Dubliner talking to a Dubliner.

Our last message will be staying on my phone.

Me. Are ya there ya bollix?

EJ. F*** off you d***. Struggling a touch. Chat soon.

Me. No bother Chief. Give me a shout when you feel up to it. X

He's irreplaceable. I miss my friend.

J.P. Fitzgerald

Professional caddy on the PGA and European tour.

I was very lucky to meet Eddie back in 1993 through Paul McGinley at Woburn Golf Club. A year later, he invited me to the Adelaide Grand Prix and said, "You have to meet my buddy, Brian Mahon – he saved me with the Sasol deal." That was Eddie. Always connecting people. Always with a story. And always at the heart of it all.

That was the start of a friendship that lasted decades.

One of my favourite memories with him came in 2011. I was caddying for Rory McIlroy when he won his first major at the US Open. It was about 1 a.m. in the States, and my phone rang. Of course, it was Eddie – 6 a.m. in England – full of excitement, telling me how much he had made me, wanting to know how much I'd made, and then, in the same breath, planning how we'd use the win to help others. He wanted a signed flag from Rory for the Click charity auction at Windsor Races in July.

We made it happen. I flew over, spent the Sunday night with Eddie, Marie, and the family – like I had many times before. He used to leave a key out for me on a Sunday night if I was late – on the condition that I didn't wake him. The next day we played golf and headed to Windsor. As always, when Eddie had the mic in his hand, he owned the room. He had us in stitches one minute and wiping our eyes the next. That night raised thousands for children's cancer care, and that's the side of Eddie that shone just as brightly as the showman – the generous heart, the deep care, the constant drive to make things better for others.

He loved life, loved people, and gave everything his full energy – whether on the golf course, the paddock, or at a charity event.

Rest in peace, Eddie. You were one of a kind.

Mike Brady

Former head of sales and marketing for Marlboro, sponsor of Eddie in his early days.

I was lucky enough to know Eddie Jordan for nearly five decades – as a colleague and a friend. I remember his stag do in

Johnny Fox's in the Dublin Mountains like it was yesterday. Different times. Great times.

We shared years of business and craic all over the world. The stories are endless, but here's one that captures the spirit of EJ.

Back in my Marlboro and Philip Morris days, we proudly backed Eddie's racing ambitions, supporting him as he built one of the most colourful and iconic teams in Formula 1. But long before the pit lane glamour, there were moments that showed exactly who he was – quick-witted, fearless, and able to turn the ordinary into the unforgettable.

31 October 1978: Munster beats the mighty All Blacks, 12–0. But the real damage was done the day before – on a soggy Limerick golf course. I was playing with EJ and my boss, Michael O'Flaherty. On the third hole, a ball whizzed past us from the group behind. No shout. It happened again on the next hole. EJ calmly pulled out a 3-wood and launched the ball back at them. That stopped it.

When we got to the clubhouse, reporters asked how the group behind us were getting on. EJ just said, "Four pricks." Turned out it was most of the All Blacks team. We left quickly.

The moral? EJ rattled the All Blacks – and the next day, Munster finished the job. Only Eddie could claim an assist on one of Irish rugby's greatest days – from a golf course.

Eddie brought that same fearless energy, humour, and mischief to everything he touched. I'll miss him hugely. But what a ride it was to be part of his story.

See ya soon, kid.

Ian Poulter

LIV professional golfer. Former European Tour and Ryder Cup player.

Eddie, as we all know, was larger than life – the small but mighty lovable rogue. Yet no matter who you were, he treated everyone with the utmost respect.

Time in his company was infectious, always filled with laughter, joy, and a wicked sense of fun. He was endlessly generous with his time and his love for friends from all walks of life.

I always admired his passion and that unstoppable urge to light up any room he walked into. He left a lasting impression on everyone he met. The stories were endless – most unrepeatable – and he always left us wanting more.

Now he rests in peace, but he still keeps us smiling every time we think of him.

Lee Mutch

Co-owner of a yacht cleaning business in Monaco. Friend and cycling buddy of Eddie.

Though I'd known of EJ through charity bike rides, we truly connected in October 2017 during a children's cancer ride in Tuscany. As we said goodbye, he turned to me and said, "Take my number – you never know, you might need it sometime." That was the start of an unforgettable friendship.

Eddie's "daily dose of aggro," as he called it, once had us chased by a man with a stick in South Africa and another time by someone with a leaf blower in Ventimiglia. He loved to stir things up – always with a wink.

From the Col de la Madone to the Cape Town Cycle Tour, we rode together whenever he was in town. One year in Cape Town was peak Eddie: land, boys' night out, early ride, dinner with Marie, 6 a.m. race, rock pool dip, quick change, and a long lunch. By Monday, we'd escape while Eddie headed off on his next adventure.

Every arrival came with a message: "Ride – 7:30 – Be at mine." He was never late.

One morning, we stopped by a man in a wheelchair. Eddie greeted him like an old friend and quietly slipped him a note. Later, I asked how they knew each other. "He lives under that tree."

Before leaving, Eddie arranged for a new wheelchair to be delivered. "If he can get around, maybe he can help himself."

In March 2025, we saw that man again – freewheeling downhill, smiling. "Life is good," he said.

Eddie, you gave your time, your heart, and made everything unforgettable.

Jake Humphrey

British television presenter and entrepreneur, best known for fronting Formula 1 coverage on the BBC and co-founding the High Performance *podcast.*

If there's one thing I carry with me from my time with Eddie Jordan, it's this: *Be the light in the room.*

Eddie had a rare gift – the ability to change the entire energy of a space the moment he stepped into it. Most people, whether they realize it or not, act like thermometers. They reflect the temperature of the room they're in. If things are tense, they become tense. If things are flat, they stay flat.

Eddie? He was a thermostat. He didn't just reflect the mood – he set it.

He could walk into a room that felt unsure, reserved, even negative – and with a flash of wit, a surge of charisma, and that unstoppable energy, he would shift the entire atmosphere. He brought rhythm, volume, warmth. He lifted people. And in doing so, he reminded us what's possible when you choose to lead with energy and optimism.

That wasn't just something he did in conversation or company – it's how he lived. It's how he did business in Formula 1. It's how he helped bring the sport alive to a whole new audience on the BBC. It's why people were drawn to him, why rooms lit up when he arrived, and why his presence made people feel like *something exciting might just happen.*

But here's the deeper truth I learned from watching Eddie: optimism is more than personality. It's the foundation of high performance. Why? Because high performance demands resilience. And the most resilient people I've ever met are the most optimistic – they believe tomorrow can be better, even when today is tough.

Eddie believed that. And he made others believe it too.

So now, every day, I remind myself of that lesson. When I walk into a room, I try to be the light. To bring that spark. That hope. That momentum.

It's not always easy, but it's always worth it. And that's what Eddie taught me.

Adrian Lazarus

Fashion film director, proprietor of Bokeh Karaoke Lounge venues in Cape Town.

I met Eddie and Marie on a golf cart heading to a Riviera party seven years ago. I had no idea who he was – dressed like a rock star, vibrant, and unmissable. Weeks later in Cape Town, jogging along the beachfront, he stopped to chat. I assumed he wouldn't remember me – but he did. He had that spark. I knew he'd leave a mark.

Soon after, while organizing the Bokeh Fashion Film Festival, our friend Reneé suggested Eddie play with his band. Bold idea – but he embraced it. He gave a welcome speech, lit up the room with Formula 1 tales, then stole the show with drums and spoons.

During COVID, we briefly lost touch. But reconnecting in Cape Town as I opened the Bokeh Karaoke Bar, Eddie returned in full force – popping in for haircuts and playing our opening night. He filled the room with energy, again.

Coffee with Eddie became ritual. He stole dessert with a wink – "Don't tell Marie" – and reminded me our wives and daughters were our Queens. He pushed me to think bigger. One comment about bar optics reshaped my Monaco lounge.

We also filmed *Point of Success* together. With guests like Gary Player and David Yarrow, Eddie took the interviewer's seat with ease. That same charisma defined *Formula For Success* – he lit up the studio and brought Formula 1's magic to life.

Eddie's mantra: keep attacking, never settle. Just before he passed, he reminded me: what truly matters is love.

Thank you, my friend. I miss you dearly.

Wade Ormsby

Professional golfer on the Asian Tour. Formerly on LIV Golf and the European Tour.

Like many boys, I followed Formula 1 with my father. My late dad, Peter, was a golf professional and golf retailer in Adelaide. Eddie, of course, told it differently: "Peter was the head pro at Royal Adelaide Golf Club," he'd insist – often getting the details wrong, but always with charm.

We met during the early '90s Australian Grands Prix. Eddie welcomed our family into the Jordan pit in exchange for golf gear and tee times – a natural deal. A friendship was born, and it lasted over 30 years.

In 2005, during the BMW PGA Championship at Wentworth, Eddie burst under the ropes on the twelfth fairway, gave me a huge hug mid-round, and insisted I come stay with them in Surrey. He left his number at the scorer's hut – classic EJ. Just like that, our bond reignited.

In the years that followed, Eddie, Marie, and their family welcomed me into their world. The dinners, the stories, the belief he gave you – it all meant the world. Two lines I'll never forget: "If you don't believe, you're f**ked" and "Stop dicking around and get going".

Eddie loved golf – as player, caddy, fan, and motivator. He travelled with me across Europe, and during the 2014 Ryder Cup at Gleneagles, he played a quiet but powerful role backing his mate, Paul McGinley.

Summers in Spain became tradition. Golf, training, laughs, and lessons. On his boat in Puerto Banús, "Captain EJ" moored like a pirate king, champagne flying. One call stands out – FaceTime from the Med, bandana on, spoons nearby, sun on his face. We laughed and remembered.

Eddie lived big. His message: Never let the old man in. A mentor, friend, and force of nature. Forever grateful.

Darren Petersen

Drummer, musical director, producer, pal, and EJ's music teacher.

Summer 2013, Cape Town. I get a call from the director of Roland Music South Africa – a request had come in from London. One of their UK touring artists needed a drum kit. Could I help?

I rocked up at this house expecting someone like Chad Smith or Roger Taylor. Instead, I met EJ. After setting up, he asked me to play a bit – then grabbed the spoons and jumped in. That moment kicked off an unforgettable ride as a Robber with Eddie and The Robbers.

That summer turned into an adventure – gigs with Luca and EJ, travelling from Cape Town to places I never dreamed I'd perform. I met incredible people and realized what's possible when you just believe. What stood out most was EJ's ability to really listen. He knew when to be the madman – charging into life – and when to step back, ask questions, observe. That balance was his superpower.

For someone so successful, his humility and hunger to learn were rare and inspiring. He also valued loyalty deeply – I felt it in every step of our friendship. He had my back. He was real, brutally honest, and always just a call away.

He'd shine a light on others, push me with his signature: "C'mon!!!"

FFS!!" – and even call himself out when wrong. That loyalty never faded. Even at the end. I am who I am today because of EJ. My time with him has filled my tank – to grow, to push, to dream bigger.

I'll always love you, EJ.

Mark Gallagher

Former senior executive at Jordan Grand Prix.

Kidlington Airport, Oxfordshire. It's early morning and the steps to the Hawker Siddeley HS125 jet sitting on the airfield's apron are down, the pilots running through their checklists, the warmth of the interior lights beckoning us on board.

By "us", I mean Eddie Jordan and I. My boss has just pulled up in his car a few minutes before our scheduled take-off. He's looking alert, dapper, and bouncing with energy. We're off to "do a few deals" in Europe.

First stop: the Netherlands, to visit the headquarters of DiverseyLever, part of the vast Unilever group. The aim is to sign a sponsorship agreement, pose for photographs with senior executives, press the flesh. I've briefed EJ and, although he's never met the company's president before, he greets him like a long-lost friend – full of bonhomie and positivity about the partnership.

Everyone, as ever, is charmed by EJ's relaxed enthusiasm. He comes across as a man on a mission. By this point, in the early 2000s, he's well established as a successful, Grand Prix–winning team boss.

From the Netherlands we move on to Germany – to Ulm, and the headquarters of fuel and lubricants specialist Liqui Moly. The company's CEO and owner, Ernst Prost, is a straight talker who opens with, "Why should I sponsor a chickenshit Formula 1 team like Jordan?" An hour with Eddie, comparing notes on running a business and challenging the big guys, and we have a deal. It's only a million – but a million more than Ernst had planned to spend on Formula 1.

"Ha ha!" quips EJ in the car back to the airfield. "We got 'im."

Back to the jet and on to Belgium. Only this time EJ asks me to stay on board while he dashes into the general aviation terminal for a short meeting with two earnest-looking men I don't recognize. He doesn't discuss it. A secret deal? A side hustle? A tentative approach from the management of a driver under contract elsewhere? Only EJ knows.

Into the air and heading back to Kidlington. Except – a glance at a text message, and EJ disappears up to the flight deck. A few radio calls later, we're diverting to Newcastle. Newcastle United are at home to EJ's beloved Coventry City, and he wants to catch the match. We land just after 7 p.m.; a hastily arranged car is waiting, and 20 minutes later, we're ushered into the VIP box at St James' Park.

Coventry are beaten, but it matters little. EJ just wanted to support them, catch up with the management. The match finishes, we're back to the jet and bound for Kidlington, landing around 10:30 p.m.

"Thanks, Mark," waves EJ – and he's gone.

Four countries, two sponsorship deals, one clandestine meeting, and a Premiership match. All in a day's work with Edmund Patrick Jordan. One of many.

Paul McGinley

Golf commentator and former European Tour and Ryder Cup professional golfer from Dublin.

I first met Eddie Jordan at the opening of the K Club in 1991. I was still an amateur golfer, just starting to find my path, and Eddie was preparing to launch his extraordinary journey into Formula 1. Even then, there was something magnetic about him – full of energy, ideas, and life.

When Ally and I moved to London in 1995, Eddie and Marie welcomed us into their world. They didn't just open their door – they opened their hearts. Their warmth made us feel at home in a new city, and from that point on, our lives became deeply intertwined. We holidayed together every year – sometimes twice. Most memories were made aboard Eddie's boat in the Med, where laughter was loud, stories long, and joy constant. Wherever we went, the experience was always elevated by Eddie's spirit.

In 2000, when our son Killian was born, Ally and I asked Marie to be his godmother. Eddie, of course, told everyone he was the godfather – typical EJ mischief. But he loved being part of that moment, and he loved our family.

I travelled to countless Grands Prix with him, watching his team rise and rise. It was special to see what he built. At the same time, our wider friendship circle grew. Ally and Marie became incredibly close, which only deepened the bond between us. Eddie also supported me in my own career in ways many don't know. He came to golf events, played in pro-ams, and charmed everyone he met. Formula 1 was a shared passion for many of the top players – and Eddie brought charisma into every room.

In 2005, I asked him to caddy for me at the BMW tournament in Munich. I was a BMW ambassador, and Eddie was constantly working them for discounted cars – so it was a win-win. But he didn't treat it as a laugh. He took it seriously. Each round had a plan: attack zones, defensive lines, like a race strategy. Every morning we'd sit down and map it out.

I needed a strong result to qualify for the World Match Play at Wentworth. I finished fifth, qualified, and reached the final – losing only to Michael Campbell, fresh from winning the US Open. A few months later, I won the Volvo Masters. Eddie was part of that journey.

Eddie Jordan was more than a friend. He was a phenomenon. The best of craic, loyal to the core, and generous in ways few ever are. I miss him deeply. His friendship meant the world to me and my family – and I'll always be grateful for the time we shared.

Michael Chester

"Chester" – a marine-engineer-turned-photographer, with motor-sport in his DNA.

The first time I came across Eddie Jordan was in the late '70s. He and Vivian Candy were running a "Grand Prix Disco" at Bective Rugby Club. They'd wait outside St Mary's College, Rathmines, handing out discounted tickets to rugby lads – the idea being, if the boys showed up, the girls from Notre Dame, St Louis, and Muckross would follow.

Eddie even gave out membership cards, guaranteeing weekend entry. No drink – just music and madness until 1 a.m. – all to raise funds for his early Mondello racing. I remember my dad bringing me to see Eddie race Formula Ford, then Formula Atlantic. He was backed by Captain America's on Grafton Street, then Marlboro Team Ireland. I still have a sticker – the tricolour above the Marlboro logo.

Later, I trained as a marine engineer and joined Irish Shipping. After it went into liquidation, I moved to Loctite and started taking motorsport photos for *Motoring News* and *Autosport*.

Through a family connection, David Marren, I wangled an invite to one of Eddie's Formula 3000 launches at Heathrow. When Jordan made it to Formula 1, I was lucky to attend some of his spectacular UK launches – including one at the Royal Albert Hall with Cirque du Soleil.

Back in Ireland, Eddie discovered I worked for Loctite and, in typical EJ style, immediately pushed for an introduction. He was after sponsorship.

I picked him up from Weston and drove him to our HQ in Tallaght. He had it all mapped out – looking for funding for the Brazil and Argentina Grands Prix. I waited in reception while he pitched our CEO. Eventually, he came out grinning, deal done. No details shared – just a wink and a lift back to Weston.

The sponsorship covered two races and aligned with our new plant opening in Brazil. I still don't know how much he secured – but he was happy, and with Eddie, that always meant a win.

Richard Hadida

British entrepreneur and investor, owner and chairman of Oyster Yachts.

The night I met Eddie, it was love at first sight. I immediately found myself "sucked" in the bosom of his family, and my life would never be the same again. I had the great fortune to spend a lot of time with him, he served on my board, and he was also the Oyster brand ambassador. When Eddie walked into a room, to use a nautical expression, it's like hitting a white squall. Mayhem and chaos in equal measure. He only had one speed and that was flat out.

I remember once we were on a chairlift in Courchevel, he asked me if I could book a table for four of us at a popular mountain restaurant at 1 p.m. I called them and they said they are full till 3 p.m. He said, "Tell them it's Eddie Jordan, I need a table for four people at 1 p.m. and I'll be there then and the table better be ready." I relayed the message, we turned up, and of course there it was. That's how he rolled, everywhere, always.

Eddie was a father to me, and a brother and a friend, all rolled into one. He could always pull rank on me if he needed, and he did sometimes and I obeyed. He's saved my skin more than once.

Eddie was up at dawn, full throttle all day, and then when 9 p.m. struck, he would do an Irish goodbye, the white squall had passed.

My life is so much quieter now.

My life will never be the same without him.

How I miss the storm.

PJ Fallon

Irish motorsport engineer and team manager.

I first met Eddie around 1973 or 1974, just as I was starting out in Formula Ford. He'd just returned from karting in Jersey during the Irish bank strike, having made a bit of money, and bought a brand-new Crosslé 30F – a big deal then. Most of us were scraping by, and there he was at Mondello Park with a gleaming new car.

Eddie was still working at the Bank of Ireland on Camden Street – always hustling, fixing deals, arranging meetings. One early scheme involved parking second-hand cars outside the bank and offering finance-and-sale packages. Ask for a car, and he'd say, "Leave it with me 48 hours" – and deliver.

There was a dark day I'll never forget. Eddie had a bad crash at Mallory Park and left me to sell his Jaguar while he recovered. I later drove his wrecked Crosslé to John Crosslé's in Northern Ireland, only to get stopped at Newry – helicopters overhead, roadblocks everywhere. It was the day of the Miami Showband massacre. Fran O'Toole, one of the victims, had been Eddie's school friend. He was devastated.

Eddie attracted serious backers – Vivian Candy, George Macken, and Marlboro, through Michael Brady and Michael O'Sullivan. He learned sponsorship from the best – he soaked it all up.

That instinct served him in Formula 1. I worked with him again in the early Jordan GP days, managing sponsors like Denis O'Brien, Eircell, and DHL. With Gary Anderson, he built the Jordan 191 – beautiful, fast, and fearless. Just like Eddie.

He was tough on drivers but helped launch careers – Irvine, Herbert, Donnelly.

In our last chat, we laughed about those mad early days – chaotic, brilliant, unforgettable.

Eddie didn't just pass through motorsport, he made it better.

Barry Grinham

Personal trainer for EJ and strength and conditioning coach for Jordan Grand Prix.

I remember it like yesterday – 1989, the first day EJ swept into my circuit weights class in North Oxford.

It started with Marie joining my Tuesday ladies' session and smashing the class rowing time on the Concept II. The "witches of North Oxford" muttered, "She doesn't work and has no kids." I'd reply, "Actually, she has four – aged three, five, seven, and nine." Their faces looked like smacked arses. No Botox in those days!

Marie asked if she could bring her husband to the Thursday class. Of course – another fiver in the sky rocket. In comes Marie, followed by "Electric Lips", already slagging me off. He didn't know I was from the darkest depths of East London and well used to market stalls and building sites. So I gave it back: "If your arse was as big as your mouth, your guts would drop out."

The class roared. He grinned. "Come to the house after – I'm building a factory. Want a gym in it."

I had no idea who he was. I thought he made furniture. In the changing rooms, someone filled me in – Formula 3000 success,

Formula 1 ambitions. I installed the gym. Drivers, staff, even the CEO used it. But Eddie still loved class, the craic, and pints at the Rose & Crown.

From Soto to sailing, ski trips to summer chaos, Eddie and Marie gave my family so much. The memories are, as he'd say, mega.

The rest is history. Right to that final day in March.

Miss you, Electric Lips – and yes, I'll FTB.

Stuart Makin

Partner at Stonehage Fleming and Trustee of the Jordan Family Trust.

I had the privilege of working closely with Eddie on a daily basis for over 20 years in relation to the Jordan Family Office Trust.

Eddie loved having a trustee as a buffer between himself and anything the family wanted to do that he was not in favour of, and I got used to being the family "bad cop". I had been pressing Eddie for months to bring his family more into the affairs of the Trust and suggested that we hold a family meeting when all were gathered for Christmas holidays in Cape Town. Eddie had pushed back, saying the Trust was for him and Marie and that the kids didn't need to know anything about it. Imagine my surprise when I got a call on Boxing Day from Eddie and was summonsed to hold a family meeting on the same day. He met me at the door when I arrived and whispered in my ear, "Good luck – you're going to need it!" One of the first questions I got was "with all the health potions that Mom is taking, I will be 85 before I see any benefit. What's the point in that?" Thanks, Eddie!

Eddie used to say, only half-jokingly, that there were five children in the Trust – his four kids, and the fifth being the portion that went to charity. It was classic Eddie: irreverent, sharp, and deeply principled all at once.

With Eddie there was never a dull moment, and life is just not the same without him. Rest in peace, my friend.

Peter Young

Jordan Grand Prix and EJ advisor since 1999.

Little did I realize that when I joined Jordan Grand Prix as an accountant in 1999, with no knowledge of or interest in Formula 1, that I would end up working for Eddie and his family as his trusted adviser, sounding board, family office, and being his friend for over 25 years. Eddie wasn't just my boss, he was an ever-present figure in my life. My wife used to joke that he was our marriage's third wheel – sometimes the first person I spoke to in the morning, and the last voice I said goodnight to!

Working for Eddie was a privilege, but it was like riding a rollercoaster – you had to embrace uncertainty and could never plan your day as you never knew what crazy idea or scheme he would be dreaming up next – no two days were ever the same. He had an ability to think completely different to most, including me, finding angles and opportunities to make a deal work that no one else could spot.

Eddie had a special charisma and magnetic energy, and everyone wanted to talk to him. There are people that enter the room and then there was Eddie! He would say what he thought rather than what he should but always got away with it with his usual Irish charm.

I believe we worked together well. We were chalk and cheese, but when combined, we formed a great team. For me, loyalty and trust were Eddie's most amazing attributes. When he liked and trusted someone, he stood by them all the way. This level of trust enabled our bond to remain until the end.

Working for Eddie was demanding and enjoyable, there was rarely a dull moment. He always had the uncanny knack to draw out the best in people. He challenged me every day – his favourite version of saying hello to me was, "Have you made any money for me yet?" He kept me on my toes and in return, as he often said, I "kept kept him out of jail".

Those who knew him all know that Eddie loved a deal, whatever it was, but it wasn't always about the money, it was more about the game, the thrill and always, the art of negotiation. His negotiating skills were second to none, which is just one of the many skills Eddie taught me. He always said, "Never put your cards on the table first and if both sides of the deal feel bruised then it's a good deal."

Eddie's passing has left a tremendous hole in my life and in that of my family, which will never be filled. Even my young daughter said that she will miss his swearing when he was on loudspeaker in the car!

RIP, Eddie, and thank you for the ride and the unwavering loyalty.

Dr Costa Kapnias

CEO of Readyroom and Eddie's doctor in Cape Town.

How do you put into words the journey I had with the enigma that is Eddie Jordan? I met him through a friend, Ian Banner, when Eddie was buying a sensor that measured body physiology. I didn't know then it would spark such a profound connection.

Eddie began as a client, became a friend, a business partner, a mentor – and ultimately, what the Greeks call *philotimo* – a deep, soulful love for a friend. I knew the public Eddie, but over the last year, I got to see the private side: raw, vulnerable, deeply loving – especially towards his family and friends.

Eddie used to call me a "soft cock", telling me to toughen up in business. But the reason he saw that in me is because, beneath the showman, that's what he was: loving, kind, passionate about people, especially young ones in whom he saw potential.

I've diagnosed many cancers, but telling Eddie and Marie was one of the hardest moments of my life. With Eddie, I didn't just give the diagnosis – I walked the journey beside him. I witnessed the fear, the courage, the pain – and the grace. In the end, he accepted that this was the final chapter. At a lunch in Clifton, surrounded by family and friends, he looked at me and said, "This is what it's all about." He died a few days later.

His final words?

"We need a seven iron, we need a nine iron, and we're not leaving until we get a hole-in-one."

So next time you're on a par three – go for the ace. Eddie's watching.

Luca Pachetti

Musician and the singer/guitarist with Eddie and The Robbers.

I met Eddie by chance while busking on Grafton Street. One of those surreal moments you can't make up. He stepped out of the crowd, left his card, and walked off. I was in my early twenties, barely spoke English, and had no idea what Formula 1 was. But that moment changed everything.

He brought me into his Magical Mystery Tour as lead singer of his band, The Robbers. From there, it was private jets, yacht parties, jamming with icons, global gigs, fundraising for brilliant causes.

Eddie did everything with full force. Whether forming a band, raising millions, or haggling over a tenner, he gave it all. It was never about the money – it was about the thrill, the story, the game. Often too good to let the truth get in the way.

I saw the real Eddie – onstage, backstage, in quiet moments between chaos. Despite the jets and the glitter, he was grounded, craving connection and energy. He didn't wait to be entertained, he was the entertainment.

He loved tension, loved the role of "agitated man". He'd test and tease you – not to intimidate, but to shake you up, to remind you not to take life too seriously. If he liked your spirit, you were in.

He ran the band like an Formula 1 team: no off switch, no half measures. Pub or stadium – same sparkle, same setup.

And at every show, there'd be that moment: a glance, a smirk, as if to say, "What more do you need? This is the best life."

Eddie had a way of stopping time. Of feeling the magic. Of being alive.

A one-off. A true master of life.

Henri Leconte

Former French tennis player and Davis Cup-winner.

Crazy Eddie,
  My legend of passion and madness.
  Heart wide open, engine roaring, always drumming to the beat of life.
  A friend like no other – wild, generous, unforgettable.
  Driven by love, laughter, and rock 'n' roll.
  Always love you 🖤 RIP
  Big kisses and Love 🖤🖤

Stefan Johansson

Swedish former Formula 1 driver. Raced for Ferrari and McLaren in the 1980s.

I WON'T IS A TRAMP
I CAN'T IS A QUITTER
I DON'T KNOW IS LAZY
I WISH I COULD IS A WISHER
I MIGHT IS WAKING UP
I WILL TRY IS ON HIS FEET
I CAN IS ON HIS WAY
I WILL IS AT WORK
I DID IS NOW THE BOSS
For Eddie, forever the BOSS!

Mick Tunney

Entrepreneur and close friend to Eddie for 50 years.

I was flicking through the *Evening Press* classifieds, looking at second-hand cars, when I stumbled on a section marked "Karts". Just one ad was listed: CHAMPIONSHIP WINNING KART FOR SALE.

I rang the number. The man said I was lucky – there'd been plenty of interest. When I told him where I lived, he said he was nearby and would swing by in 20 minutes.

Five minutes later, an open-top pink MGB pulled up, a kart strapped to the boot. Out jumped a man in a tweed jacket and deerstalker hat. It was 1971 – and that was my first encounter with Edmund Jordan.

He wasn't keen to unload the kart, claiming he had another viewing. A quick look revealed it was in bad shape – misaligned steering, dodgy brakes, awkward seat. After some coaxing, we got it down. The engine wouldn't start.

Two hours later, we'd re-tracked the steering, fixed the brakes, and half rebuilt the thing. Of course, there was no other viewing.

When I asked what championship it had won, he said, "It's a Tecno – a kart like this won the world championship."

"So this one hasn't?"

"No, but I'm showing its potential."

I didn't buy it, but said if he ever needed help, I'd be happy to. And so it began.

One early race weekend he drove the wrong way round a kart circuit in cowboy boots and underpants, crashed, and ended up in Drogheda Hospital – transported in a hearse borrowed from a fellow racer who was also an undertaker.

When a doctor tried to cut off his boot, he bellowed:

"You don't understand – I just bought those f***ing boots!" That was Eddie.

With his leg in a cast after the crash, he spent weeks at my house. He grew close to my mum, who kept him fuelled with her homemade shortbread – always packed in a Jacob's tin – while we worked through the nights.

Years later, when Eddie was very ill, he told me:

"I woke up . . . and all I could taste was your mother's shortbread. It brought everything back."

Fierce. Loyal. Irrepressible.

Eddie Jordan – one of a kind.

Michael D. Higgins

President of Ireland.

I would like to take this opportunity to acknowledge the immense contribution that Eddie made to Irish sport, not only through his remarkable achievements in the world of motor racing, but also in the inspiration and pride he brought to so many people in Ireland and beyond. No Irish motorsport fan could ever forget Eddie's infectious energy and determination, and the wonderful memories that the Jordan Formula 1 team gave to countless people in Ireland and around the world. Eddie's loss will be so deeply felt.

Enda Kenny

Former Taoiseach of Ireland.

Eddie Jordan was a man of vision, courage, and irrepressible energy. He took on the world of Formula 1 with the same determination and belief that has always defined the best of Ireland. I got on really well with Eddie and was happy to support him whenever possible – including during my time in government in the 1990s, when Jordan Grand Prix carried our flag to the grid against the biggest names in world motorsport. Eddie never forgot that support, and I never forgot the way he repaid it – by building a team that was competitive, spirited, and utterly true to himself. He was an outstanding ambassador for Ireland, bringing our name to millions around the world, not just through racing, but through his music, his business, and his generosity. It was always to the Irish pits that fans flocked after races, whether in Buenos Aires, Tokyo, or Dubai. His Jordan race may be over and he has taken the chequered flag of life, but the legend lives on.

Micheál Martin

Taoiseach of Ireland.

Eddie Jordan was a true original – a man whose energy, creativity, and passion brought Irish talent to the world stage. Eddie lived life to the full, facing his final days with the same courage and tenacity displayed throughout many years as an entrepreneur, F1 pioneer and TV pundit. There were few like him.

From the paddocks of Formula 1 and through his love of

music, he represented Ireland with pride, charm, and unmistakable spirit. He was not only a trailblazer in sport and business, but also a generous supporter of people and causes close to his heart. Eddie had that rare ability to connect with everyone he met, from world champions to young people starting out, always offering encouragement and belief. Ireland has lost a great ambassador. My thoughts are with Marie, his family, and all who loved him.

Appendices

About the Eddie Jordan Foundation

Founded on the principles that defined his life – courage, energy, generosity, and a sense of fun – the Eddie Jordan Foundation is a living legacy to the values of one of motorsport's great mavericks. Established to harness the power of sport, music, and mentorship to inspire and uplift, the Foundation supports causes close to Eddie's heart: young people, education, healthcare, and the transformative effect of opportunity.

At its core, the Eddie Jordan Foundation believes in giving people a chance. Just as Eddie spotted and backed young talent like Michael Schumacher and Damon Hill before the world knew their names, the Foundation seeks to champion individuals and organizations with big potential but little access. Whether it's helping to fund medical research, supporting youth programmes in underprivileged communities, or providing scholarships for the next generation of engineers, innovators, and creators, the Foundation's work reflects Eddie's belief that talent is everywhere – opportunity is not.

The Foundation also uses this book as part of its mentoring programme. The 25 principles shared in these pages form the core curriculum for workshops, training sessions, and personal development programmes, helping people build confidence, resilience, creativity, and ambition. It's a practical toolkit for anyone who wants to make their mark.

A portion of proceeds from Eddie's businesses, including ventures in sport, entertainment, and electric mobility, flow into the Foundation, making every deal a force for good. True to Eddie's ethos, the Foundation partners with people who think differently and aren't afraid to break the mould. Music has always been central to Eddie's life, and fundraising events often fuse his love of performance with his passion for philanthropy – bringing together musicians, sportspeople, and entrepreneurs in support of meaningful change.

The Eddie Jordan Foundation doesn't follow the rulebook. It backs the bold, lifts the overlooked, and thrives on the idea that a little bit of chaos, handled with heart, can change lives. It's not about legacy, it's about movement. Energy. Forward motion. Just like Eddie.

Eddie never gave to tick a box – he gave because he believed in people. This Foundation is his way of inspiring the next generation to go for it.

To learn more, get involved, or donate, visit **www.ej.foundation** or scan the QR code below.

How to Support the Mission

The Eddie Jordan Foundation exists to turn belief into action – to take the spirit of Eddie's fearless, generous, and unconventional approach to life and channel it into real impact for people and communities. If Eddie's story, this book, or the Foundation's mission inspires you, there are many ways you can help us keep the momentum going.

1. **Volunteer Your Time or Expertise:** We welcome mentors, trainers, speakers, and creative professionals to contribute to our programmes. Whether it's running a workshop, designing a session, or coaching a young person with potential, your time and knowledge can help someone take the next big step in their life.
2. **Donate:** *Every donation – big or small – fuels life-changing programmes* ... in education, healthcare, entrepreneurship, and the arts. One hundred per cent of your donation goes directly to the Foundation's work on the ground. Whether it's a one-off contribution or regular giving, your support fuels scholarships, training programmes, and grassroots initiatives that give people a fighting chance. You can donate directly at **www.ej.foundation**.

3. **Partner with Us:** Are you part of a company, brand, or organization that shares Eddie's values? We are always open to creative, purpose-driven partnerships – whether through corporate giving, cause-related marketing, co-branded events, or long-term CSR collaboration. Eddie believed in making deals with heart. If your business does too, we'd love to hear from you.

4. **Sponsor a Programme or Fund a Principle:** The Foundation runs a growing series of workshops and mentoring sessions based on the 25 principles outlined in this book. You or your business can sponsor the delivery of a full course, a single principle, or a dedicated programme for a school, youth group, or community centre. You'll be directly involved in shaping the journey of those who need a hand up.

5. **Host or Attend a Fundraising Event:** From music nights and sporting dinners to charity auctions and leadership breakfasts, our fundraising events are as lively and generous in spirit as Eddie himself. Host an event in your city, join one of our annual galas, or simply come along, get inspired, and bring a few friends. Keep an eye on our events calendar at **www.ej.foundation**.

6. **Share the Message:** Sometimes support is as simple as spreading the word. If this book speaks to you, if Eddie's legacy moves you, tell someone. Share it online, give it as a gift, or post about the Foundation and our work. The more people who hear the message, the more impact we can make.

7. **Leave a Legacy:** For those who want to make a lasting difference, legacy giving is a powerful way to ensure the Foundation continues its mission for generations to come. If you'd like to include the Eddie Jordan Foundation in your will or estate planning, we can guide you through the process with care and clarity.

How to Support the Mission

Every act of support is an act of belief. Eddie always said the best investment you can make is in people. By supporting the Eddie Jordan Foundation, you're not just honouring his memory – you're helping the next underdog get to the grid.

To find out more or get involved,

visit **www.ej.foundation**

or email us directly at

info@ej.foundation

Get Checked (JFDI)

Why Waiting is Not Brave. It's Dangerous.

Eddie Jordan didn't write this book – but he inspired every word of it. And in the final months of his life, he had a message that mattered more than any business lesson or racing story: get yourself checked. For cancer. For your heart. For anything that can sneak up and take you out of the game too early.

He shared his own cancer diagnosis on the *Formula For Success* podcast with David Coulthard – not for sympathy, but as a wake-up call to anyone still pretending they're invincible. He wanted men and women to stop messing around, to take their health seriously, and to live long enough to enjoy the full ride.

So this appendix is here because Eddie wanted to make sure people don't take things for granted and know how important it is to get checked regularly If one person reads this and books a check-up, he'll still be doing his job.

Get Checked (JFDI)

What You Need to Check (and When)

For Men:

- **Prostate Check:** From **age 50** (or earlier if there's family history). A simple **PSA blood test** is the starting point. Quick. Easy. Essential.
- **Testicular Self-Exams: Once a month**, in the shower. Feel for lumps, swelling, or anything unusual. It takes seconds.
- **Bowel Cancer Screening:** Most countries offer screening from **age 60**. If you get a test kit through the door – *do it.*
- **Heart Health:** From your **40s**, get a basic blood panel annually – **cholesterol, blood pressure, glucose**. Prevention is power.

For Women:

- **Cervical Screening (Smear Test):** From **age 25**, every **three years** – then every **five years** from ages 50 to 64. It's awkward, but it's how lives are saved.
- **Breast Screening:** From **age 50**, book a **mammogram** every one to three years. It finds what your hands can't.
- **Self-Checks:** Get to know your body. Do a **monthly breast exam**. Any change – don't wait.
- **Ovarian Awareness:** Look out for bloating, pressure in the pelvis, feeling full quickly – subtle signs, easy to miss.
- **Heart Health:** Heart disease affects women just as much. **Annual blood pressure and cholesterol checks** should be standard.

For Everyone:

- **Skin Checks:** Especially important if you've spent time in the sun. Get any mole that looks odd checked by a dermatologist **once a year**.
- **Get a Full Physical Each Year.** Don't wait for something to feel wrong. Make it routine.
- **Know Your Family History.** Tell your doctor if a parent or sibling had cancer, heart issues, or anything genetic. It changes your risk profile.
- **Mental Health Is Health.** If you're not sleeping, anxious, feeling low – talk to someone. There's no shame. You're not alone.
- **Have the Conversation.** Talk to your mates. Your partner. Your kids. Normalize it. Especially the awkward bits.

> *"Don't be stupid. Don't wait or put it off.*
> *Go and get tested."*
> – Eddie Jordan

No Excuses.

You've read this far because you believe in doing things properly, so don't be lazy with the one thing you can't replace – *yourself.*
Book the check-up. Ask the questions. Make the time.

Online Workbook:
Reflect and Apply The Jordan Code

Ready to put The Jordan Code into action?

Go to **www.ej.foundation** and create your account. Once you're in, you'll get access to the interactive online workbook built around the 25 principles in this book.

It's designed to help you turn ideas into action – and keep going.

- **Explore each principle** in depth with tailored content and real-life examples.
- **Complete exercises** that challenge your thinking and apply the lessons to your life.
- **Track your progress** with built-in tools that show how you're developing over time.
- **Set goals and build habits** that reflect who you want to be.
- **Receive personalized insights** that adapt to your pace and path.

We're continually updating the content, adding fresh perspectives, new exercises, and evolving support. It's not a course, it's a co-pilot. For now, and for a very long time to come. Start today and commit to becoming the best version of yourself!

FTB!

How to Play the Spoons

For a bit of fun, here is an insight into how to play the spoons. It will take some practice to play them like EJ, but it's always fun.

How to Play the Spoons (Like a Lunatic but with Rhythm)

You don't need a fancy instrument to get the party going. Sometimes, all you need is two old dessert spoons, a pint or two, and a bit of Irish madness. Playing the spoons is about rhythm, fun, and making noise that people *feel* more than hear. I've seen a table come alive just from the beat of cutlery and chaos. It's not refined – and that's the point.

Step 1: Find Your Weapons

Grab two metal spoons. Soup spoons are an excellent option and create a great tone – dessert spoons work well also. They need to be the same size and have a bit of flex. Nothing too posh. Nothing too heavy. Think old-school canteen gear, not your mother's silver wedding set.

Step 2: Grip Like You Mean It

Start with your dominant hand – for most of us, that's the right hand. Pick up your first spoon and lay it across the middle knuckle of your index (pointer) finger, so the bowl of the spoon and your thumb are both facing upwards.

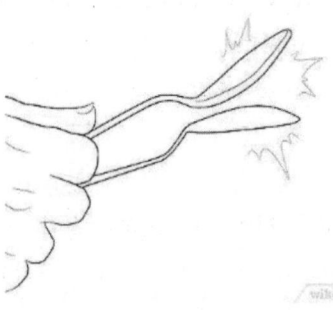

Now curl that pointer finger down into a loose fist. The tip of your finger should grip the flared end of the spoon's handle, pinning it gently against your palm. Your thumb presses across the top of the handle, helping to lock it in place. The spoon should cross the knuckle about half an inch in from the end of the handle.

Next, take your second spoon. This one sits between your index and middle fingers, also across the middle knuckle – but this time the bowl faces down, so the backs of the spoons are facing each other with a small gap between them.

Curl your middle finger into a relaxed grip, catching the end of the second spoon's handle just like you did with your pointer finger. Again, it should cross the knuckle about an inch from the back of the handle, creating that perfect springy tension between the two spoons.

If you've done it right, the spoons should act like a clapper – when you flick or tap your wrist, they bounce off one another with a sharp click. That's your rhythm machine, that's your entry into Irish pub legend.

Hold the two spoons back-to-back so the curved sides face out and there's a little gap between the bowls – just enough for your knuckles to fit between. One spoon rests on your index finger, the other behind it. Your thumb wraps around to hold it all snug.

It should feel like you're holding a spring-loaded clapper. Because that's what it is.

Step 3: Use Your Body (This is Important)

You're not just tapping spoons together – you're bouncing them off your knee, your hand, your chest if you're brave enough. Start with your knee: sit down and hold your spoons over your thigh. Then tap-tap-tap with a flick of the wrist, letting the spoons click against your leg and the top of your other hand in rhythm.

Flick, flick, tap. Flick, flick, tap. Get into a groove.

Step 4: Rhythm is King

Find the beat. Let your wrist do the work – not your whole arm, or you'll look like a seal trying to conduct an orchestra. It's wristy, snappy, percussive. Think *bodhrán* meets back-alley chaos. Add some foot stomping. That's your drum kit now.

Step 5: Turn Heads (Or at Least Raise Eyebrows)

Once you're in rhythm, mix it up. Knees, thighs, hands, elbows. If you're really feeling it (and you're not in a tuxedo), you can use your forehead! Let it be messy. Let it be loud. Let it be *you*.

Acknowledgements

First and foremost, my deepest gratitude to Marie Jordan – for her warmth, grace, and unwavering support throughout this journey. Her love and partnership with Eddie were the heartbeat of his extraordinary life, and her encouragement has meant the world.

To Zoe, Miki, Zak, and Kyle – this book, and the Eddie Jordan Foundation, are dedicated to continuing your dad's remarkable legacy. Eddie's energy, spirit, and values are woven into every page, and it is with deep respect and sincerity that I hope this honours both his memory and the profound loss you carry.

Special thanks to Greg Venning and Paul Adamson for their sharp editorial insight and tireless attention to detail. To Rae Feather and Julie Reynolds – thank you for being generous sounding boards, offering thoughtful feedback when it mattered most. Darren McGrath, your encouragement, design contributions, and belief in this project added energy and clarity to every phase. Frankie Woods, Reneé and Len Feinstein – thank you for your unwavering support and encouragement.

Acknowledgements

I'm grateful to Danielle O'Sullivan, Mike Brady, Damon Hill, and all who have helped gather the voices that shaped this tribute. To Espen Baklid, thank you for the beautiful Eddie Jordan Foundation logo that now represents a legacy of impact. Keith Sutton, thank you for the photos. David Luxton and Richard Milner, and everyone at Quercus – thank you for your belief and for helping this book become a reality. To Liam and Mike, thank you for your patience and brilliance with the audiobook recording.

And to everyone who contributed in even the smallest way – your presence helped this become what it is. Roisin O'Shea, thank you for helping champion the Eddie Jordan Foundation. Zoe Willis, thank you so much for all your support and encouragement.

Finally, to my daughters – Jill, for your brilliant editing eye, and Mia and Ella, for your support, humour, and love – thank you for keeping me grounded and inspired. To Barry, Jean, Kevin, and Paul – thank you for everything always.

About the Author

Keith O'Loughlin is an entrepreneur, strategist, and storyteller with a career spanning global technology, sport, and investment. A long-time friend and business partner of Eddie Jordan, Keith has led major companies, advised iconic brands, and built ventures at the intersection of innovation and instinct.

He is the founder of JKO Capital, which he founded with Eddie Jordan. He has worked across sectors as diverse as gaming, mobility, and retail. Passionate about people, purpose, and performance, Keith brings a sharp eye for what drives success – and a deep belief in the power of doing things differently. *Full Throttle: Lessons from a Life of Motorsport, Money and Mischief* is his tribute to the man who broke the rules, backed the underdog, and proved that energy and belief can take you anywhere.